DATA BOOK ON
HYDROCARBONS

Books from the

STANDARD OIL DEVELOPMENT COMPANY
Research Affiliate of Standard Oil Company (New Jersey)

MAXWELL, J. B.—Data Book on Hydrocarbons

STEARNS, R. F., JACKSON, R. M., JOHNSON, R. R., and LARSON, C. A.—Flow Measurement with Orifice Meters

"The Esso Series"
Published by D. VAN NOSTRAND COMPANY, INC.

DATA BOOK ON
HYDROCARBONS

APPLICATION TO PROCESS ENGINEERING

by

J. B. MAXWELL

NINTH PRINTING

D. VAN NOSTRAND COMPANY, INC.
PRINCETON, NEW JERSEY

TORONTO   MELBOURNE
LONDON

Van Nostrand Regional Offices: *New York, Chicago, San Francisco*

D. Van Nostrand Company, Ltd., *London*

D. Van Nostrand Company (Canada), Ltd., *Toronto*

D. Van Nostrand Australia Pty. Ltd., *Melbourne*

Library of Congress Catalog Card No. 68-20910

First Published February 1950
*Reprinted March 1951, January 1955,
February 1957, March 1958, December 1960,
November 1962, June 1965, February 1968*

PRINTED IN THE UNITED STATES OF AMERICA

PREFACE

The primary purpose of this book is to provide (1) basic data on hydrocarbons and petroleum fractions, (2) methods of applying these data to process engineering, including illustrative examples and some fundamental theory, and (3) applications of a few of the unit operations of chemical engineering used extensively in the petroleum industry.

Earlier editions of the present volume have been used in the Standard Oil Development Company and other affiliates of the Standard Oil Company (New Jersey). Because this book has proved to be quite valuable to technical personnel, the Standard Oil Development Company has decided to make it available for practicing engineers and students of petroleum technology.

The author is very much indebted to many associates in the preparation of this book and, in particular, to W. H. Hatch for invaluable assistance in editing the text and preparing the charts for publication, to C. O. Rhys, Sr., for the derivation of the Mollier diagrams and other charts, to C. J. Robrecht for constructive criticism and advice during the preparation of the manuscript. Furthermore, any list of acknowledgments would be incomplete without mentioning R. S. Piroomov who was responsible for the early development of a company data book.

J. B. MAXWELL

Standard Oil Development Company
Linden, New Jersey

CONTENTS

PHYSICAL DATA

CONTENTS

Section 1

PHYSICAL CONSTANTS

In the following tables the more common physical constants are given for hydrocarbons, certain other organic series, and miscellaneous gases. While these constants, in general, are based upon reliable data, estimated values were included in a few instances where available data were considered questionable. Where no reasonably good basis was available for either estimating or calculating the constants, they are omitted.

The density, boiling point, melting point, and heat of combustion for most of the hydrocarbons are those given in the *Bureau of Standards Circular C461*.[1]

GENERAL REFERENCES

Annual Tables of Physical Constants, Nat. Research Council (1941, 1942).

Beattie, Poffenberger and Hadlock, *J. Chem. Phys.* **3**, 96 (1935).

Beattie, Simard and Su, *J. Am. Chem. Soc.* **61**, 24 (1939); **61**, 924 (1939).

Cole and Cole, *J. Chem. Phys.* **9**, 341 (1941).

Doss, "Physical Constants of the Principal Hydrocarbons," 4th Edition, The Texas Co., New York, N.Y. (1943).

Ginnings, *J. Am. Chem. Soc.* **62**, 1923 (1940).

Ginnings and Baum, *J. Am. Chem. Soc.* **59**, 1111 (1937).

Ingersoll, Thesis, Mass. Inst. Tech. (1930).

International Critical Tables, Vols. I and III.

Kay, *Ind. Eng. Chem.* **30**, 459 (1938).

Kharasch, *J. Research Nat. Bur. Standards* **2**, 359 (1929).

Krase and Goodman, *Ind. Eng. Chem.* **22**, 13 (1930).

Meyers, Scott, Brickwede and Rands, Unpublished Data, Nat. Bur. Standards.

Pickering, *Bur. Standards Sci. Paper 541* (1926).

Rintelen, Gross and Saylor, *J. Am. Chem. Soc.* **62**, 1923 (1940).

Tables annuelles de constantes et donnée numerique, Vols. VII to XIII (1925–1939).

[1] "Selected Values of Properties of Hydrocarbons," *Nat. Bur. Standards Circular C461* (1947).

PHYSICAL CONSTANTS OF HYDROCARBONS

	FORMULA	MOLEC. WT.	BOILING POINT °F	MELTING POINT °F	DENSITY			CRITICAL CONSTANTS			HEAT OF COMBUSTION @ 60°F—BTU/lb	
					°API	Sp Gr 60°/60°	Lb/gal	t °F	P Atm	D G/ml	Gross	Net
NORMAL PARAFFINS												
Methane	CH₄	16.0	−258.9	−296.5	340	0.30	2.50	−116.3	45.8	0.162	23,860g	21,500g
Ethane	C₂H₆	30.1	−128.0	−297.8	247	.374	3.11	+90.1	48.2	.203	22,300g	20,420g
Propane	C₃H₈	44.1	−43.8	−305.7	147	.508	4.23	206.3	42.0	.226	21,650g	19,930g
Butane	C₄H₁₀	58.1	+31.1	−216.9	111	.584	4.86	306	37.4	.225	21,290g	19,670g
Pentane	C₅H₁₂	72.1	96.9	−201.5	92.7	.631	5.25	386.5	32.6	.232	21,070g	19,500g
Hexane	C₆H₁₄	86.2	155.7	−139.5	81.6	.664	5.53	455.0	29.4	.234	20,780	19,240
Heptane	C₇H₁₆	100.2	209.2	−131.1	74.2	.688	5.73	512.5	26.8	.234	20,670	19,160
Octane	C₈H₁₈	114.2	258.2	−70.3	68.6	.707	5.89	565	24.6	.233	20,590	19,100
Nonane	C₉H₂₀	128.2	303.4	−64.5	64.5	.722	6.01	612c	23v	---	20,530	19,050
Decane	C₁₀H₂₂	142.3	345.2	−21.5	61.3	.734	6.11	654c	22v	---	20,480	19,020
Undecane	C₁₁H₂₄	156.3	384.4	−14.1	58.7	.744	6.19	695c	20v	---	20,450	19,000
Dodecane	C₁₂H₂₆	170.3	421.3	+14.7	56.4	.753	6.27	731c	18v	---	20,420	18,980
ISO-PARAFFINS												
Isobutane	C₄H₁₀	58.1	10.9	−255.0	120	.563	4.69	275	36	.234	21,240g	19,610g
2-Methylbutane (Isopentane)	C₅H₁₂	72.1	82.2	−255.5	94.9	.625	5.20	369.5	32.4	.234	21,030g	19,450g
2,2-Dimethylpropane (Neopentane)	C₅H₁₂	72.1	49.0	+2.1	105	.597	4.97	329c	35v	---	20,960g	19,330g
2-Methylpentane (Isohexane)	C₆H₁₄	86.2	140.5	−245	83.5	.658	5.48	437c	31v	---	20,750	19,210
3-Methylpentane	C₆H₁₄	86.2	145.9	−180	80.0	.669	5.57	443c	30v	---	20,760	19,220
2,2-Dimethylbutane (Neohexane)	C₆H₁₄	86.2	121.5	−147.6	84.9	.654	5.44	415c	31v	---	20,700	19,160
2,3-Dimethylbutane (Diisopropyl)	C₆H₁₄	86.2	136.4	−198.8	81.0	.666	5.54	441	31	.241	20,740	19,200
2-Methylhexane (Isoheptane)	C₇H₁₆	100.2	194.1	−180.8	75.7	.683	5.68	496	28v	---	20,650	19,140
3-Methylhexane	C₇H₁₆	100.2	197.5	−182.9	73.0	.692	5.76	504	28.5v	---	20,660	19,150
3-Ethylpentane	C₇H₁₆	100.2	200.2	−181.5	69.8	.703	5.85	508v	28.5	---	20,670	19,160
2,2-Dimethylpentane	C₇H₁₆	100.2	174.6	−190.8	77.2	.678	5.64	475c	28.5	---	20,600	19,090
2,3-Dimethylpentane	C₇H₁₆	100.2	193.6	---	70.6	.700	5.83	498c	29	---	20,640	19,130
2,4-Dimethylpentane	C₇H₁₆	100.2	176.9	−183.1	77.2	.678	5.64	477	28.5v	---	20,620	19,110
3,3-Dimethylpentane	C₇H₁₆	100.2	186.9	−211.0	71.2	.698	5.81	487c	28v	---	20,620	19,110

	Formula	Mol. wt.									Heat of comb. (liquid)	Heat of comb. (gas)
2,2,3-Trimethylbutane (Triptane)	C_7H_{16}	100.2	177.6	− 13.0	72.1	0.695	5.78	480[b]	29.5	—	20,620	19,110
2-Methylheptane (Isoöctane)	C_8H_{18}	114.2	243.8	−165.1	70.1	.702	5.84	549[c]	25[v]	—	20,570	19,080
3-Ethylhexane	C_8H_{18}	114.2	245.4	—	65.6	.718	5.98	551[c]	25[v]	—	20,570	19,080
2,5-Dimethylhexane (Di-isobutyl)	C_8H_{18}	114.2	228.4	−130	71.2	.698	5.81	530	25	0.237	20,550	19,060
2,4-Trimethylpentane ("Isoöctane")	C_8H_{18}	114.2	210.6	−161.2	71.8	.696	5.79	515[c]	27[v]	—	20,540	19,050
OLEFINS												
Ethylene	C_2H_4	28.0	−154.7	−272.5	273	.35	2.91	50	51	.22	21,640[b]	20,290[b]
Propylene	C_3H_6	42.1	53.9	−301.4	140	.522	4.35	196.5	45.4	.233	21,040[b]	19,690[b]
Butene-1	C_4H_8	56.1	20.7	—	104	.601	5.00	293[c]	39[c]	—	20,840[b]	19,490[b]
Cis-Butene-2	C_4H_8	56.1	38.6	−218.0	94.2	.627	5.22	316[c]	37[v]	—	20,780[b]	19,430[b]
Trans-Butene-2	C_4H_8	56.1	33.6	−157.7	100	.610	5.08	310[c]	37[v]	—	20,750[b]	19,400[b]
Isobutene	C_4H_8	56.1	19.6	−220.5	104	.600	4.99	292.5	39.5	.234	20,720[b]	19,370[b]
Pentene-1 (Amylene)	C_5H_{10}	70.1	86.2	−216.4	87.2	.647	5.38	385[c]	36[v]	—	20,710[b]	19,360[b]
Cis-Pentene-2	C_5H_{10}	70.1	98.6	−290.2	82.6	.661	5.50	398[c]	35[v]	—	20,660[b]	19,310[b]
Trans-Pentene-2	C_5H_{10}	70.1	96.8	−211.0	84.9	.654	5.44	396[c]	35[v]	—	20,640[b]	19,290[b]
2-Methylbutene-1	C_5H_{10}	70.1	88.0	—	84.5	.655	5.45	387[c]	36[v]	—	20,610[b]	19,260[b]
3-Methylbutene-1 (Iso-amylene)	C_5H_{10}	70.1	68.4	−292.0	92.0	.633	5.27	363[c]	37[v]	—	20,660[b]	19,310[b]
2-Methylbutene-2	C_5H_{10}	70.1	101.2	−207.0	80.6	.667	5.55	401[c]	35[v]	—	20,570[b]	19,220[b]
Hexene-1	C_6H_{12}	84.2	146.4	−218.0	77.2	.678	5.64	463[c]	34[v]	—	20,450	19,100
Cis-Hexene-2	C_6H_{12}	84.2	155.4	−231.0	73.9	.689	5.73	473[c]	34[v]	—	20,420	19,070
Trans-Hexene-2	C_6H_{12}	84.2	154.2	−207.0	75.7	.683	5.68	472[c]	34[v]	—	20,400	19,050
Cis-Hexene-3	C_6H_{12}	84.2	153.7	−211.0	75.4	.684	5.69	472[c]	34[v]	—	20,420	19,070
Trans-Hexene-3	C_6H_{12}	84.2	154.6	−171	76.0	.682	5.68	473[c]	34[v]	—	20,400	19,050
DIOLEFINS												
Propadiene	C_3H_4	40.1	−30.1	−213.0	106	.595	4.95	249	70	—	20,880[b]	19,930[b]
Butadiene-1,2	C_4H_6	54.1	+ 50.5	—	83.5	.658	5.48	343[c]	—	—	—	—
Butadiene-1,3	C_4H_6	54.1	24.1	−164.0	94.2	.627	5.22	308	45	—	20,230[b]	19,180[b]
Pentadiene-1,2	C_5H_8	68.1	112.8	− 85.0	71.5	.697	5.80	420[c]	—	—	—	—
Cis-Pentadiene-1,3	C_5H_8	68.1	111.6	—	71.8	.696	5.79	420[c]	—	—	20,150[b]	19,040[b]
Trans-Pentadiene-1,3	C_5H_8	68.1	108.1	—	76.0	.682	5.68	415[c]	—	—	20,150[b]	19,040[b]
Pentadiene-1,4	C_5H_8	68.1	78.9	−234.0	81.3	.665	5.53	350[c]	—	—	20,320[b]	19,210[b]
3-Methylbutadiene-1,2	C_5H_8	68.1	104	−184.0	82.9	.685	5.70	410[c]	—	—	—	—
2-Methylbutadiene-1,3 (Isoprene)	C_5H_8	68.1	93.3	−231.0	74.8	.686	5.71	395[c]	—	—	20,060[b]	18,950[b]

a Heat of combustion as a gas—otherwise as a liquid. c Critical temperature-boiling point correlation. * Mixture of cis- and trans-isomers.
b Estimated. v Vapor pressure curve or correlation. ** Sublimes.

PHYSICAL CONSTANTS OF HYDROCARBONS (Cont.)

	FORMULA	MOLEC. WT.	BOILING POINT °F	MELTING POINT °F	DENSITY			CRITICAL CONSTANTS			HEAT OF COMBUSTION @ 60°F—BTU/lb	
					°API	Sp Gr 60°/60°	Lb/gal	t °F	P Atm	D G/ml	Gross	Net
DIOLEFINS (Cont.)												
Hexadiene-1,2	C_6H_{10}	82.1	172	—	64.5	0.722	6.01	495[e]	—	—	—	—
Hexadiene-1,3*	C_6H_{10}	82.1	163	—	67.8	.710	5.91	485[e]	—	—	—	—
Hexadiene-1,4*	C_6H_{10}	82.1	149	—	70.6	.700	5.83	470[e]	—	—	—	—
Hexadiene-1,5	C_6H_{10}	82.1	139.3	-221.4	71.8	.696	5.79	454	—	—	20,130	18,980
Hexadiene-2,3	C_6H_{10}	82.1	154.4	—	75.1	.685	5.70	475[e]	—	—	—	—
Hexadiene-2,4*	C_6H_{10}	82.1	176	—	63.7	.725	6.03	500[e]	—	—	—	—
3-Methylpentadiene-1,2	C_6H_{10}	82.1	158	—	65.0	.720	5.99	480[e]	—	—	—	—
4-Methylpentadiene-1,2	C_6H_{10}	82.1	158.0	—	67.0	.713	5.93	480[e]	—	—	—	—
2-Methylpentadiene-1,3*	C_6H_{10}	82.1	169	—	63.9	.724	6.03	490[e]	—	—	—	—
3-Methylpentadiene-1,3*	C_6H_{10}	82.1	171	—	59.7	.740	6.16	495[e]	—	—	—	—
4-Methylpentadiene-1,3	C_6H_{10}	82.1	169.3	-94.0	63.9	.724	6.03	490[e]	—	—	—	—
2-Methylpentadiene-1,4	C_6H_{10}	82.1	133	—	70.9	.699	5.82	445[e]	—	—	—	—
2-Methylpentadiene-2,3	C_6H_{10}	82.1	162.0	—	66.1	.716	5.96	485[e]	—	—	—	—
2,3-Dimethylbutadiene-1,3	C_6H_{10}	82.1	155.7	-105	62.1	.731	6.08	475[e]	—	—	19,880	18,730
2-Ethylbutadiene-1,3	C_6H_{10}	82.1	167	—	61.0	.735	6.12	490[e]	—	—	—	—
ACETYLENES												
Acetylene	C_2H_2	26.0	-119**	-114	209	.416	3.46	103.5	62.0	0.231	21,470[g]	20,740[g]
Methylacetylene	C_3H_4	40.1	9.8	-153	94.9	.625	5.20	275[e]	65[v]	—	20,810[g]	19,860[g]
Butyne-1 (Ethylacetylene)	C_4H_6	54.1	+47.7	-188.5	86.2	.650	5.41	375	65[v]	—	20,650[g]	19,600[g]
Butyne-2 (Dimethylacetylene)	C_4H_6	54.1	80.4	26.0	71.2	.698	5.81	420	60[v]	—	20,510[g]	19,460[g]
Pentyne-1 (Propylacetylene)	C_5H_8	68.1	104.4	-159	71.8	.696	5.79	429	—	—	20,550[g]	19,440[g]
Pentyne-2	C_5H_8	68.1	132.8	-148	66.1	.716	5.96	460[e]	—	—	20,450[g]	19,340[g]
3-Methylbutyne-1 (Isopropylacetylene)	C_5H_8	68.1	82	—	79.7	.670	5.58	410[e]	—	—	20,500[g]	19,390[g]
Hexyne-1 (Butylacetylene)	C_6H_{10}	82.1	160.9	-205.6	65.0	.720	5.99	—	—	—	—	—
Hexyne-2	C_6H_{10}	82.1	184.1	-126.4	60.8	.736	6.13	—	—	—	—	—
Hexyne-3	C_6H_{10}	82.1	179.2	-149.8	63.1	.727	6.05	—	—	—	—	—
4-Methylpentyne-1	C_6H_{10}	82.1	142.1	-157.1	67.5	.711	5.92	—	—	—	—	—
4-Methylpentyne-2	C_6H_{10}	82.1	162	—	65.3	.719	5.98	—	—	—	—	—
3,3-Dimethylbutyne-1	C_6H_{10}	82.1	100.0	-114.2	78.7	.673	5.60	—	—	—	—	—
OLEFINS-ACETYLENES												
Buten-3-yne-1 (Vinylacetylene)	C_4H_4	52.1	42	—	73.9	.689	5.73	365[e]	75[v]	—	—	—

Penten-1-yne-3	C5H6	66.1	138.6	—	58.7	0.744	6.19					—
Penten-1-yne-4 (Allylacetylene)	C5H6	66.1	107	—	49.4	.782	6.51					
2-Methylbuten-1-yne-3	C5H6	66.1	90	—	—	—	—					
Hexen-1-yne-3	C6H8	80.1	185	—	56.4	.753	6.27					
Hexen-1-yne-5	C6H8	80.1	158	—	32.8	.861	7.17					
2-Methylpenten-1-yne-3	C6H8	80.1	169	—	—	—	—					
3-Methylpenten-3-yne-1[*]	C6H8	80.1	156	—	—	—	—					
AROMATICS												
Benzene	C6H6	78.1	176.2	41.9	28.6	.884	7.36	551.3	47.9	0.304	17,990	17,270
Toluene	C7H8	92.1	231.1	-139.0	30.8	.872	7.26	609.1	41.6	.292	18,270	17,450
o-Xylene	C8H10	106.2	292.0	-13.3	28.4	.885	7.37	675	37	.288[b]	18,500	17,610
m-Xylene	C8H10	106.2	282.4	-54.2	31.3	.869	7.24	655[b]	36[v]	.288[b]	18,500	17,610
p-Xylene	C8H10	106.2	281.0	+55.9	31.9	.866	7.21	652	35[v]	.270[b]	18,430	17,540
Ethylbenzene	C8H10	106.2	277.1	-138.9	30.8	.872	7.26	655	38	—	18,490	17,600
1,2,3-Trimethylbenzene	C9H12	120.2	349.0	-13.8	25.7	.900	7.49	720[c]	32[v]	—	—	—
1,2,4-Trimethylbenzene (Pseudocumene)	C9H12	120.2	336.5	-47.3	29.1	.881	7.34	708[b]	33	—	18,570	17,620
1,3,5-Trimethylbenzene (Mesitylene)	C9H12	120.2	328.3	-48.6	31.1	.870	7.24	700[b]	33	—	18,620	17,670
Propylbenzene	C9H12	120.2	318.6	-147.1	31.9	.866	7.21	690	34[v]	—	18,660	17,710
Isopropylbenzene (Cumene)	C9H12	120.2	306.3	-140.8	31.9	.866	7.21	680[c]	35[v]	—	18,670	17,720
1-Methyl-2-Ethylbenzene	C9H12	120.2	329.2	-126.6	28.7	.883	7.35	702[c]	34[v]	—	—	—
1-Methyl-3-Ethylbenzene	C9H12	120.2	322.7	—	31.1	.870	7.24	695[c]	34[v]	—	—	—
1-Methyl-4-Ethylbenzene	C9H12	120.2	324.5	-82.7	31.5	.868	7.23	696[c]	34[v]	—	—	—
CYCLOPARAFFINS												
Cyclopropane	C3H6	42.1	-27.0	-196.6	98.6	.615	5.12	256	54	—	—	—
Cyclobutane	C4H8	56.1	+54.7	-58.0	74.8	.686	5.71	385[b]	50[v]	—	—	—
Cyclopentane	C5H10	70.1	120.7	-136.7	56.9	.751	6.25	470[b]	46[v]	—	20,350[b]	19,000[v]
Methylcyclopentane	C6H12	84.2	161.3	-224.4	56.2	.754	6.28	520[b]	42[v]	—	20,110	18,760
1,1-Dimethylcyclopentane	C7H14	98.2	189.5	-105	54.7	.760	6.33	550[b]	42[v]	—	—	—
1,2-Dimethylcyclopentane-cis	C7H14	98.2	210.7	62	50.4	.778	6.48	570[b]	40[v]	—	20,020	18,670
1,2-Dimethylcyclopentane-trans	C7H14	98.2	197.4	-182	55.4	.757	6.30	560[b]	41[v]	—	20,020	18,670
1,3-Dimethylcyclopentane-trans	C7H14	98.2	195.4	-213	57.2	.750	6.24	555[b]	41[v]	—	—	—
Ethylcyclopentane	C7H14	98.2	218.2	-217	52.0	.771	6.42	580[b]	40[v]	—	20,110	18,760
Cyclohexane	C6H12	84.2	177.3	+44	49.0	.784	6.53	538	40.4	.273	20,030	18,680
Methylcyclohexane	C7H14	98.2	213.6	-195.6	51.3	.774	6.44	575	40[v]	—	20,000	18,650

[a] Heat of combustion as a gas—otherwise as a liquid. [b] Estimated. [c] Critical temperature-boiling point correlation. [v] Vapor pressure curve or correlation. * Mixture of cis- and trans- isomers. ** Sublimes.

PHYSICAL CONSTANTS OF ORGANIC COMPOUNDS

FORMULA	MOLEC. WT.	BOILING POINT °F	MELTING POINT °F	DENSITY Sp Gr 60°/60°	DENSITY Lb/gal	CRITICAL CONSTANTS t °F	CRITICAL CONSTANTS P Atm	CRITICAL CONSTANTS D G/ml	HEAT OF VAPORIZ. @B.P. BTU/lb	HEAT OF COMBUSTION @ 60°F—BTU/lb Gross	HEAT OF COMBUSTION @ 60°F—BTU/lb Net
ALCOHOLS											
Methanol (Methyl Alcohol) CH_3OH	32.0	148.1	−143.7	0.796	6.63	464.0	78.7	0.272	474	9760	8580
Ethanol (Ethyl Alcohol) CH_3CH_2OH	46.1	173.0	−174	.794	6.61	469.6	63.1	.275	361	12,780	11,550
Propanol-1 (Normal Propyl Alcohol) $CH_3CH_2CH_2OH$	60.1	207.0	−195	.808	6.73	506.7	50.0	.273	296	14,450	13,190
Propanol-2 (Isopropyl Alcohol) $(CH_3)_2CHOH$	60.1	180.2	−129	.789	6.57	—	—	—	289	14,350	13,090
Butanol-1 (Normal Butyl Alcohol) $CH_3(CH_2)_2CH_2OH$	74.1	243.9	−129.6	.814	6.78	549			254	15,500	14,220
Butanol-2 (Sec. Butyl Alcohol) $CH_3CH_2CH(OH)CH_3$	74.1	211.1	—	.811	6.75		48		242	—	—
2-Methylpropanol-1 (Isobutyl Alcohol) $(CH_3)_2CHCH_2OH$	74.1	226.4	−162	.806	6.71				249	15,450	14,170
2-Methylpropanol-2 (Tert. Butyl Alcohol) $(CH_3)_3COH$	74.1	180.7	77.9	(.793)	(6.60)				235	15,290	14,010
Pentanol-1 (Normal Amyl Alcohol) $CH_3(CH_2)_3CH_2OH$	88.1	280.4	−109.8	.819	6.82				223*	16,220	14,930
Pentanol-2 (Sec. Amyl Alcohol) $CH_3(CH_2)_2CH(OH)CH_3$	88.1	247.1	—	.814	6.78				213*	—	—
Pentanol-3 (Diethyl Carbinol) $(CH_3CH_2)_2CHOH$	88.1	240	—	.826	6.88				211*	—	—
2-Methylbutanol-1 (Sec. Butyl Carbinol) $CH_3CH_2CH(CH_3)CH_2OH$	88.1	264	—	.820–.825	6.83–6.87				218*	—	—
2-Methylbutanol-2 (Tert. Amyl Alcohol) $CH_3CH_2C(OH)(CH_3)_2$	88.1	215.8	15	.815	6.79				203*	16,030	14,740
3-Methylbutanol-1 (Isoamyl Alcohol) $(CH_3)_2CHCH_2CH_2OH$	88.1	269.2	−179	.814	6.78				216	16,150	14,860
3-Methylbutanol-2 (Methyl Isopropyl Carbinol) $(CH_3)_2CHCH(OH)CH_3$	88.1	233	—	.825	6.87				209*	—	—
2,2-Dimethylpropanol-1 (Tert. Butyl Carbinol) $(CH_3)_3CCH_2OH$	88.1	236	120–125	—	—				210*	—	—
GLYCOLS AND GLYCEROL											
Ethanediol-1,2 (Ethylene Glycol) $CH_2(OH)CH_2OH$	62.1	387.5	9	1.118	9.31	—	—	—	344	8250	7340

Propanediol-1,2 (Propylene Glycol)	$CH_3CH(OH)CH_2OH$	76.1	371	—	1.042	8.68				273*	10,350	9350
Propanediol-1,3 (Trimethylene Glycol)	$CH_2(OH)CH_2CH_2(OH)$	76.1	350 (appr.)	—						266*	10,450	9450
Propanetriol-1,2,3 (Glycerol)	$CH_2(OH)CH(OH)CH_2OH$	92.1	554	65.0	1.265	10.53			0.271	—	7760	6940
ETHERS												
Methyl Ether	CH_3OCH_3	46.1	−11.5	−217	.719	—	260	52	.262	187	13,570[g]	12,340[g]
Ethyl Ether	$CH_3CH_2OCH_2CH_3$	74.1	94.1	−177.3	.752	5.99	381	35		151	15,840	14,560
Propyl Ether	$CH_3(CH_2)_2O(CH_2)_2CH_3$	102.2	194.2	−188	.729	6.26				129	16,930	15,630
Isopropyl Ether	$(CH_3)_2CHOCH(CH_3)_2$	102.2	155.3	−122	.773	6.07				120	16,870	15,570
Butyl Ether	$CH_3(CH_2)_3O(CH_2)_3CH_3$	130.2	288.0	−144	.760	6.44				115*	17,560	16,250
Sec. Butyl Ether	$[CH_3CH_2CH(CH_3)]_2O$	130.2	250	—		6.33				109*	—	—
ALDEHYDES												
Methanal (Formaldehyde)	$HCHO$	30.0	−3	−180	.786	—				320*	8050[g]	7420[g]
Ethanal (Acetaldehyde)	CH_3CHO	44.0	68.5	−190.3	.812	6.54				257*	11,400	10,540
Propanal (Propionaldehyde)	CH_3CH_2CHO	58.1	120	−114	.809	6.76				215*	13,400	12,420
Butanal (Butyraldehyde)	$CH_3CH_2CH_2CHO$	72.1	167.2	−144	.799	6.74				189*	14,640	13,590
2-Methylpropanal (Isobutyraldehyde)	$(CH_3)_2CHCHO$	72.1	142	−87	.795	6.65				180*	14,600	13,550
KETONES												
Propanone (Acetone)	CH_3COCH_3	58.1	133.0	−138.8	.810	6.62				220	13,260	12,280
Butanone (Methyl Ethyl Ketone)	$CH_3COCH_2CH_3$	72.1	175.5	−123.5	.812	6.74				190	14,540	13,490
Pentanone-2 (Methyl Propyl Ketone)	$CH_3COCH_2CH_2CH_3$	86.1	216.1	−108.0	.820	6.76				168*	15,430	14,330
Pentanone-3 (Diethyl Ketone)	$(CH_3CH_2)_2CO$	86.1	215.2	−40	.820	6.83				168*	15,380	14,280
3-Methylbutanone-2 (Methyl Isopropyl Ketone)	$CH_3COCH(CH_3)_2$	86.1	200.7	−134	.806	6.83				165*	15,350	14,250
4-Methyl Pentanone-2 (Methyl Isobutyl Ketone)	$CH_3COCH_2CH(CH_3)_2$	100.2	240.6	−119		6.71				152*	15,980	14,840

* Calculated or estimated with a probable accuracy of ±2%.

[g] Heat of combustion as a gas—otherwise as a liquid.

PHYSICAL CONSTANTS OF GASES

	FORMULA	MOLEC. WT.	BOILING POINT °F	MELTING POINT °F	DENSITY			CRITICAL CONSTANTS			HEAT OF COMBUSTION @ 60°F—BTU/lb	
					°API	Sp Gr 60°/60°	Lb/gal	t °F	P Atm	D G/ml	Gross	Net
Ammonia	NH_3	17.0	− 28.1	−107.9	97.5	0.617	5.15	270.3	111.5	0.235	9670	8000
Carbon Dioxide	CO_2	44.0	−109.3*	− 69.9	42.0	.815	6.78	88.0	73.0	.460	—	—
Carbon Monoxide	CO	28.0	−312.7	−337.0	—	—	—	−220.4	34.5	.301	4345	4345
Chlorine	Cl_2	70.9	− 30	−151	—	—	—	291	76	.57	—	—
Ethyl Chloride	C_2H_5Cl	64.5	54.1	−214	25.5	.901	7.51	369	51.6	.33	—	—
Hydrogen	H_2	2.0	−423.0	−434.5	—	—	—	−400	12.8	.031	61,100	51,600
Hydrogen Chloride	HCl	36.5	−121.0	−173.6	—	—	—	124.5	81.6	.42	—	—
Hydrogen Sulfide	H_2S	34.1	− 76.5	−122.0	46.0	.797	6.64	212.7	88.9	—	7100	6550
Methyl Chloride	CH_3Cl	50.5	− 11.6	−143.8	20.3	.931	7.76	289.6	65.8	.37	—	—
Nitrogen	N_2	28.0	−320.5	−346.0	—	—	—	−232.8	33.5	.31	—	—
Oxygen	O_2	32.0	−297.4	−362.0	—	—	—	−181.9	49.7	.43	—	—
Sulfur Dioxide	SO_2	64.1	14.0	− 98.9	—	1.394	11.62	315.0	77.7	.52	—	—

* Sublimes.

Section 2

CHARACTERISTICS OF PETROLEUM FRACTIONS

Average Boiling Point of Petroleum Fractions

Many physical properties of pure hydrocarbons can be correlated with specific gravity and normal boiling point as independent variables. However, for use in the petroleum industry, these correlations must also be applicable to petroleum fractions which are mixtures of a large number of components, usually having a wide variation in boiling points.

While the average specific gravity is a property of the petroleum fraction which can be measured directly, just as in the case of pure compounds, there is not an analogous average normal boiling point for a mixture. By integrating or averaging its distillation curve (temperature vs. liquid volume percent distilled), a volume average boiling point can be determined for the mixture. However, as Watson and Nelson[1] and Smith and Watson[2] have pointed out, this has no special significance as a true average boiling point and many physical properties can be better correlated by the use of some other average boiling point, i.e., weight average, molal average, etc. Consequently, in all correlations involving boiling points of petroleum fractions, the proper average should be used. For the following physical properties, these are:

Average Boiling Point	*Physical Property*
Volume average	Viscosity
	Liquid specific heat
Weight average	True critical temperature
Molal average	Pseudo-critical temperature
	Thermal expansion of liquids
Mean average	Molecular weight
	Characterization factor
	Specific gravity
	Pseudo-critical pressure
	Heat of combustion

[1] Watson and Nelson, *Ind. Eng. Chem.* **25**, 880 (1933).
[2] Smith and Watson, *Ind. Eng. Chem.* **29**, 1408 (1937).

Since a distillation curve is usually available and a volume average boiling point is readily obtained therefrom, the other average boiling points are given as a function of these data. The chart on page 14 is based on an assay (True Boiling Point) distillation[3] of the whole crude, while the chart on page 15 refers to the 10% (or ASTM) distillation of the fraction itself.

The chart on page 14 was derived empirically from crude assay fractions of a number of crudes. For narrow boiling fractions, all of the average boiling points approach each other and the volume average boiling point may be used for any of the others. Then, by appropriately combining the volume average boiling points of the narrow cuts, the various average boiling points of wider cuts were determined. The weight and molal average boiling points of the wider cuts were calculated directly by combining the narrow cuts on the basis of their weight and mole fractions, respectively. The mean average boiling point could not be calculated in the same manner since it is not a direct average or integral of its fractional parts. As used herein, mean average boiling point is defined as the boiling point which best correlates the molecular weight of petroleum fractions. Consequently, the mean average boiling point for wider cuts was determined indirectly from the generalized molecular weight chart on page 21.

Although Smith and Watson proposed a cubic average boiling point for the correlation of characterization factor, specific gravity-boiling point relations for the different crudes indicate that the present mean average boiling point can be used for correlating gravity, and consequently characterization factor. Smith and Watson also used cubic average boiling point for correlating viscosity, but the present data indicate that the volume average is the proper boiling point.

Since these boiling point correlations were developed directly from crude assay distillations, this chart should always be used[4] if an assay is available. Otherwise, the 10% (or ASTM) distillation of the fraction may be used in conjunction with the other chart. The latter was derived from the crude assay chart and an empirical correlation between the two types of distillation curves. The difference between the two sets of curves at zero slope represents the thermometer stem corrections for the 10% distillations.

In the case of light hydrocarbon mixtures, where the analysis is known, the volume, weight, and molal average boiling points can be calculated directly from the boiling points of the components and their volume, weight, and mole fractions, respectively. On the other hand, the mean average boiling point must be determined indirectly from the average molecular weight of the mixture. Up to an

[3] Approximately 15 theoretical plates and 5 to 1 reflux ratio.
[4] Below slopes of 2°F/% for low boiling fractions (V.A.B.P. < 500°F) and 3°F/% for high boiling fractions (V.A.B.P. > 500°F), the volume average may be used for the other average boiling points with very little error.

average molecular weight of 80, the molecular weight-boiling point relation for normal paraffins (page 20) may be used for this purpose, but for higher molecular weights the generalized chart on page 21 should be employed.

Characterization Factor

Watson and Nelson[1] introduced characterization factor as an index of the chemical character of pure hydrocarbons and petroleum fractions. The characterization factor of a hydrocarbon is defined as the cube root of its absolute boiling point in °R divided by its specific gravity (60°F/60°F), or

$$\text{Characterization Factor} = \sqrt[3]{T_B}/\text{Sp Gr}$$

Characterization factor is given on page 16 as a function of gravity in °API and boiling point in °F for hydrocarbons and petroleum fractions.

That characterization factor is only an approximate index of the chemical nature of hydrocarbons is indicated by its variation with boiling point both for members of a homologous series and for fractions from the same crude (page 17). However, it has considerable value in that it can be applied to the entire boiling range of a crude and it has been generally accepted by the petroleum industry.

Typical Crude Fractions

For approximate use when there are insufficient data, several correlations have been developed for typical crude fractions grouped according to characterization factor and viscosity index.[5] These groups are numbered in order of decreasing paraffinicity and each may be considered representative of the crude fractions within its characterization factor or viscosity index range. The five groups were arbitrarily selected as follows:

Group	Characterization Factor	Viscosity Index of Lube Fractions[6]
I	12.1–12.6	80–100
II	11.9–12.2	60–80
III	11.7–12.0	40–60
IV	11.5–11.8	20–40
V	11.3–11.6	0–20

Fractions from some of the more common crudes are classified in the following table:

[5] See page 156.
[6] Dewaxed to +20°F pour.

	TYPICAL GROUP	
CRUDE	White Products	Gas Oils and Heavier
Pennsylvania	I	I
Rodessa	I	I
Panhandle	II	I
Mid-Continent	II	II
Kuwait	I–II	II–III
Iraq	II	II–III
Iranian	II	II–III
East Texas	III	II
South Louisiana	III	II
Jusepin	III	III
West Texas	III	III
Tia Juana (Med. and 102)	III	IV
Colombian	IV	IV
Lagunillas	V	V

Since, in the case of some crudes, the lower boiling fractions belonged in a different group than the higher boiling fractions, they were classified separately—that is, into white products having an average boiling point less than 500°F, and gas oils and heavier having an average boiling point greater than 500°F.

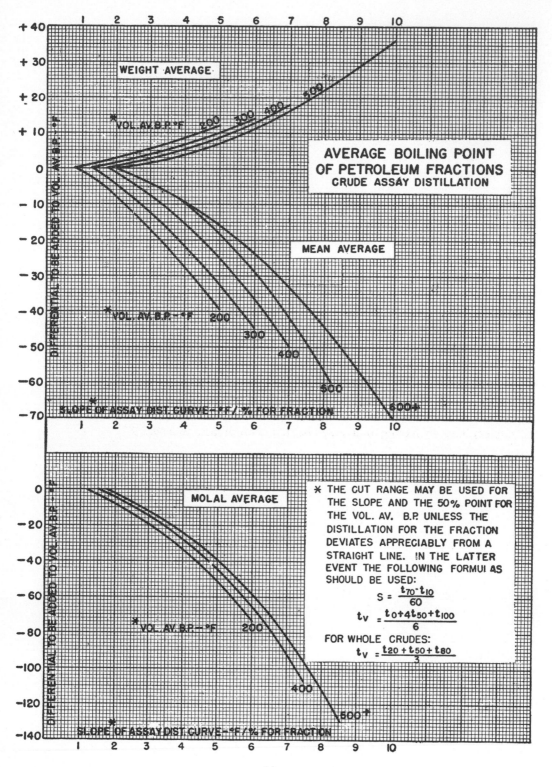

AVERAGE BOILING POINT
OF PETROLEUM FRACTIONS
CRUDE ASSAY DISTILLATION

WEIGHT AVERAGE

MEAN AVERAGE

MOLAL AVERAGE

* THE CUT RANGE MAY BE USED FOR
THE SLOPE AND THE 50% POINT FOR
THE VOL. AV. B.P. UNLESS THE
DISTILLATION FOR THE FRACTION
DEVIATES APPRECIABLY FROM A
STRAIGHT LINE. IN THE LATTER
EVENT THE FOLLOWING FORMULAS
SHOULD BE USED:

$$S = \frac{t_{70} - t_{10}}{60}$$

$$t_V = \frac{t_0 + 4t_{50} + t_{100}}{6}$$

FOR WHOLE CRUDES:

$$t_V = \frac{t_{20} + t_{50} + t_{80}}{3}$$

14

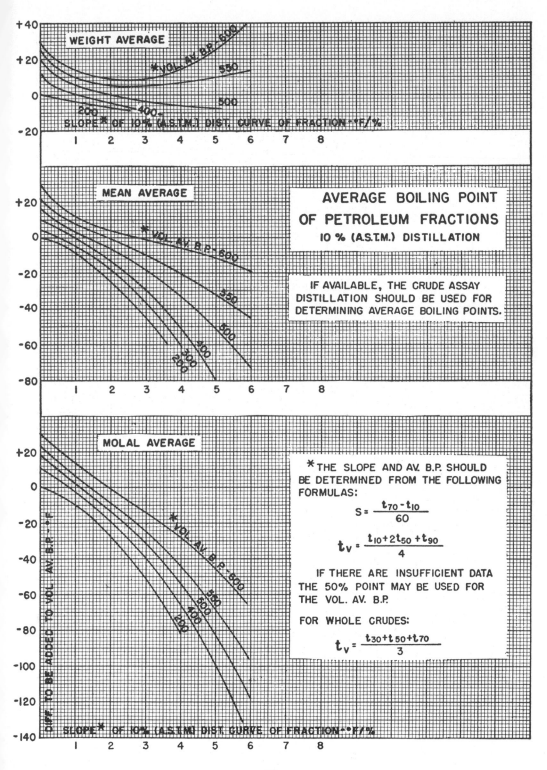

AVERAGE BOILING POINT
OF PETROLEUM FRACTIONS
10 % (A.S.T.M.) DISTILLATION

IF AVAILABLE, THE CRUDE ASSAY
DISTILLATION SHOULD BE USED FOR
DETERMINING AVERAGE BOILING POINTS.

* THE SLOPE AND AV. B.P. SHOULD
BE DETERMINED FROM THE FOLLOWING
FORMULAS:

$$S = \frac{t_{70} - t_{10}}{60}$$

$$t_V = \frac{t_{10} + 2t_{50} + t_{90}}{4}$$

IF THERE ARE INSUFFICIENT DATA
THE 50% POINT MAY BE USED FOR
THE VOL. AV. B.P.

FOR WHOLE CRUDES:

$$t_V = \frac{t_{30} + t_{50} + t_{70}}{3}$$

15

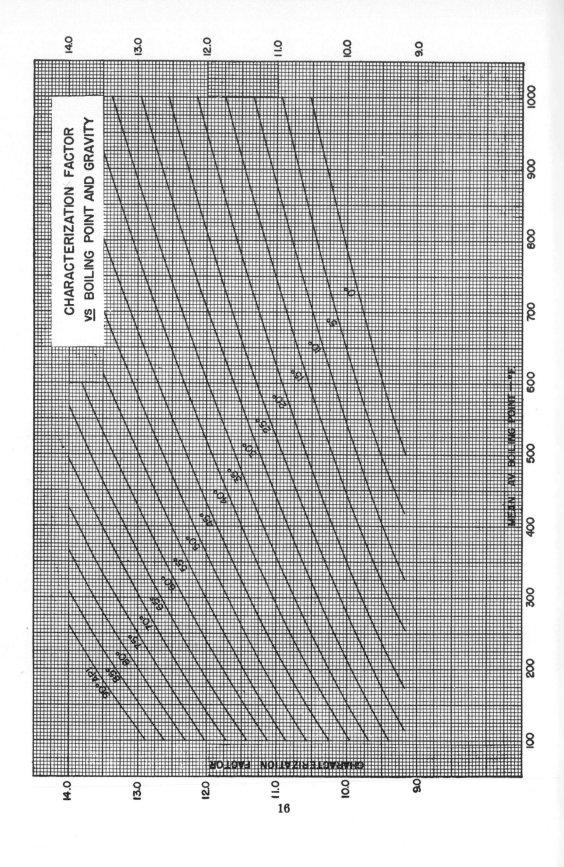

CHARACTERIZATION FACTOR
vs BOILING POINT AND GRAVITY

MEAN AV BOILING POINT — °F.

CHARACTERIZATION FACTOR

16

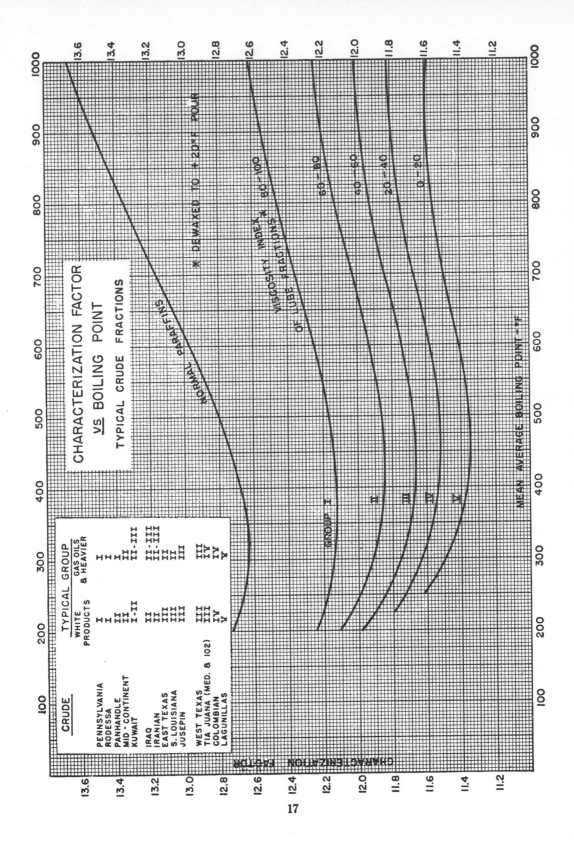

CHARACTERIZATION FACTOR
vs BOILING POINT

TYPICAL CRUDE FRACTIONS

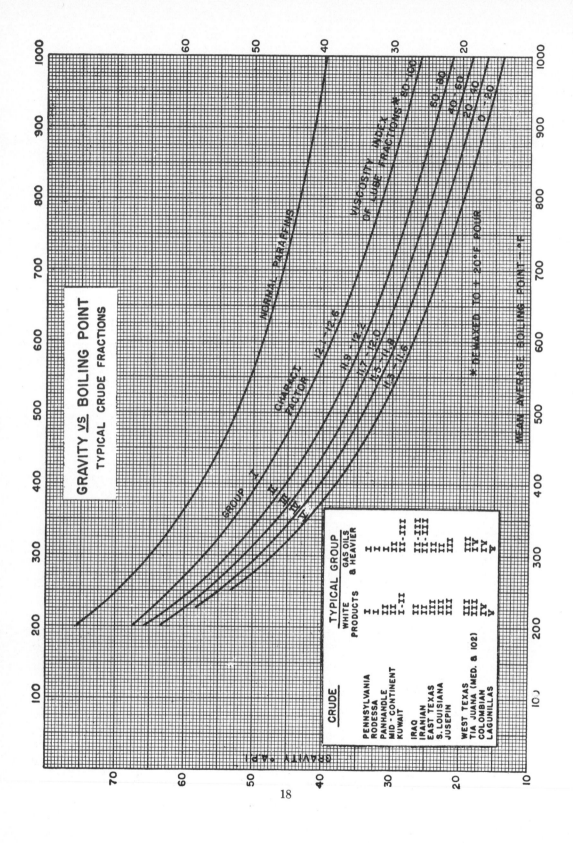

GRAVITY vs BOILING POINT
TYPICAL CRUDE FRACTIONS

NORMAL PARAFFINS

CHARACT. FACTOR

12. - 12.6
11.9 - 12.4
11.7 - 11.0
11.5 - 10.9
11.3 - 11.6

GROUP I
II
III
IV
V

VISCOSITY INDEX
OF LUBE FRACTIONS*

80 - 100
60 - 80
40 - 60
20 - 40
0 - 20

* DEWAXED TO + 20°F POUR

MEAN AVERAGE BOILING POINT—°F

GRAVITY - °API

CRUDE	TYPICAL GROUP	
	WHITE PRODUCTS	GAS OILS & HEAVIER
PENNSYLVANIA	I	I
RODESSA	I	I
PANHANDLE	II	II
MID - CONTINENT	I - II	II - III
KUWAIT	II	II - III
IRAQ	III	III - III
IRANIAN	III	III
EAST TEXAS	III	III
S. LOUISIANA	III	III
JUSEPIN	III	III
WEST TEXAS	III	III
TIA JUANA (MED. & 102)	IV	IV
COLOMBIAN	V	V
LAGUNILLAS	V	V

18

Section 3

MOLECULAR WEIGHT

The molecular weight chart for petroleum fractions on page 21 was derived from an empirical correlation of molecular weight and the function, $T_m/s^{0.40}$, where T_m is the mean average boiling point of the fraction in °R, and s, the specific gravity at 60°F/60°F. The average deviation for about one hundred petroleum fractions from 75 to 500 molecular weight is $\pm 2\%$.

Up to a molecular weight of about 300 this correlation applies equally well to pure hydrocarbons, with the exception of normal paraffins, which have lower molecular weights than predicted by the chart. Above 300 molecular weight most pure hydrocarbons for which data are available deviate from the correlation in the same direction as the normal paraffins. An explanation of this incongruity may be that these particular high molecular weight compounds have relatively long chains and consequently should fall somewhere between the normal paraffins and the multibranched and multicyclic hydrocarbons in petroleum fractions.

The molecular weight of crude fractions is given as an independent function of mean average boiling point, page 22, and also of gravity, page 23, for approximate use when only one of these variables is known. Examination of these charts shows that the boiling point chart is much less susceptible to variations with type of crude than the gravity chart and, consequently, will usually give a better approximation than the latter. However, in general, gravity rather than the boiling point will be available.

GENERAL REFERENCES

API Research Project 42.
Bridgeman, *Proc. API* **10**, No. 2, p. 124 (1929).
Doss, "Physical Properties of the Principal Hydrocarbons," 4th Edition, The Texas Co., New York, N.Y. (1943).
Fitzsimons and Thiele, *Ind. Eng. Chem. (Anal. Ed.)* **7**, 11 (1935).
Francis and Wood, *J. Chem. Soc.* **48**, 1420 (1926).
Kay, *Ind. Eng. Chem.* **28**, 1014 (1936).
Mair and Schicktanz, *J. Research Nat. Bur. Standards* **17**, 909 (1936).
Mair and Willingham, *J. Research Nat. Bur. Standards* **21**, 535, 565, 581 (1938).
Rosenbaum, *J. Chem. Phys.* **9**, 295 (1941).
Shepard, *J. Am. Chem. Soc.* **53**, 1948 (1931).

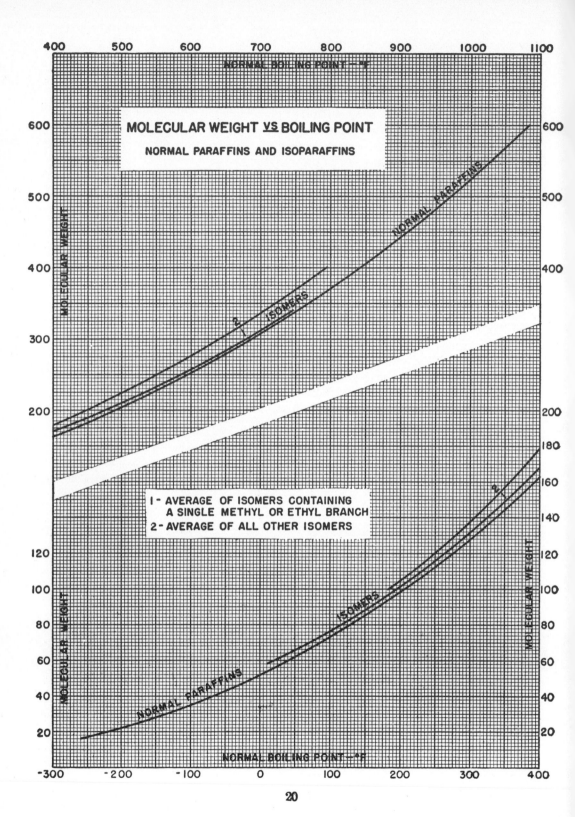

MOLECULAR WEIGHT VS BOILING POINT

NORMAL PARAFFINS AND ISOPARAFFINS

1 - AVERAGE OF ISOMERS CONTAINING
A SINGLE METHYL OR ETHYL BRANCH
2 - AVERAGE OF ALL OTHER ISOMERS

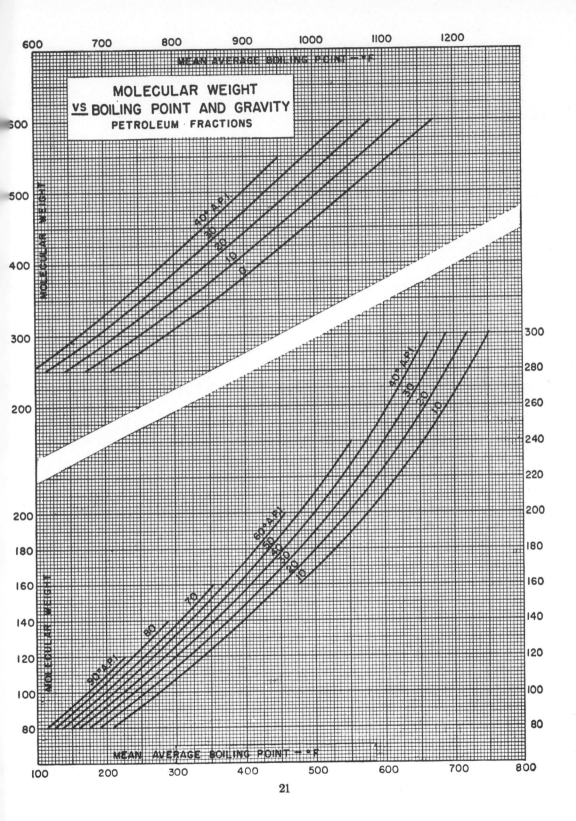

MOLECULAR WEIGHT
VS BOILING POINT AND GRAVITY
PETROLEUM · FRACTIONS

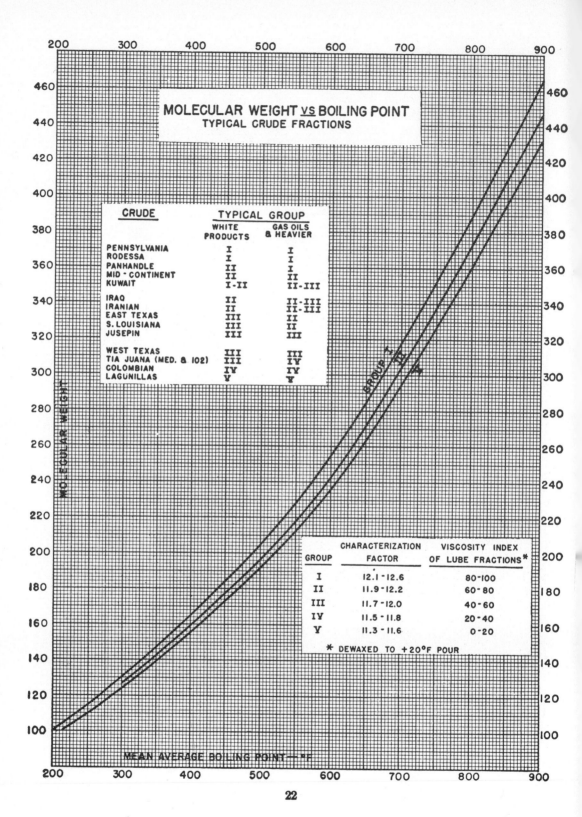

MOLECULAR WEIGHT vs BOILING POINT
TYPICAL CRUDE FRACTIONS

CRUDE	TYPICAL GROUP	
	WHITE PRODUCTS	GAS OILS & HEAVIER
PENNSYLVANIA	I	I
RODESSA	I	I
PANHANDLE	II	I
MID-CONTINENT	II	II
KUWAIT	I-II	II-III
IRAQ	II	II-III
IRANIAN	II	II-III
EAST TEXAS	III	II
S. LOUISIANA	III	II
JUSEPIN	III	III
WEST TEXAS	III	III
TIA JUANA (MED. & 102)	III	IV
COLOMBIAN	IV	IV
LAGUNILLAS	V	V

GROUP	CHARACTERIZATION FACTOR	VISCOSITY INDEX OF LUBE FRACTIONS*
I	12.1-12.6	80-100
II	11.9-12.2	60-80
III	11.7-12.0	40-60
IV	11.5-11.8	20-40
V	11.3-11.6	0-20

* DEWAXED TO +20°F POUR

MOLECULAR WEIGHT

MEAN AVERAGE BOILING POINT—°F

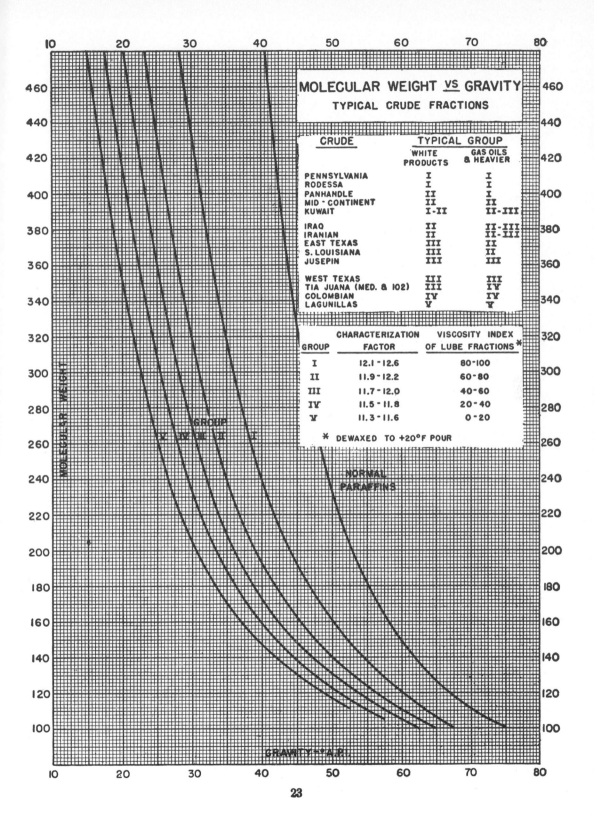

MOLECULAR WEIGHT VS GRAVITY
TYPICAL CRUDE FRACTIONS

CRUDE	TYPICAL GROUP	
	WHITE PRODUCTS	GAS OILS & HEAVIER
PENNSYLVANIA	I	I
RODESSA	I	I
PANHANDLE	II	I
MID - CONTINENT	II	II
KUWAIT	I-II	II-III
IRAQ	II	II-III
IRANIAN	II	II-III
EAST TEXAS	III	II
S. LOUISIANA	III	II
JUSEPIN	III	III
WEST TEXAS	III	III
TIA JUANA (MED. & 102)	III	IV
COLOMBIAN	IV	IV
LAGUNILLAS	V	V

GROUP	CHARACTERIZATION FACTOR	VISCOSITY INDEX OF LUBE FRACTIONS *
I	12.1 - 12.6	80-100
II	11.9 - 12.2	60-80
III	11.7 - 12.0	40-60
IV	11.5 - 11.8	20-40
V	11.3 - 11.6	0-20

* DEWAXED TO +20°F POUR

MOLECULAR WEIGHT

GROUP
V IV III II I

NORMAL PARAFFINS

GRAVITY - °A.P.I.

Section 4

VAPOR PRESSURE

In developing the vapor pressure curves for most of the individual hydrocarbons, the reciprocals of the absolute temperatures were plotted against those of a reference compound (ethane, butane, or hexane) at the same vapor pressures.[1] With one or two exceptions, this relation was linear over the entire range of the data, but if a slight curvature was indicated, as in the case of benzene vs. hexane, a straight line was not imposed upon the data. The vapor pressure curves for methane and the reference compounds were developed directly from the data by plotting vapor pressures against reciprocal temperatures. Most of the reliable data fell within $\pm 1°F$ of the correlations, and this may be considered as about the accuracy of solid portions of the vapor pressure curves. Normal boiling points in all cases were taken from "Selected Values of Properties of Hydrocarbons."[2]

While vapor pressure is meaningless above the critical temperature, the curves were extrapolated beyond this point so that other properties in the liquid phase could be calculated in the absence of any other data. For example, these extrapolated curves may be used to make rough approximations of the fugacity, density, and enthalpy of hydrocarbon vapors in solutions at temperatures above the critical.

The generalized vapor pressure charts for hydrocarbons were also derived from the linear reciprocal temperature relation with hexane used as the reference compound. The pressure scales correspond to the vapor pressure of hexane as a function of reciprocal temperature. The temperature scales were based on the reciprocal relation up to 700°F, but above 700°F it was necessary to modify the scale to secure better agreement with data on high boiling hydrocarbons and petroleum fractions.[3]

The slopes of the normal boiling point lines on the rectilinear chart and the corresponding points on the alignment charts were based on normal paraffins. However, with the exception of some of the lowest boiling members of the various series, there is a good indication that these charts apply to hydrocarbons in general. In API Research Project 42, the boiling points of a large number of

---

[1] This is the most nearly linear of the simple vapor pressure relations, with the exception of a similar one where the reciprocal temperatures are plotted at the same reduced vapor pressures.

[2] *Nat. Bur. Standards Circular C461* (1947).

[3] Beale and Docksey, *J. Inst. Petr. Tech.* **21**, 860 (1935).

different high boiling hydrocarbons were determined at 0.5 mm, 1.0 mm, and 760 mm, and these were checked against the low-pressure alignment chart. The average deviation was about 2°F over an average extrapolation of around 400°F, and there was no trend between the paraffins and other hydrocarbons.

The extrapolation of the vapor pressure scale below the hexane data has been checked indirectly by the Clapeyron equation using thermal data on hexane at low temperatures. Also, low-pressure data (below 0.001 atm) on petroleum fractions are in good agreement with this correlation.

GENERAL REFERENCES

Aston, Kennedy and Schumann, *J. Am. Chem. Soc.* **62**, 2059 (1940).

Aston and Messerly, *J. Am. Chem. Soc.* **62**, 1917 (1940).

Beale, *J. Inst. Petr. Tech.* **22**, 311 (1937).

Beattie, Hadlock and Poffenberger, *J. Chem. Phys.* **3**, 93 (1935).

Beattie, Poffenberger and Hadlock, *J. Chem. Phys.* **3**, 96 (1935).

Beattie, Simard and Su, *J. Am. Chem. Soc.* **61**, 24 (1939).

Beattie, Su and Simard, *J. Am. Chem. Soc.* **61**, 924 (1939).

Bekhedahl, Wood and Wojciechowski, *J. Research Nat. Bur. Standards* **17**, 883 (1936).

Benoliel, Thesis, Pennsylvania State College (1941).

Benson, *Ind. Eng. Chem., Anal. Ed.* **13**, 502 (1941).

Brown and Coats, *Univ. of Mich. Res. Circ. Series* 2 (1928).

Communication from The M. W. Kellogg Co., New York, N.Y.

Dana, Jenkins, Burdick and Timm, *Refrig. Eng.* **12**, 387 (1926).

Doss, "Physical Constants of the Principal Hydrocarbons," 4th Edition, The Texas Co., New York, N.Y. (1943).

Egan and Kemp, *J. Am. Chem. Soc.* **59**, 1264 (1937).

Francis and Robbins, *J. Am. Chem. Soc.* **55**, 4339 (1933).

Frolich and Copson, *Ind. Eng. Chem.* **21**, 1116 (1929).

Garner, Adams and Stuchell, *Refiner* **21**, 321 (1942).

Heisig, *J. Am. Chem. Soc.* **55**, 2304 (1933).

Heisig and Davis, *J. Am. Chem. Soc.* **57**, 339 (1935).

Heisig and Hurd, *J. Am. Chem. Soc.* **55**, 3485 (1933).

Ingersoll, Thesis, Mass. Inst. Tech. (1930).

International Critical Tables, Vol. III.

Kassel, *J. Am. Chem. Soc.* **58**, 670 (1936).

Kay, *Ind. Eng. Chem.* **30**, 459 (1938).

Kistiakowsky and Rice, *J. Chem. Phys.* **8**, 610 (1940).

Kistiakowsky, Ruhoff, Smith and Vaughan, *J. Am. Chem. Soc.* **57**, 876 (1935); **58**, 146 (1936).

Krase and Goodman, *Ind. Eng. Chem.* **22**, 13 (1930).

Lamb and Roper, *J. Am. Chem. Soc.* **62**, 806 (1940).

Kinder, *J. Phys. Chem.* **35**, 531 (1931).

Livingston and Heisig, *J. Am. Chem. Soc.* **52**, 2409 (1930).

Loomis and Walters, *J. Am. Chem. Soc.* **48**, 2051 (1926).

Maxwell, *Ind. Eng. Chem.* **24**, 502 (1932).

Morehouse and Maass, *Can. J. Research* **5**, 307 (1931); **11**, 637 (1934).

Nieuwland, Calcott, Downing and Carter, *J. Am. Chem. Soc.* **53**, 4197 (1931).
Pitzer and Scott, *J. Am. Chem. Soc.* **65**, 803 (1943).
Rintelen, Saylor and Gross, *J. Am. Chem. Soc.* **59**, 1129 (1937).
Sage, Lacey and Schaafsma, *Ind. Eng. Chem.* **26**, 214, 1218 (1934).
Sage, Webster and Lacey, *Ind. Eng. Chem.* **29**, 658 (1937).
Schmidt, Thesis, Paris (1934).
Stuckey and Saylor, *J. Am. Chem. Soc.* **62**, 2922 (1940).
Vaughan, *J. Am. Chem. Soc.* **54**, 3863 (1932).
Vaughan and Graves, *Ind. Eng. Chem.* **32**, 1252 (1940).
Wiebe and Breevoort, *J. Am. Chem. Soc.* **52**, 622 (1930).
Wiebe, Hubbard and Breevoort, *J. Am. Chem. Soc.* **52**, 611 (1930).

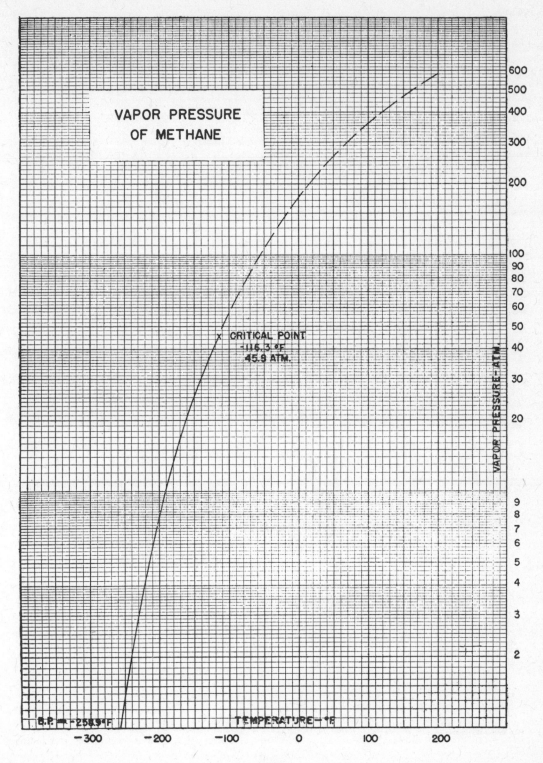

VAPOR PRESSURE
OF METHANE

CRITICAL POINT
-116.3 °F
45.8 ATM.

VAPOR PRESSURE-ATM.

B.P. = -258.9°F

TEMPERATURE—°F

27

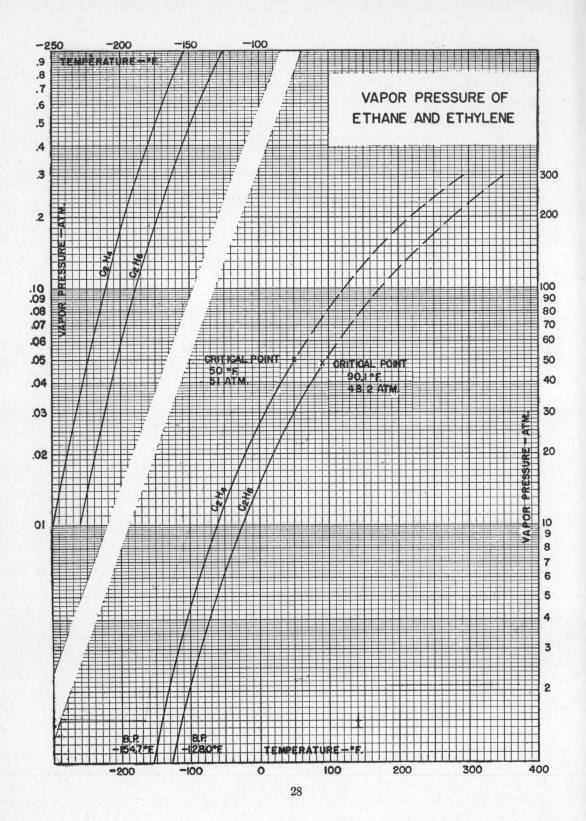

VAPOR PRESSURE OF
ETHANE AND ETHYLENE

CRITICAL POINT
50 °F.
51 ATM.

CRITICAL POINT
90.1 °F.
48.2 ATM.

TEMPERATURE —°K.

VAPOR PRESSURE —ATM.

VAPOR PRESSURE — ATM.

TEMPERATURE —°F.

B.P.
-154.7°F.

B.P.
-128.0°F.

C₂H₄

C₂H₆

28

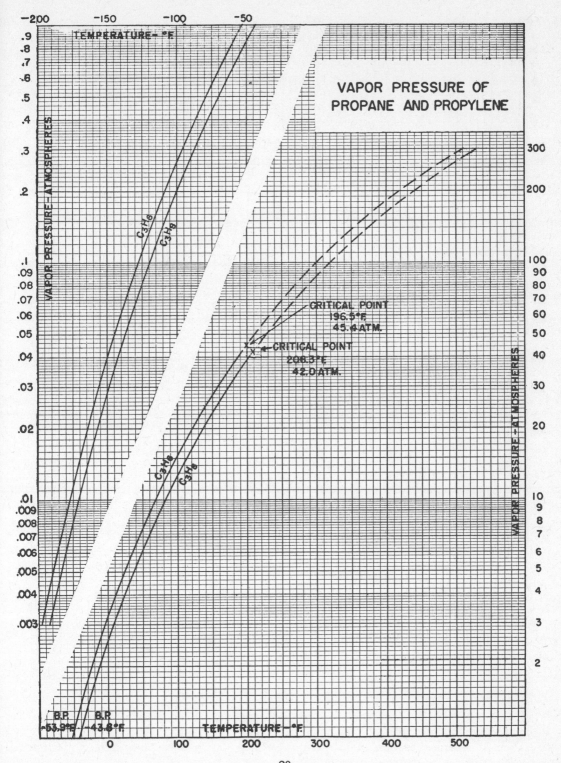

VAPOR PRESSURE OF PROPANE AND PROPYLENE

CRITICAL POINT
196.5°F
45.4 ATM.

CRITICAL POINT
208.3°F
42.0 ATM.

TEMPERATURE-°F

VAPOR PRESSURE-ATMOSPHERES

VAPOR PRESSURE-ATMOSPHERES

C₃H₆

C₃H₈

C₃H₆

C₃H₈

B.P. -53.9°F   B.P. -43.8°F

TEMPERATURE-°F

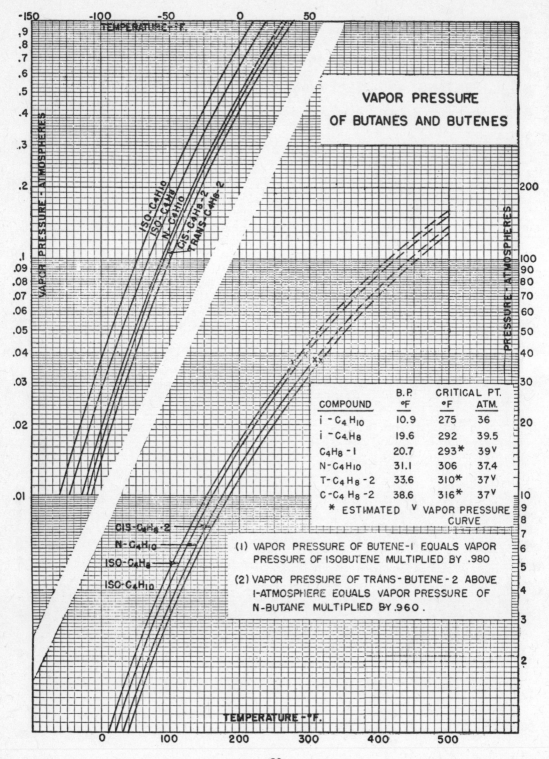

VAPOR PRESSURE
OF BUTANES AND BUTENES

COMPOUND	B.P. °F	CRITICAL PT. °F	ATM.
i - C_4H_{10}	10.9	275	36
i - C_4H_8	19.6	292	39.5
C_4H_8 - 1	20.7	293*	39^V
N - C_4H_{10}	31.1	306	37.4
T - C_4H_8 - 2	33.6	310*	37^V
C - C_4H_8 - 2	38.6	316*	37^V

* ESTIMATED ^{V} VAPOR PRESSURE CURVE

(1) VAPOR PRESSURE OF BUTENE-1 EQUALS VAPOR PRESSURE OF ISOBUTENE MULTIPLIED BY .980

(2) VAPOR PRESSURE OF TRANS-BUTENE-2 ABOVE 1-ATMOSPHERE EQUALS VAPOR PRESSURE OF N-BUTANE MULTIPLIED BY .960 .

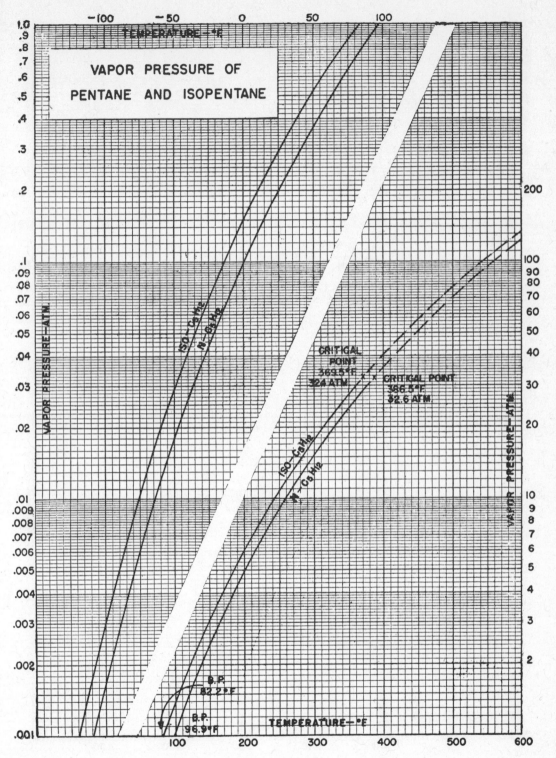

VAPOR PRESSURE OF
PENTANE AND ISOPENTANE

TEMPERATURE—°F

VAPOR PRESSURE—ATM.

ISO—C5H12

N—C5H12

CRITICAL
POINT
369.5°F
324 ATM.

CRITICAL POINT
366.5°F
32.6 ATM.

ISO—C5H12

N—C5H12

B.P.
82.2°F

B.P.
96.9°F

TEMPERATURE—°F

VAPOR PRESSURE—ATM.

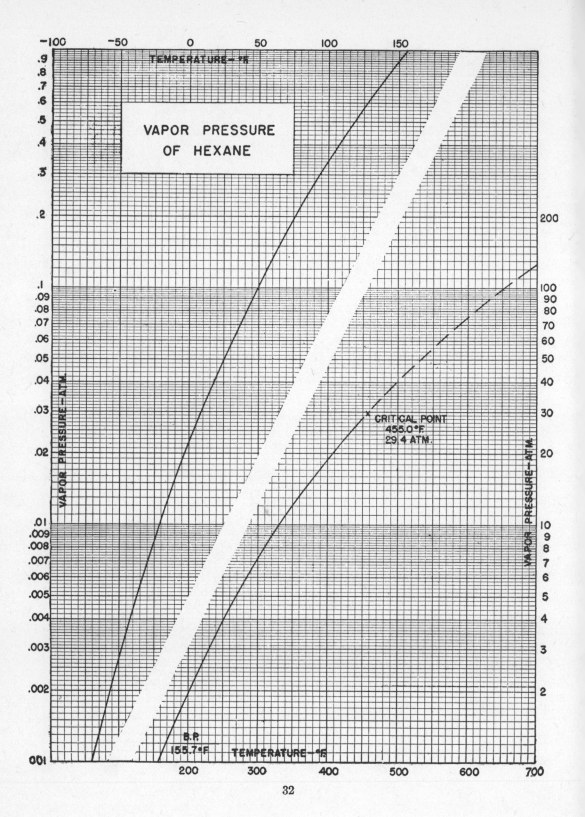

VAPOR PRESSURE
OF HEXANE

TEMPERATURE – °F

VAPOR PRESSURE – ATM.

CRITICAL POINT
455.0°F
29.4 ATM.

B.P.
155.7°F

TEMPERATURE – °F

VAPOR PRESSURE – ATM.

32

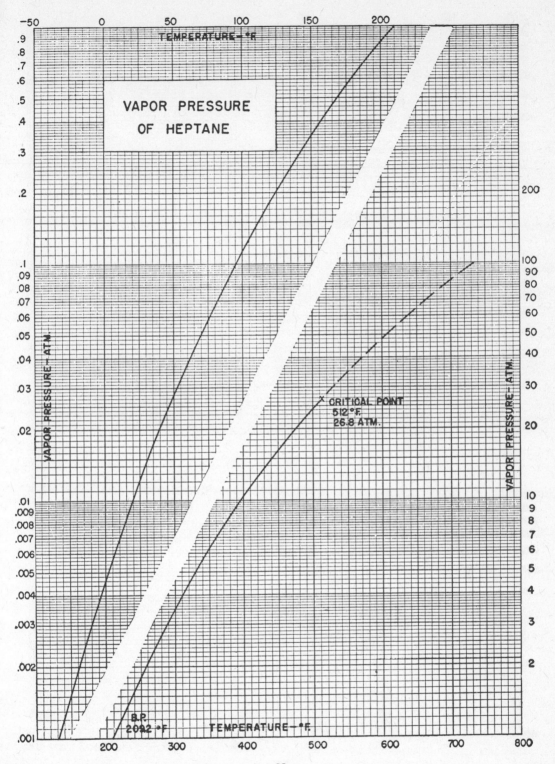

VAPOR PRESSURE
OF HEPTANE

CRITICAL POINT
512°F.
26.8 ATM.

B.P.
209.2 °F

TEMPERATURE—°F.

TEMPERATURE—°F

VAPOR PRESSURE—ATM.

VAPOR PRESSURE—ATM.

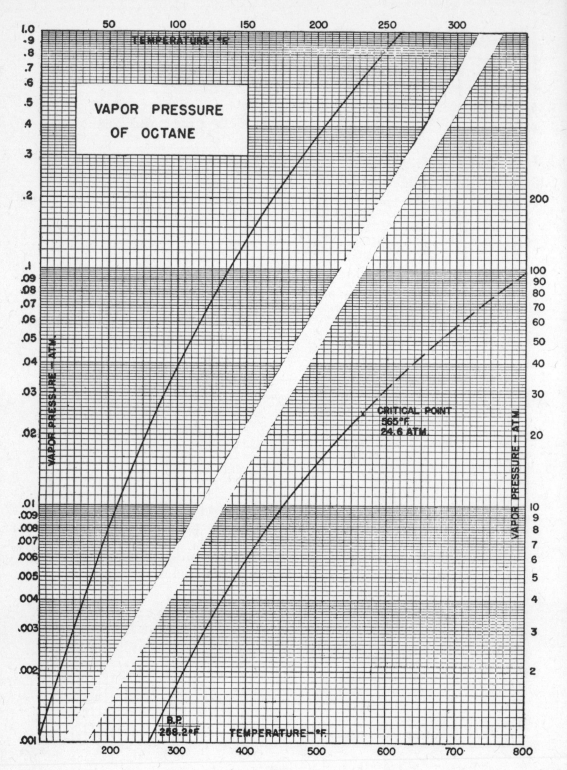

VAPOR PRESSURE
OF OCTANE

CRITICAL POINT
565°F
24.6 ATM.

VAPOR PRESSURE — ATM.

VAPOR PRESSURE — ATM.

TEMPERATURE —°F

TEMPERATURE —°F.

B.P.
258.2°F

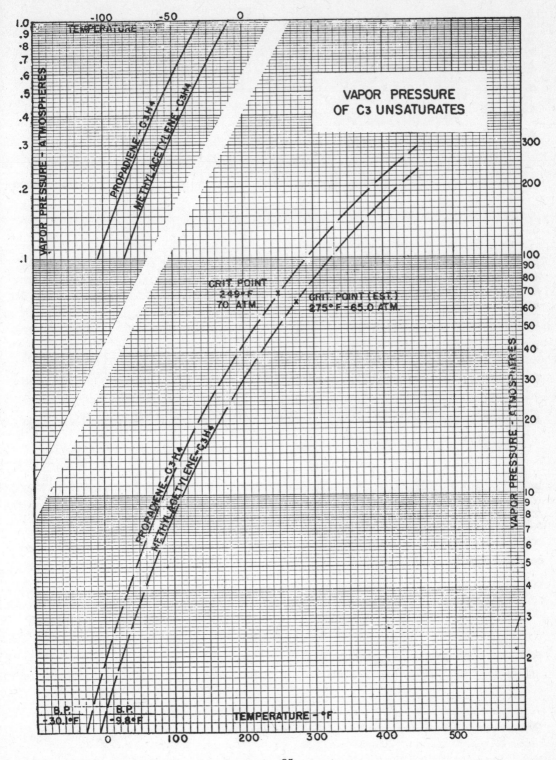

VAPOR PRESSURE
OF C3 UNSATURATES

TEMPERATURE - °F

VAPOR PRESSURE - ATMOSPHERES

PROPADIENE - C3H4

METHYLACETYLENE - C3H4

CRIT. POINT
249°F
70 ATM.

CRIT. POINT (EST.)
275°F - 65.0 ATM.

PROPADIENE - C3H4

METHYLACETYLENE - C3H4

VAPOR PRESSURE - ATMOSPHERES

B.P.
-30.1°F

B.P.
-9.8°F

TEMPERATURE - °F

35

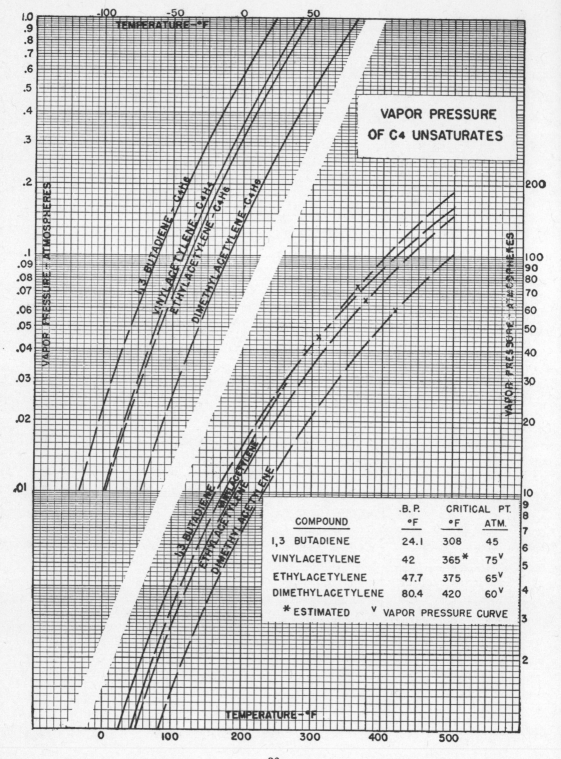

VAPOR PRESSURE
OF C4 UNSATURATES

COMPOUND	.B.P. °F	CRITICAL PT. °F	ATM.
1,3 BUTADIENE	24.1	308	45
VINYLACETYLENE	42	365*	75[V]
ETHYLACETYLENE	47.7	375	65[V]
DIMETHYLACETYLENE	80.4	420	60[V]

*ESTIMATED   [V] VAPOR PRESSURE CURVE

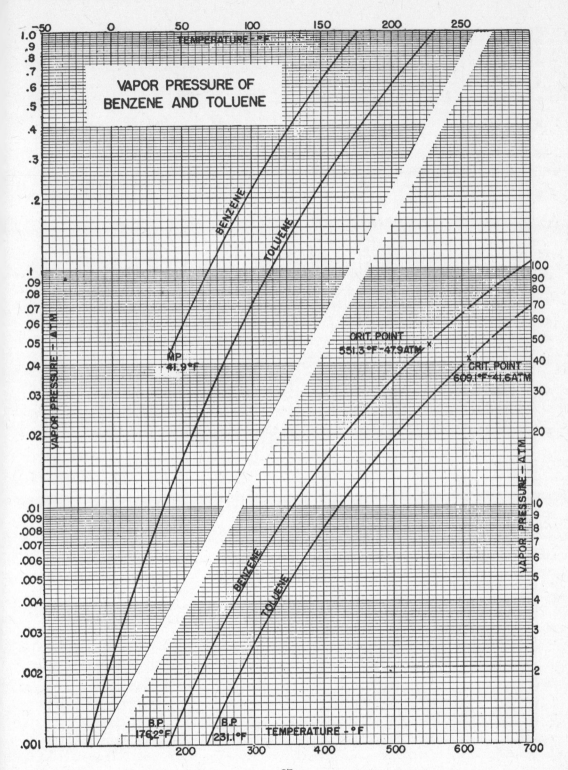

VAPOR PRESSURE OF
BENZENE AND TOLUENE

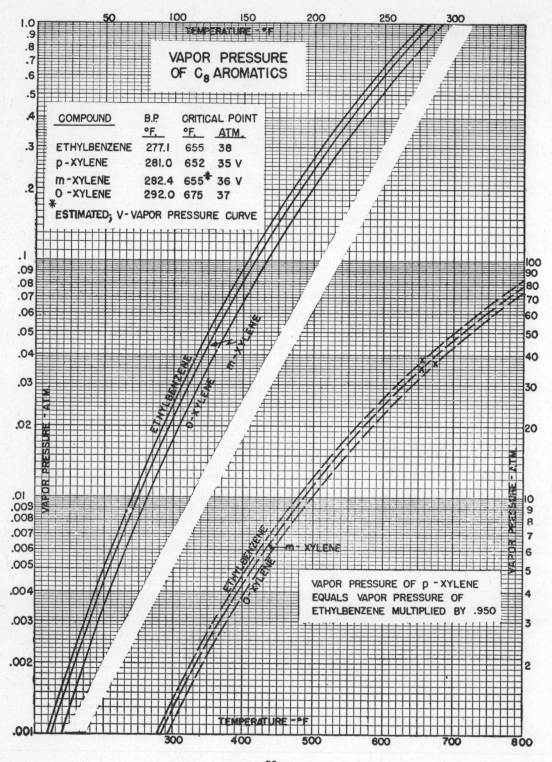

VAPOR PRESSURE
OF C$_8$ AROMATICS

COMPOUND	B.P. °F.	CRITICAL POINT	
		°F.	ATM.
ETHYLBENZENE	277.1	655	38
p-XYLENE	281.0	652	35 V
m-XYLENE	282.4	655*	36 V
O-XYLENE	292.0	675	37

* ESTIMATED; V- VAPOR PRESSURE CURVE

TEMPERATURE - °F

VAPOR PRESSURE - ATM

ETHYLBENZENE
O-XYLENE
m-XYLENE

VAPOR PRESSURE OF p-XYLENE
EQUALS VAPOR PRESSURE OF
ETHYLBENZENE MULTIPLIED BY .950

TEMPERATURE - °F

VAPOR PRESSURE - ATM

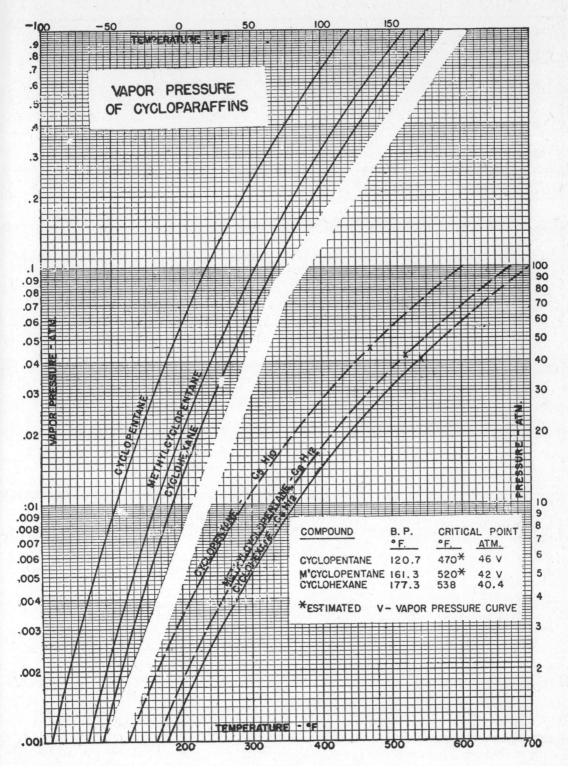

VAPOR PRESSURE
OF CYCLOPARAFFINS

COMPOUND	B. P.	CRITICAL POINT	
	°F.	°F.	ATM.
CYCLOPENTANE	120.7	470*	46 V
M'CYCLOPENTANE	161.3	520*	42 V
CYCLOHEXANE	177.3	538	40.4

*ESTIMATED   V - VAPOR PRESSURE CURVE

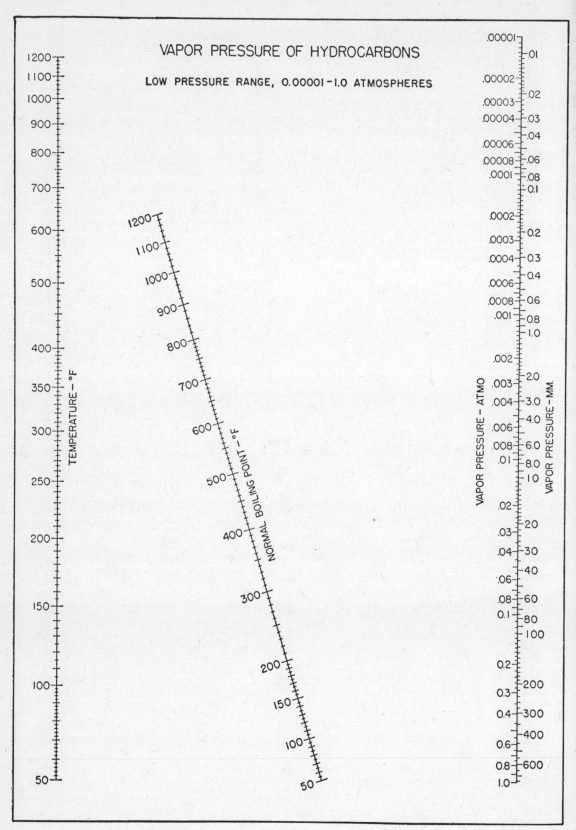

VAPOR PRESSURE OF HYDROCARBONS

LOW PRESSURE RANGE, 0.00001 – 1.0 ATMOSPHERES

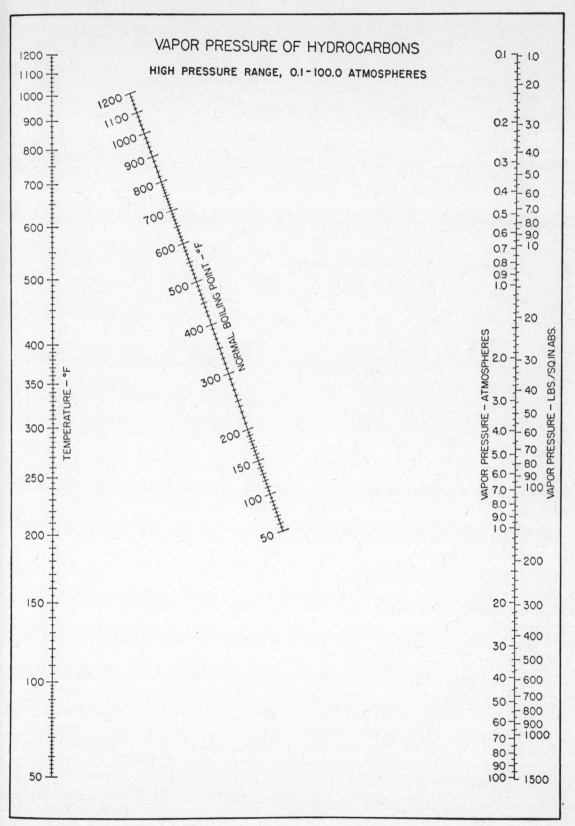

VAPOR PRESSURE OF HYDROCARBONS

HIGH PRESSURE RANGE, 0.1-100.0 ATMOSPHERES

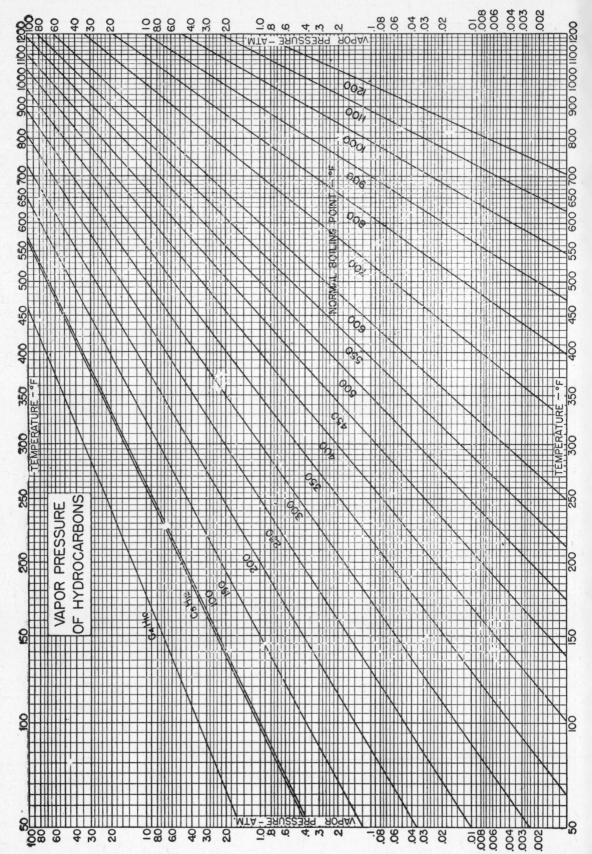

VAPOR PRESSURE
OF HYDROCARBONS

42

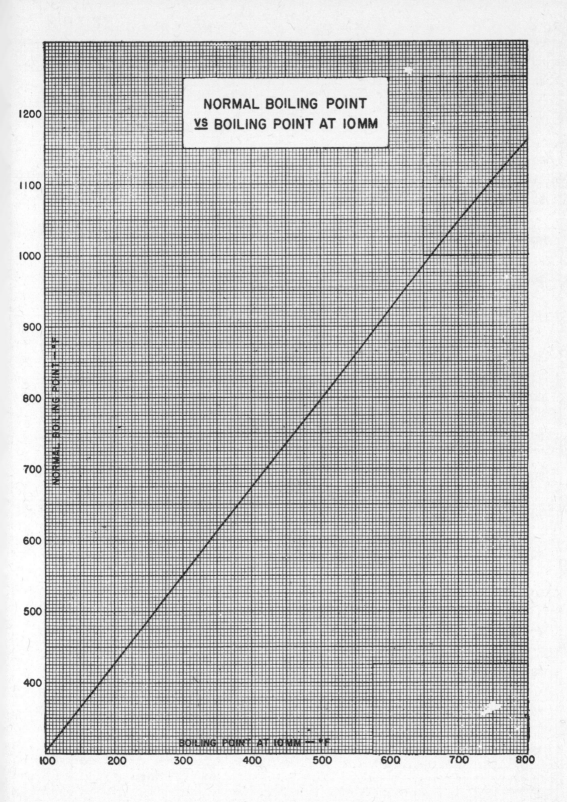

NORMAL BOILING POINT
VS BOILING POINT AT 10MM

NORMAL BOILING POINT —°F

BOILING POINT AT 10MM —°F

VAPOR PRESSURE OF GASOLINES

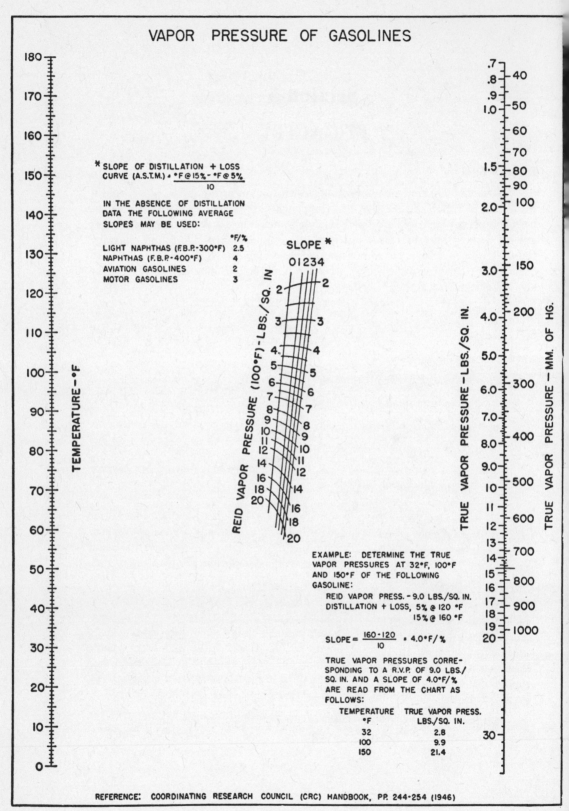

* SLOPE OF DISTILLATION + LOSS
  CURVE (A.S.T.M.) = $\dfrac{°F @ 15\% - °F @ 5\%}{10}$

IN THE ABSENCE OF DISTILLATION
DATA THE FOLLOWING AVERAGE
SLOPES MAY BE USED:

	°F/%
LIGHT NAPHTHAS (F.B.P.-300°F)	2.5
NAPHTHAS (F.B.P.-400°F)	4
AVIATION GASOLINES	2
MOTOR GASOLINES	3

EXAMPLE: DETERMINE THE TRUE
VAPOR PRESSURES AT 32°F, 100°F
AND 150°F OF THE FOLLOWING
GASOLINE:

REID VAPOR PRESS.- 9.0 LBS./SQ. IN.
DISTILLATION + LOSS, 5% @ 120 °F
15% @ 160 °F

SLOPE = $\dfrac{160-120}{10}$ = 4.0°F/%

TRUE VAPOR PRESSURES CORRE-
SPONDING TO A R.V.P. OF 9.0 LBS./
SQ. IN. AND A SLOPE OF 4.0°F/%
ARE READ FROM THE CHART AS
FOLLOWS:

TEMPERATURE °F	TRUE VAPOR PRESS. LBS./SQ. IN.
32	2.8
100	9.9
150	21.4

REFERENCE: COORDINATING RESEARCH COUNCIL (CRC) HANDBOOK, PP. 244-254 (1946)

Section 5

FUGACITY

Raoult's Law

If two or more compounds form an ideal solution in the liquid phase, and if the saturated vapors of the individual components are perfect gases, the system has been termed an ideal system.[1] For such a system the partial vapor pressure of any component may be calculated from the composition of the liquid phase by Raoult's Law and from the composition of the vapor phase by Dalton's Law. An equation of these two expressions gives the liquid-vapor equilibrium relation for any component, i where $i = 1, 2, \cdots, n$:

$$p_i = P_i x_i = \pi y_i \tag{1}$$

or
$$y_i/x_i \doteq P_i/\pi = K_i \tag{2}$$

where p_i = partial pressure of i

P_i = saturated vapor pressure of i

x_i = mole fraction of i in the liquid phase

y_i = mole fraction of i in the vapor phase

π = total (vapor) pressure of the system

K_i = vapor-liquid equilibrium constant for i at the temperature and pressure of the system

The above equation, usually referred to as the Raoult's Law relation, is true only for ideal systems, as defined above. However, it is usually a good approximation for mixtures of homologues and, in general, for mixtures of chemically similar compounds, if none of the saturated vapors at the equilibrium temperature deviate too greatly from a perfect gas.

Up to moderate pressures (several atmospheres) hydrocarbon mixtures frequently fall within the scope of the Raoult's Law relation. However, its application to these mixtures is rather limited because of the wide differences usually encountered between the boiling points of the most volatile and least volatile components. This results in equilibrium temperatures at which the saturated vapors of the lowest boiling components deviate considerably from a perfect gas, even though the equilibrium pressure of the system may be relatively low.

[1] Gamson and Watson, *Nat. Petroleum News, Technical Section* **36**, R-258 (1944).

Fugacity Functions

In order to improve the accuracy in predicting vapor-liquid equilibrium constants for hydrocarbons at higher pressures, Lewis and Luke[2] and other investigators replaced the pressures in equations (1) and (2) by analogous fugacities for any component, i, whereby:

$$f_i = f_{Pi}x_i = f_{\pi i}y_i \tag{3}$$

or
$$y_i/x_i = f_{Pi}/f_{\pi i} = K_i \tag{4}$$

where f_i = fugacity of i in either phase of the system

$\quad f_{Pi}$ = fugacity of i as a pure saturated liquid (or vapor) at its vapor pressure corresponding to the equilibrium temperature of the system

$\quad f_{\pi i}$ = fugacity of i as a pure vapor at the equilibrium temperature and pressure of the system

Generalized correlations have been developed for the ratio of fugacity to pressure for pure hydrocarbons as a function of reduced temperature and reduced pressure. A correlation of this type (pages 62 and 63) was used in conjunction with the vapor pressure charts to develop the fugacity function charts for individual hydrocarbons.[3] The fugacity function given by these charts, $\pi f_P/f_\pi$, may be considered a corrected vapor pressure and used in place of the latter in any equation pertaining to liquid-vapor equilibrium such as equations (1) and (2).

These simple fugacity relations greatly extend the pressure range for which liquid-vapor equilibria for hydrocarbon systems may be predicted with confidence, and can be used up to equilibrium pressures of 20 to 25 atm with a fair degree of accuracy. Beyond these pressures and especially as the critical point of the mixture is approached, serious deviations from true equilibrium conditions are encountered. Under these circumstances, the assumptions of ideal mixtures no longer hold and the fugacities of the individual compounds are dependent upon the compositions of the liquid and vapor phases as well as temperature and pressure.

In the region where the simple fugacity relations no longer apply and consequently beyond the scope of the present charts, there are data in the literature on a number of specific binary and multicomponent hydrocarbon systems. Also, The M. W. Kellogg Co.[4] has published an excellent correlation for light paraffin and olefin hydrocarbons in which the fugacities of the individual compounds are given as a function of the molal average boiling points of the liquid and vapor

[2] Lewis and Luke, *Trans. Am. Soc. Mech. Engrs.* **54**, 55 (1932).

[3] This method was actually used only up to the critical temperature of each compound. Beyond this point values were calculated from more general fugacity correlations developed by The M. W. Kellogg Co. to avoid using extrapolated vapor pressure curves.

[4] "Liquid-Vapor Equilibria in Mixtures of Light Hydrocarbons," The M. W. Kellogg Co., New York, N. Y. (1950).

phases in addition to the equilibrium temperature and pressure. The Kellogg correlation was derived from the application of exact thermodynamic relations to a comprehensive equation of state for pure hydrocarbon vapors and liquids and their mixtures.[5]

If, in addition to hydrocarbon vapors, other gases (air, H_2, CO_2, etc.) are present in the vapor phase, it is recommended that an effective pressure, equal to the product of the total pressure multiplied by the square root of the mole fraction of the entire hydrocarbon portion of the vapor, or $\pi\sqrt{y_{HC}}$, be used in determining the fugacities of the individual hydrocarbons. Fragmentary data have indicated that this effective pressure gives better results than either the total pressure, π, or partial hydrocarbon pressure, πy_{HC}, for determining individual fugacities. Then, after the fugacities or fugacity functions have been read from the charts, the total pressure is again used as a basis for all equilibrium calculations. The following example illustrates the application of the fugacity function charts when other gases are present in the vapor phase:

Example 1. Determine the pressure and composition of the liquid phase in equilibrium with a vapor of the following composition at 90°F:

Component	Vapor Mole Fract.	1st Trial $\pi = 25$ atm $\pi_e = 21.5$ atm		2nd Trial $\pi = 20$ atm $\pi_e = 17.2$ atm		Interpolation $\pi = 21.8$ atm
		F, atm	x	F, atm	x	x
Air	0.040	*	—	*	—	—
H_2	.220	*	—	*	—	—
CH_4	.280	180	0.039	180	0.031	0.034
C_2H_6	.175	38.0	.115	36.0	.097	.104
C_3H_8	.160	13.5	.296	12.7	.252	.269
C_4H_{10}	.125	4.9	.637	4.4	.568	.593
	1.000		1.087		0.948	1.000

* In this example, the fugacity functions of air and H_2 are considered to be infinite.

where π = total equilibrium pressure

$\pi_e = \pi\sqrt{0.740}$ = effective pressure used to determine fugacity functions

$F = \pi f_P/f_\pi$ = fugacity function for pure hydrocarbons

$x = \pi y/F$

Relative Volatility

Since relative volatility is quite useful in fractionation problems, curves for the relative volatilities of light unsaturates and isoparaffins to the corresponding normal paraffins are given on pages 64 to 66. The curves for the C_4 unsaturates

[5] Benedict, Webb and Rubin, *J. Chem. Phys.* **8**, 334 (1940); **10**, 7474 (1942).

may also be used in conjunction with the normal butane fugacity chart to predict fugacity functions for these compounds.

Except for butadiene and the normal butenes, these relative volatility curves were derived from the Kellogg fugacity correlation. Composition was indirectly taken into account to some extent since the fugacities for each pair of compounds were read at the same liquid and vapor molal average boiling points as well as at the same temperatures and pressures.

In general, the relative volatility charts may be considered to have a somewhat greater range of applicability than the simple fugacity charts. They may be used up to 25 atm, irrespective of the composition of the liquid and vapor phases of the mixture; beyond this pressure their application is limited to systems in which there is a difference of at least 75°F between the molal average boiling points of the two phases, but under no circumstances should the curves be extrapolated. While all of the curves may be considered to be accurate within 25% for *the relative volatility minus one* ($\alpha - 1$), deviations from the solid curves rarely exceed 15% for this difference.

Chemical Structure and Liquid Activity Coefficients

When components in a hydrocarbon mixture are quite dissimilar chemically, the liquid phase may deviate appreciably from an ideal solution. This effect of chemical structure is not taken into account in any of the fugacity correlations heretofore considered. It has been mentioned that in correlations of the Kellogg type, fugacity is a function of the liquid and vapor compositions, but only with respect to components of similar chemical structure.

To correct for chemical dissimilarity in solutions of light hydrocarbons in absorber oils, liquid activity coefficients are given for these light hydrocarbons on page 67. Within the range of the data these activity coefficients were practically independent of temperature (100°F and 220°F) and pressure (500 psia and 1000 psia).

GENERAL REFERENCES

Brown, Souders and Smith, *Ind. Eng. Chem.* **24,** 513 (1932).
Dean and Tooke, *Ind. Eng. Chem.* **38,** 389 (1946).
Hadden, *Chem. Eng. Progress* **44,** 37 (1948).
Kay, *Chem. Revs.* **29,** 501 (1941).
Lewis, *Ind. Eng. Chem.* **28,** 257 (1936).
Lewis and Kay, *Oil and Gas J.* **32,** 40 (1934).
Lewis and Randall, "Thermodynamics," pp. 190–198, McGraw-Hill Book Co. (1923).
Nelson and Bonnell, *Ind. Eng. Chem.* **35,** 204 (1943).
Sage and Lacey, *Ind. Eng. Chem.* **30,** 1296 (1938).

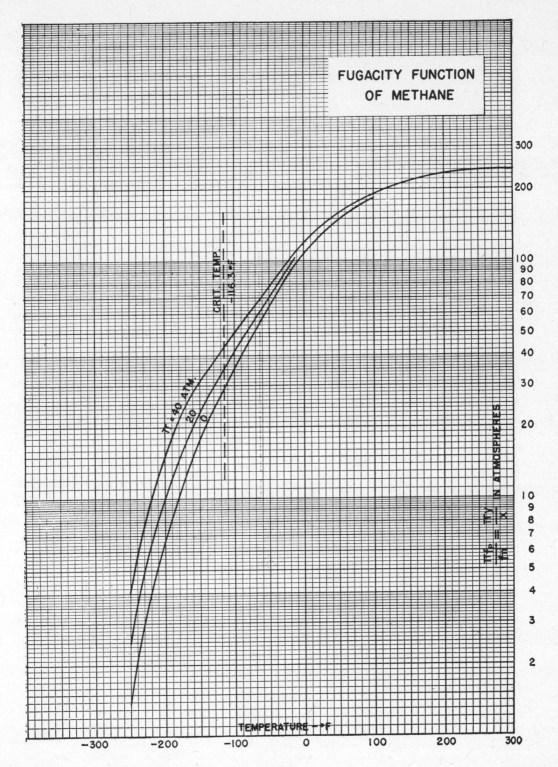

FUGACITY FUNCTION
OF METHANE

CRIT. TEMP. -116.3°F

$\pi = 40$ ATM.
20
0

$\dfrac{fugacity}{x} = \dfrac{f}{\pi}$ IN ATMOSPHERES

TEMPERATURE →°F

-300   -200   -100   0   100   200   300

49

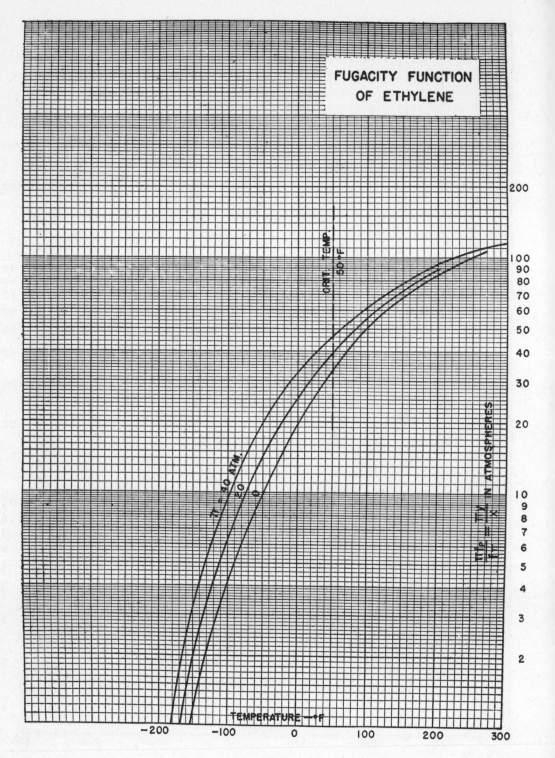

FUGACITY FUNCTION
OF ETHYLENE

TEMPERATURE —°F

CRIT. TEMP.
50°F

$\frac{\pi p}{f} = \frac{\pi v}{x}$, IN ATMOSPHERES

$\pi = 40$ ATM.

20

0

200
100
90
80
70
60
50
40
30
20
10
9
8
7
6
5
4
3
2

-200   -100   0   100   200   300

50

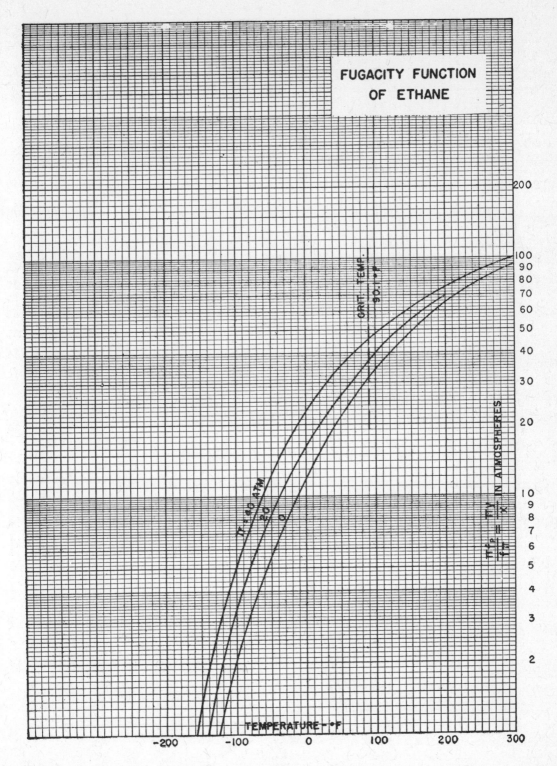

FUGACITY FUNCTION
OF ETHANE

CRIT. TEMP.
90.1°F

$\dfrac{\pi f_p}{f_m} = \dfrac{f_y}{x}$ IN ATMOSPHERES

$\pi = 40$ ATM
2.0
0

TEMPERATURE - °F

-200   -100   0   100   200   300

200
100
90
80
70
60
50
40
30
20
10
9
8
7
6
5
4
3
2

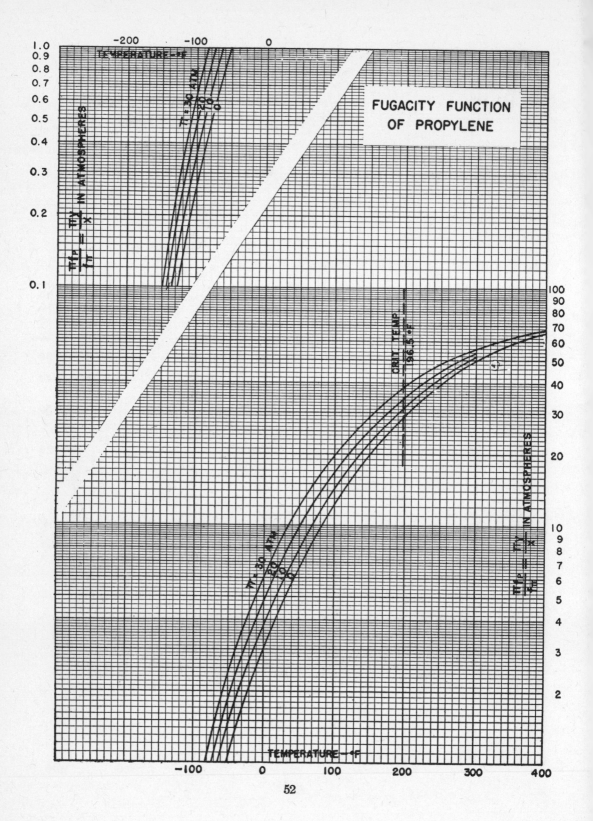

FUGACITY FUNCTION
OF PROPYLENE

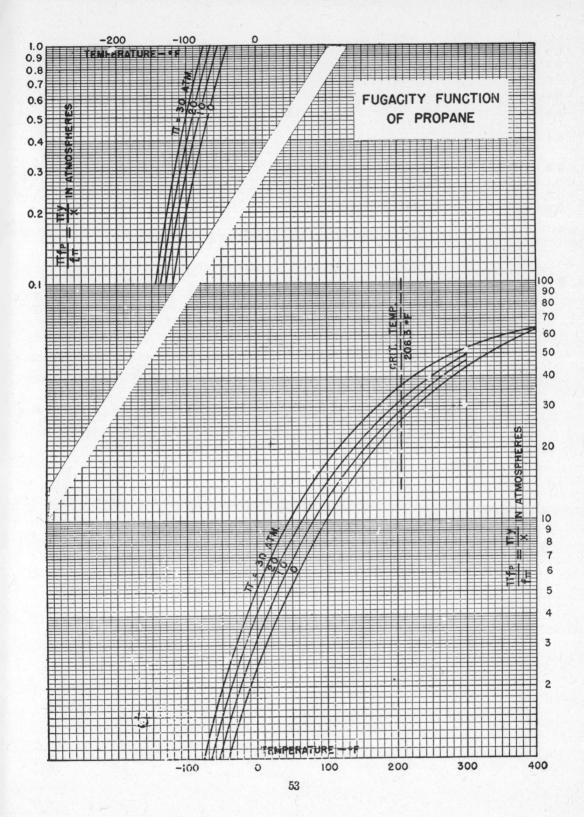

FUGACITY FUNCTION OF PROPANE

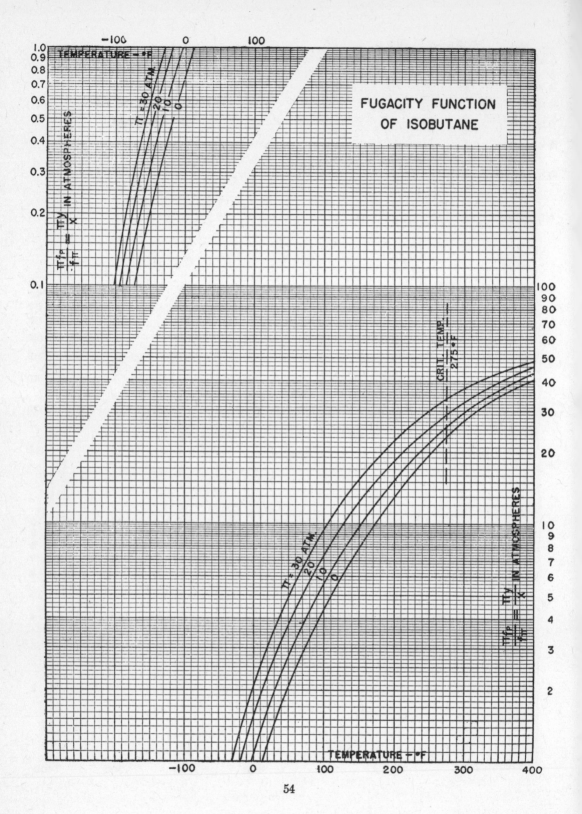

FUGACITY FUNCTION
OF ISOBUTANE

54

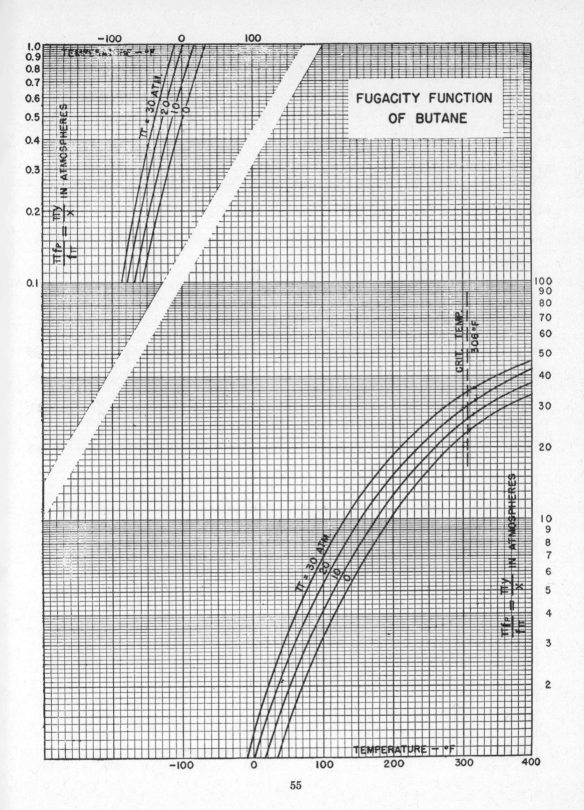

FUGACITY FUNCTION
OF BUTANE

TEMPERATURE — °F

$\dfrac{\pi f_p}{f_\pi} = \dfrac{\pi y}{x}$ IN ATMOSPHERES

$\pi = 30$ ATM

20

10

0

CRIT. TEMP.
306°F

$\dfrac{\pi f_p}{f_\pi} = \dfrac{\pi y}{x}$ IN ATMOSPHERES

55

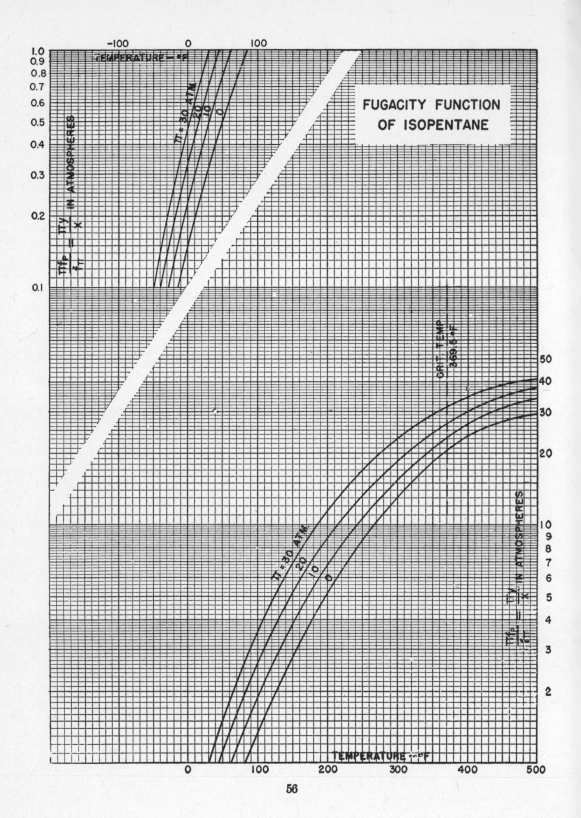

FUGACITY FUNCTION OF ISOPENTANE

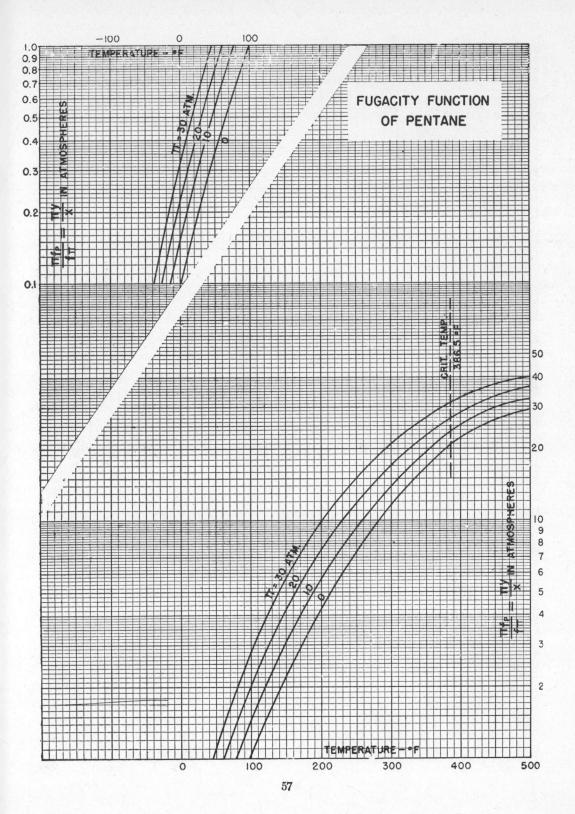

FUGACITY FUNCTION
OF PENTANE

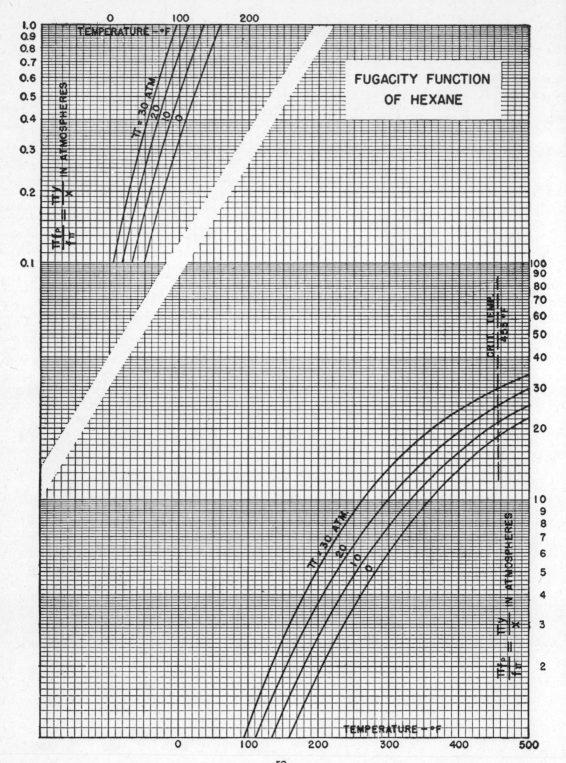

FUGACITY FUNCTION
OF HEXANE

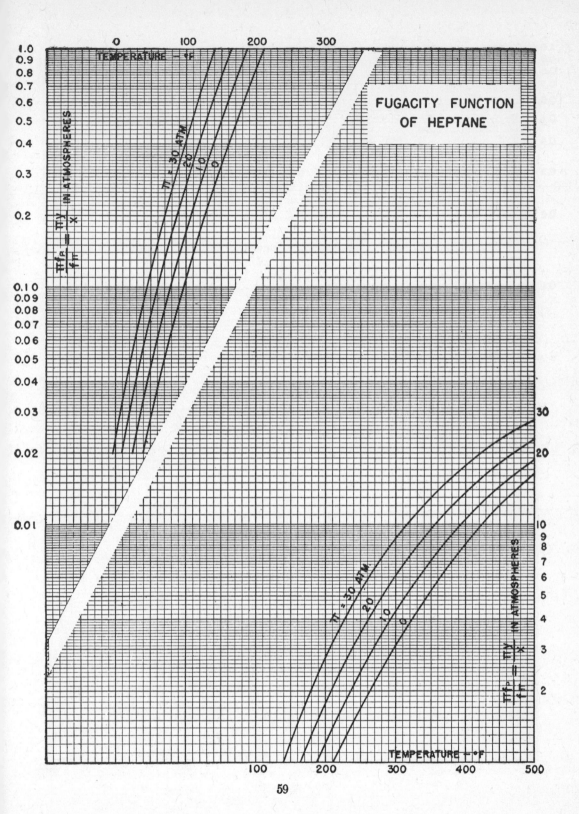

FUGACITY FUNCTION
OF HEPTANE

TEMPERATURE — °F

$\dfrac{\pi f_P}{f_\pi} = \dfrac{\pi y}{x}$ IN ATMOSPHERES

$\pi = 30$ ATM
20
10
0

$\pi = 30$ ATM
20
10
0

$\dfrac{\pi f_P}{f_\pi} = \dfrac{\pi y}{x}$ IN ATMOSPHERES

TEMPERATURE — °F

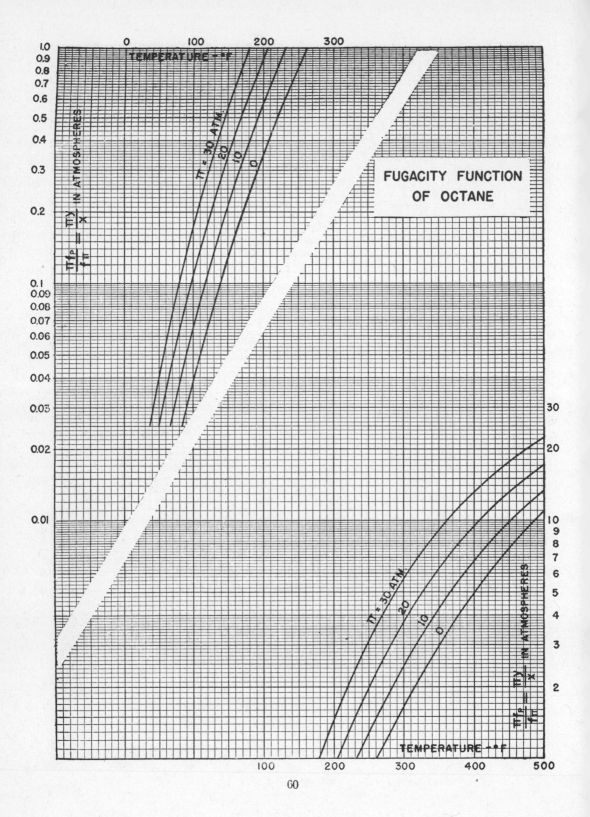

FUGACITY FUNCTION OF OCTANE

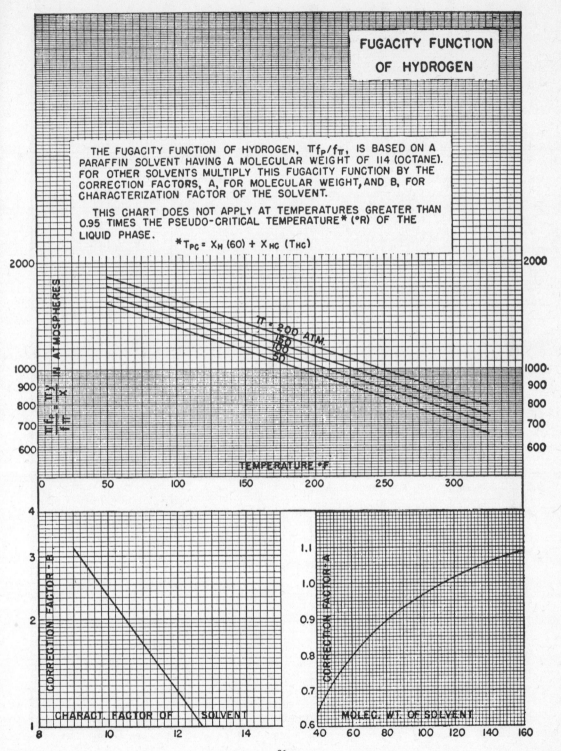

FUGACITY FUNCTION OF HYDROGEN

THE FUGACITY FUNCTION OF HYDROGEN, $\pi f_P / f_\pi$, IS BASED ON A PARAFFIN SOLVENT HAVING A MOLECULAR WEIGHT OF 114 (OCTANE). FOR OTHER SOLVENTS MULTIPLY THIS FUGACITY FUNCTION BY THE CORRECTION FACTORS, A, FOR MOLECULAR WEIGHT, AND B, FOR CHARACTERIZATION FACTOR OF THE SOLVENT.

THIS CHART DOES NOT APPLY AT TEMPERATURES GREATER THAN 0.95 TIMES THE PSEUDO-CRITICAL TEMPERATURE* (°R) OF THE LIQUID PHASE.

$*T_{PC} = X_H (60) + X_{HC} (T_{HC})$

$\frac{\pi f_P}{f_\pi} = \frac{\pi \gamma}{X}$, IN ATMOSPHERES

$\pi = 800$ ATM.
150
100
50

TEMPERATURE °F

CORRECTION FACTOR-B

CHARACT. FACTOR OF SOLVENT

CORRECTION FACTOR-A

MOLEC. WT. OF SOLVENT

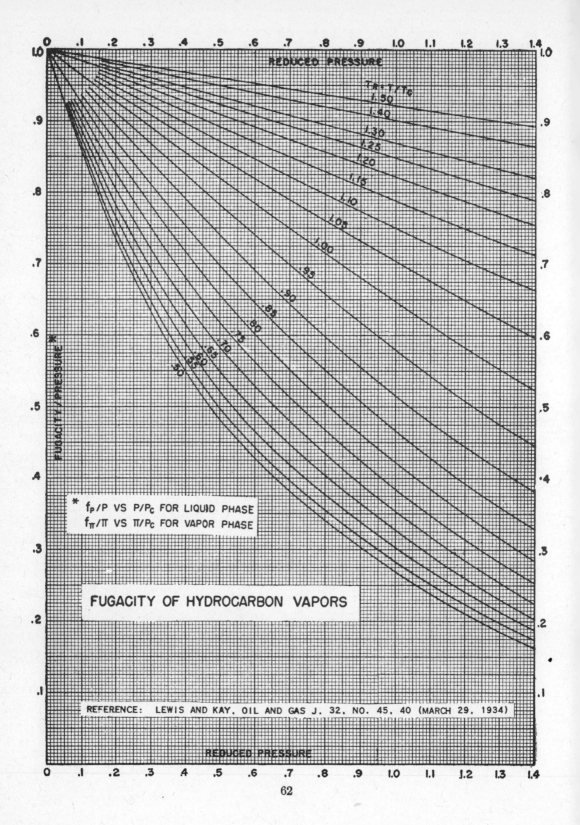

FUGACITY OF HYDROCARBON VAPORS

* f_P/P VS P/P_C FOR LIQUID PHASE
f_π/π VS π/P_C FOR VAPOR PHASE

REFERENCE: LEWIS AND KAY, OIL AND GAS J. 32, NO. 45, 40 (MARCH 29, 1934)

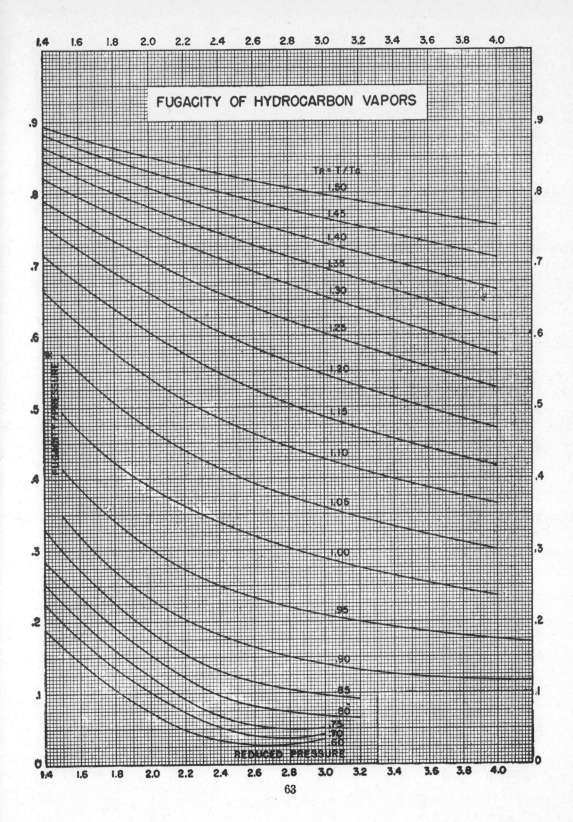

FUGACITY OF HYDROCARBON VAPORS

$T_R = T/T_C$

1.50
1.45
1.40
1.35
1.30
1.25
1.20
1.15
1.10
1.05
1.00
.95
.90
.85
.80
.75
.70
.60

FUGACITY PRESSURE

REDUCED PRESSURE

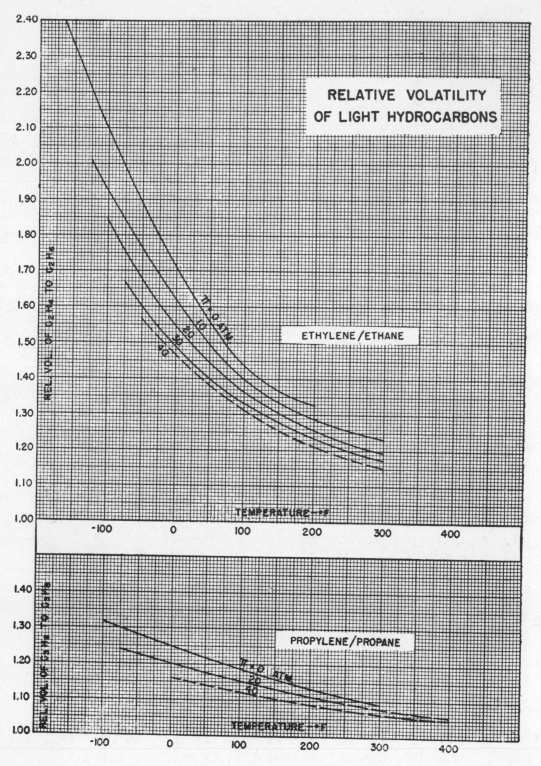

RELATIVE VOLATILITY
OF LIGHT HYDROCARBONS

ETHYLENE/ETHANE

PROPYLENE/PROPANE

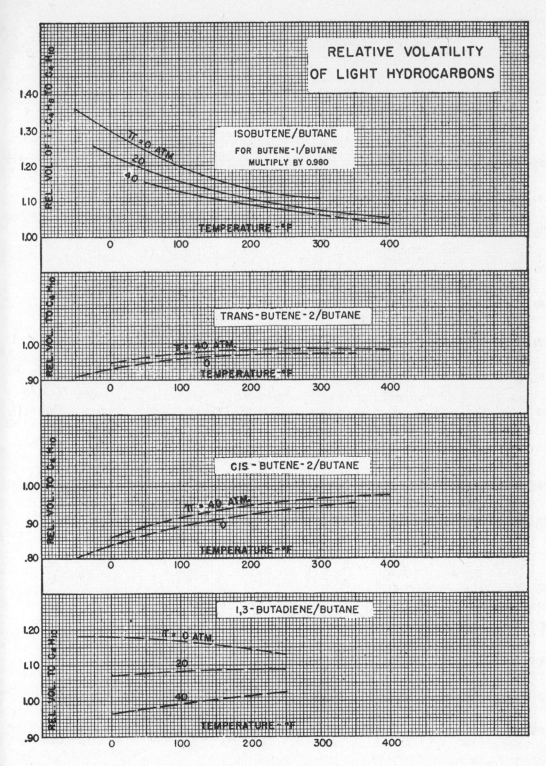

RELATIVE VOLATILITY OF LIGHT HYDROCARBONS

ISOBUTENE/BUTANE
FOR BUTENE-1/BUTANE
MULTIPLY BY 0.980

TRANS-BUTENE-2/BUTANE

CIS-BUTENE-2/BUTANE

1,3-BUTADIENE/BUTANE

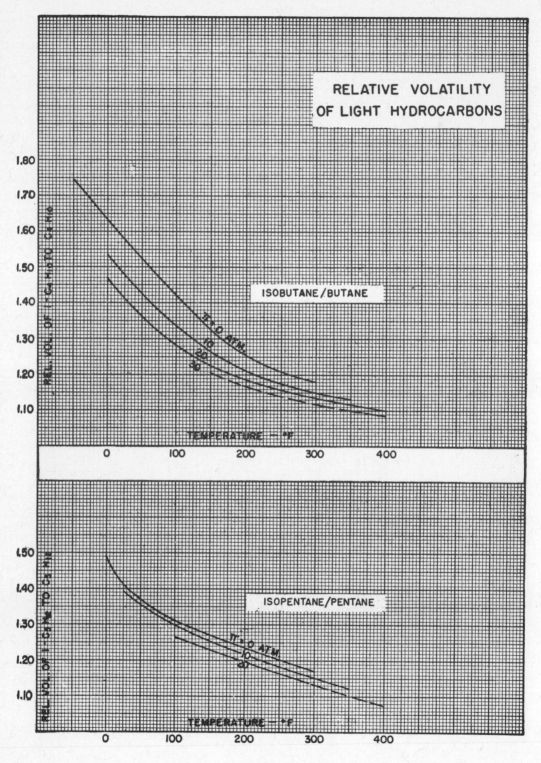

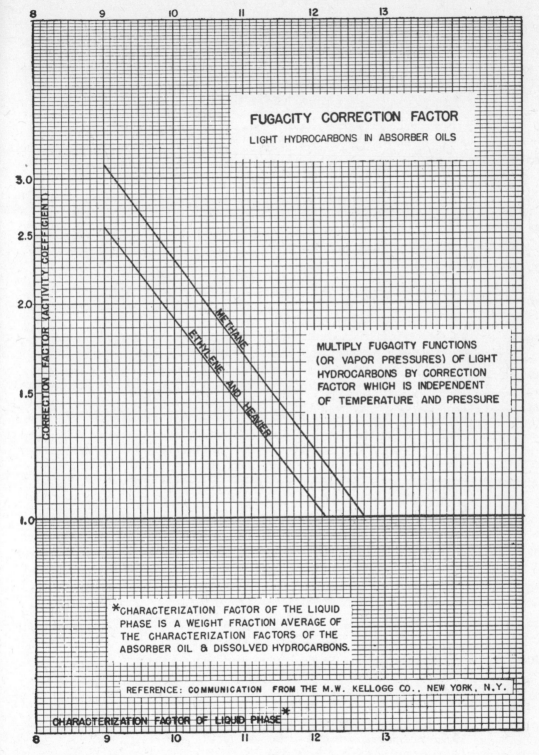

Section 6
CRITICAL PROPERTIES

Analogous to pure substances, the true critical point of a mixture is a unique point on the phase envelope where the density and composition of the vapor phase are identical with those of the liquid phase. Since the compositions of the two phases are the same, fractionation of a mixture is impossible at the critical point. Consequently, the degree of approach to the critical point of a mixture sometimes serves as a rough guide to the feasibility of separating the components by fractionation.

For pure hydrocarbons, it has been found that a number of physical properties may be correlated by reduced temperature, T/T_c, and reduced pressure, P/P_c. Various data have shown conclusively that none of these correlations apply to mixtures if the true critical temperature and pressure of the mixture are used to determine the reduced conditions. This difficulty has been overcome by the introduction by Kay[1] of the concept of pseudo-critical temperature and pressure. By using the pseudo-critical temperature and pressure to predict the reduced conditions, Kay found that compressibility data on pure hydrocarbons could be applied to mixtures. Although Kay determined the pseudo-critical point by averaging the critical properties directly for known mixtures and from the average molecular weight for petroleum fractions, it has been found that much better results can be obtained by using the average boiling point method proposed by Smith and Watson.[2]

As Smith and Watson pointed out, the true and pseudo-critical points must approach each other as the boiling range of a fraction approaches zero and must coincide for pure compounds. These conditions are fulfilled by the charts in this section applying to petroleum fractions. Smith and Watson's relation between the true and pseudo-critical pressures on page 74 has been checked by the true critical data of Kay on ethane-heptane[3] and ethane-butane[4] systems. These data confirm Smith and Watson's curve well into the region of their recommended extrapolation.

GENERAL REFERENCES

Doss, "Physical Properties of the Principal Hydrocarbons," 4th Edition, The Texas Co., New York, N.Y. (1943).
International Critical Tables, Vol. III.
Roess, *J. Inst. Petr. Tech.* **22**, 665 (1936).

[1] Kay, *Ind. Eng. Chem.* **28**, 1014 (1936).
[2] Smith and Watson, *Ind. Eng. Chem.* **29**, 1408 (1937).
[3] Kay, *Ind. Eng. Chem.* **30**, 459 (1938).
[4] Kay, *Ind. Eng. Chem.* **32**, 353 (1940).

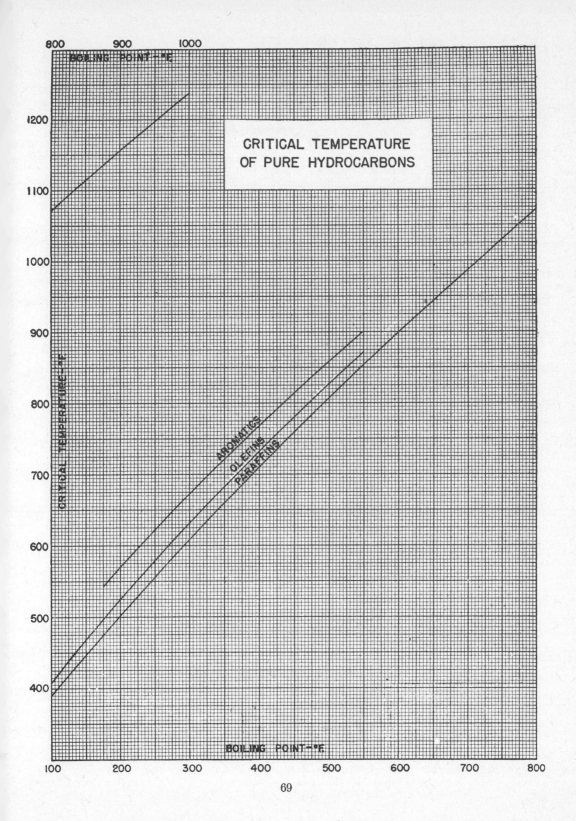

CRITICAL TEMPERATURE
OF PURE HYDROCARBONS

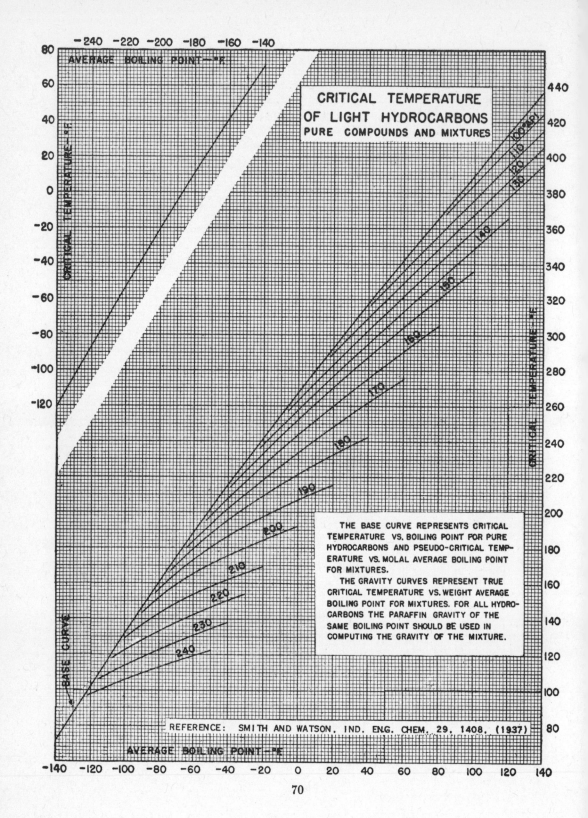

CRITICAL TEMPERATURE
OF LIGHT HYDROCARBONS
PURE COMPOUNDS AND MIXTURES

THE BASE CURVE REPRESENTS CRITICAL
TEMPERATURE VS. BOILING POINT FOR PURE
HYDROCARBONS AND PSEUDO-CRITICAL TEMP-
ERATURE VS. MOLAL AVERAGE BOILING POINT
FOR MIXTURES.

THE GRAVITY CURVES REPRESENT TRUE
CRITICAL TEMPERATURE VS. WEIGHT AVERAGE
BOILING POINT FOR MIXTURES. FOR ALL HYDRO-
CARBONS THE PARAFFIN GRAVITY OF THE
SAME BOILING POINT SHOULD BE USED IN
COMPUTING THE GRAVITY OF THE MIXTURE.

REFERENCE: SMITH AND WATSON, IND. ENG. CHEM, 29, 1408, (1937)

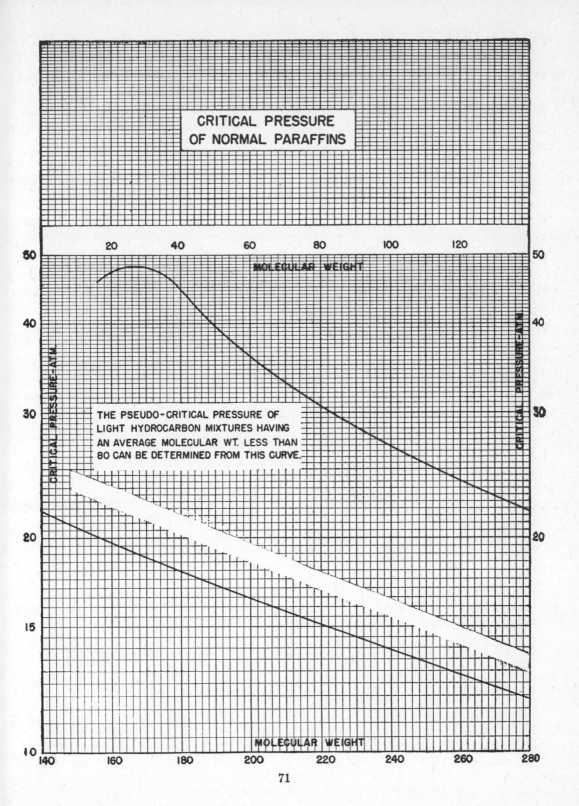

CRITICAL PRESSURE
OF NORMAL PARAFFINS

MOLECULAR WEIGHT

CRITICAL PRESSURE-ATM.

CRITICAL PRESSURE-ATM

THE PSEUDO-CRITICAL PRESSURE OF
LIGHT HYDROCARBON MIXTURES HAVING
AN AVERAGE MOLECULAR WT. LESS THAN
80 CAN BE DETERMINED FROM THIS CURVE.

MOLECULAR WEIGHT

71

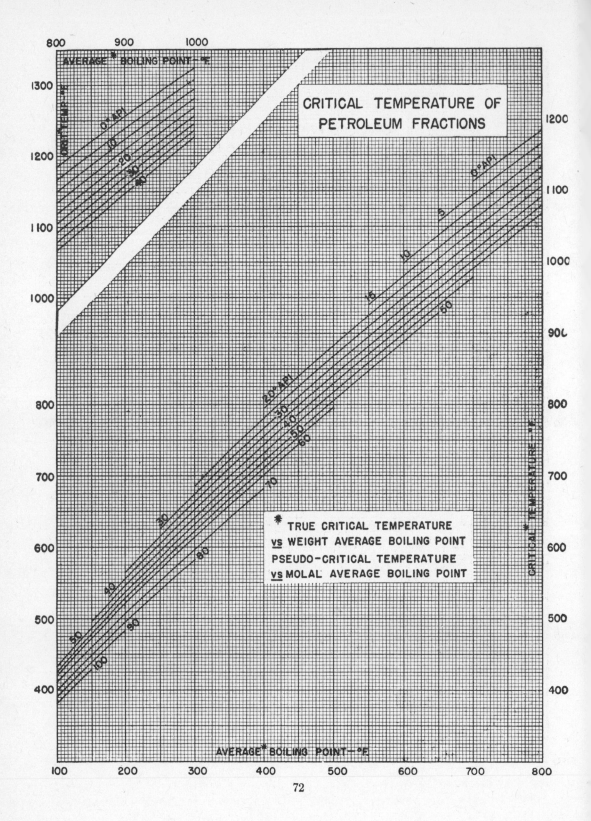

CRITICAL TEMPERATURE OF
PETROLEUM FRACTIONS

* TRUE CRITICAL TEMPERATURE
vs WEIGHT AVERAGE BOILING POINT
PSEUDO-CRITICAL TEMPERATURE
vs MOLAL AVERAGE BOILING POINT

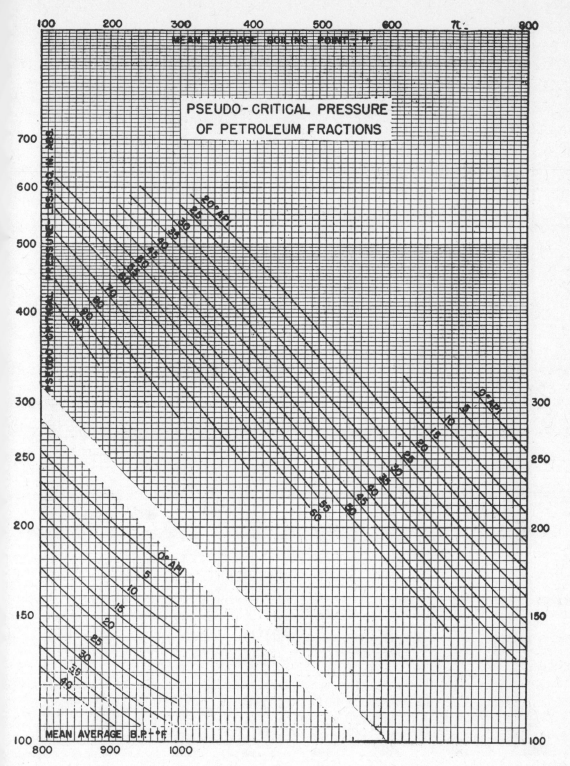

PSEUDO-CRITICAL PRESSURE
OF PETROLEUM FRACTIONS

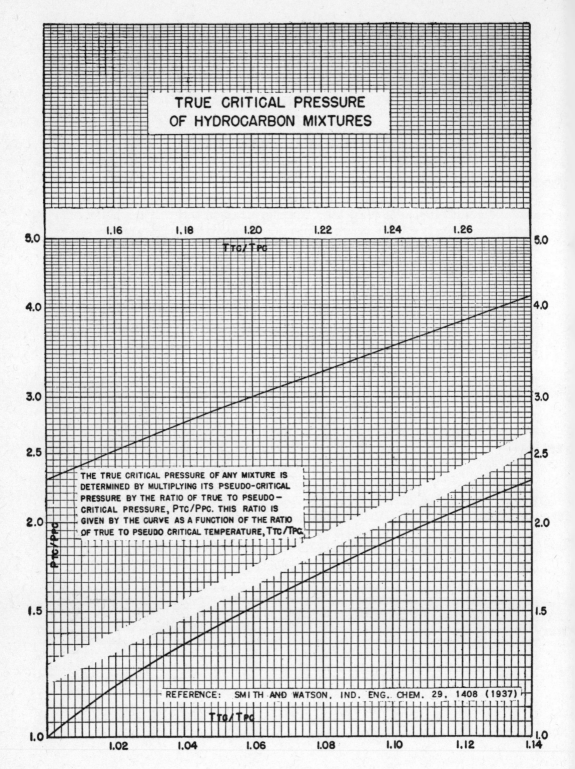

TRUE CRITICAL PRESSURE
OF HYDROCARBON MIXTURES

THE TRUE CRITICAL PRESSURE OF ANY MIXTURE IS
DETERMINED BY MULTIPLYING ITS PSEUDO-CRITICAL
PRESSURE BY THE RATIO OF TRUE TO PSEUDO-
CRITICAL PRESSURE, P_{TC}/P_{PC}. THIS RATIO IS
GIVEN BY THE CURVE AS A FUNCTION OF THE RATIO
OF TRUE TO PSEUDO CRITICAL TEMPERATURE, T_{TC}/T_{PC}.

REFERENCE: SMITH AND WATSON, IND. ENG. CHEM. 29, 1408 (1937)

74

Section 7

THERMAL PROPERTIES

Specific Heat

Since hydrocarbon vapors deviate considerably from a perfect gas, except at low pressures, their specific heats are a function of pressure as well as temperature. However, vapor specific heats at higher pressures have limited application as enthalpy correlations may be more readily used for thermal calculations. For this reason, the specific heat charts for gases and vapors (pages 88 to 91) are given only for low pressures (0–1 atm) where deviations from a perfect gas are so small that specific heat may be considered to be a function of temperature alone. The specific heat of a mixture of two or more gases at low pressures may be calculated from either their weight fractions multiplied by their specific heats or their mole fractions by their molal heat capacities (MC_p).

Two charts are given for the specific heat of petroleum vapors, one on page 90 for crude fractions and another on page 91 of more general application to both pure hydrocarbons and petroleum fractions.[1] The chart for crude fractions is a modification of the Bahlke and Kay correlation[2] and the other the same type as a chart developed by Fallon and Watson.[3] Both charts are believed to be somewhat more accurate than the previous correlations and are also representative of additional data.

The change in enthalpy of hydrocarbon vapors with pressure at constant temperature may be calculated from the chart on page 92. While the ordinate refers to the difference in enthalpy from the vapor at infinite dilution, this may be construed as any low pressure (0–1 atm). This chart was used to compute the enthalpy of hydrocarbon[4] and petroleum vapors at elevated pressures in the development of the enthalpy charts. Since the change in enthalpy at constant

[1] These correlations for petroleum fractions are not quite consistent with the additive rule for mixtures. Since these curves apply directly to mixtures, the additive rule would hold only if the specific heats either were independent of the liquid specific gravity or varied linearly with its reciprocal (directly with °API). With neither of these conditions fulfilled, the petroleum vapor correlations have a fundamental inconsistency but the resulting errors are imperceptible as far as the data are concerned.

[2] Bahlke and Kay, *Ind. Eng. Chem.* **21**, 942 (1929).

[3] Fallon and Watson, *Nat. Petroleum News, Technical Section*, R-372 (1944).

[4] For the light hydrocarbons below hexane, there was a slight trend with molecular weight in the change of enthalpy with pressure at constant temperature. This was taken into account by the use of other unpublished correlations by Gilliland (see reference on the chart on page 92) for these low-boiling hydrocarbons.

temperature can be read directly from the latter charts, this generalized chart has little direct application but is included as one of the fundamental correlations.

The chart for the specific heat of hydrocarbon liquids was developed[5] directly from liquid specific heat data on pure hydrocarbons and petroleum fractions. Since liquid specific heats were not used in the development of the enthalpy charts, this chart is independent of and not necessarily consistent with the latter correlations.[6] For the sake of consistency, the enthalpy charts usually will be used in preference to this specific heat chart but, at the same time, it is desirable to include an independent correlation of such a fundamental thermal property.

Latent Heat of Vaporization

The latent heat of vaporization of any compound is the difference in enthalpy between its saturated vapor and its saturated liquid at constant temperature and may be expressed either as a function of temperature or as a function of vapor pressure. The latent heats of low-boiling hydrocarbons and, also, higher-boiling normal paraffins of even boiling point are plotted against vapor pressure on pages 94 to 97. While the use of temperature instead of vapor pressure as the correlating variable would have advantages, it would also result in the curves crossing each other, thus making the plots difficult to read.

The latent heat charts were derived by using a direct proportionality between the molal heats of vaporization of any two hydrocarbons at the same reduced pressures.[7] For the lower boiling hydrocarbons, the latent heat data were smoothed out and extrapolated by the use of a reference compound (ethane, butane, or hexane). Where no data were available, as in the case of a few of the light hydrocarbons and all of the higher-boiling normal paraffins, the latent heats were calculated directly from this reduced pressure relationship. The slope or proportionality constant was predicted from the normal boiling point of the hydrocarbon.

The latent heat of vaporization of other hydrocarbons may be calculated from the normal paraffin curves by the use of this same relation. That is, the unknown compound will have the same molal heat of vaporization as a paraffin of the same normal boiling point at the same reduced pressure. In the case of petroleum fractions, the mean average boiling point is used for the normal boiling point and the reduced pressure is computed from the pseudo-critical pressure of the mixture. The "vapor pressure" of the fraction corresponds to that of a pure

[5] A modification of a correlation by The M. W. Kellogg Co., New York, N.Y.

[6] The enthalpy charts were derived from: (1) the vapor specific heat correlations (0-1 atm); (2) the generalized chart for change of enthalpy with pressure; and (3) the latent heat relations. Inasmuch as the inaccuracies of all three correlations accumulate in the liquid enthalpies or specific heats, the agreement with the liquid specific heat chart may be considered quite good as average deviations between the two are around ±3% with a maximum of about 6%.

[7] Maxwell, *Ind. Eng. Chem.* **24**, 502 (1932).

hydrocarbon of the same normal boiling point at the temperature of the fraction and *never refers to the bubble point, dew point, or operating pressure of the system.*

Since the difference in enthalpy between the liquid and the saturated vapor of a petroleum fraction always involves change of enthalpy of the vapor at constant temperature in addition to latent heat, except at low pressures, the enthalpy correlations are much more convenient to use than these individual thermal properties.

The following examples illustrate the use of the latent heat charts:

Example 1. Compute the latent heat of benzene at 1 atm.

The boiling point of benzene is 176.2°F and its critical pressure is 47.9 atm. The molecular weight of a normal paraffin boiling at 176.2°F is 91.5 and its critical pressure 28.3 atm. The vapor pressure of the normal paraffin corresponding to a reduced pressure of 1/47.9 (= 0.0209) is 0.0209 × 28.3 = 0.59 atm.

The molal heat of vaporization of the normal paraffin at 0.59 atm is 91.5 × (146 BTU/lb) = 13,360 BTU/mole.

The latent heat of benzene at 1 atm is then equal to 13,360 BTU/mole or 171 BTU/lb. *The Bureau of Standards Circular C461* gives 169.3 BTU/lb as the latent heat of vaporization of benzene at 1 atm.

Example 2. Determine the latent heat of vaporization of the following gas oil at 500°F.

10% Distillation	Gravity
10% @ 430°F	35°API
50% @ 540°F	
70% @ 605°F	
90% @ 680°F	

Vol. Av. B.P. = 547°F; Slope = 2.9°F/%
Mean Av. B.P. = 547 − 9 = 538°F
Molec. wt.   = 214
Vapor pressure (538°F normal B.P.) = 0.63 atm. at 500°F
Pseudo-critical pressure = 266 psia ≈ 18.1 atm

Molec. wt. of normal paraffin (538°F normal B.P.) = 222
Critical pressure of normal paraffin = 15.0 atm
Vapor pressure of normal paraffin = (15.0/18.1)0.63 = 0.52 atm
Latent heat of normal paraffin = 104 BTU/lb

Latent heat of vaporization of the gas oil at 500°F

$$= \frac{222 \times 104}{214} = 108 \ BTU/lb$$

Enthalpy of Light Hydrocarbons

The enthalpy[8] or heat content of low-boiling paraffins, olefins, and aromatics is given by the charts on pages 98 to 113. These charts can be applied to mixtures of light hydrocarbons on the basis of the following assumptions:

1. The enthalpies of individual components of a mixture are additive in the liquid phase, that is, the molal heat content of the mixture equals the sum of the products of the molal heat contents of the components by their mole fractions.

2. The enthalpies of individual components are additive in the vapor phase at low pressures (0–1 atm).

3. The change in enthalpy of the vapor with pressure at constant temperature is the same for a mixture as for a single compound having the same molecular weight as the mixture.

The first assumption is substantially true for hydrocarbon mixtures (especially for homologous series) at temperatures below the critical regions of all components. At temperatures near to or above the critical temperatures of any of the components, the liquid mixture is no longer an ideal solution of its components and there is some deviation from the rule of additive heat contents. However, since these deviations are not too serious, and since no other simple method has been developed for determining the heat content of a liquid mixture, the rule of additive enthalpies should be used for all hydrocarbon mixtures irrespective of the critical temperatures and chemical composition of the components.

The second assumption is strictly true only for vapor mixtures at infinite dilution (0 atm) but is a very close approximation for pressures up to 1 atm.

The third assumption is empirical but has been shown indirectly to give quite accurate results for mixtures of homologous series and petroleum fractions. Also, the use of the average molecular weight to determine the change of enthalpy with pressure is the simplest average which can be used.

Above the critical temperature a dashed line is shown for the heat content of the gas in solution. This line was based on the assumption that the gas in solution at any temperature would have the same partial density and enthalpy as the pure compound at a pressure corresponding to an extrapolation of its vapor pressure curve above the critical point. Obviously, this is only a rough approximation since both a vapor pressure curve and an ideal liquid solution are meaningless in this region.

Example 3. Determine the difference in enthalpy between the liquid at 100°F and the vapor at 500°F and 20 atm for a mixture having the following composition:

[8] Based on an enthalpy of zero for the saturated liquid at −200°F.

Component	Mole Fraction
C_2H_6	0.100
C_3H_8	.500
C_4H_{10}	.100
C_2H_4	.050
C_3H_6	.250
	1.000

The enthalpy of the mixture as a liquid at 100°F and as a vapor at 500°F and 0–1 atm is computed from the individual components as tabulated below:

Component	Mole Fract.	Molec. Wt. Lb/Mole of Mixture	Enthalpy of Liquid 100°F		Enthalpy of Vapor 500°F and 0–1 atm	
			BTU/lb	BTU/Mole of Mixture	BTU/lb	BTU/Mole of Mixture
C_2H_6	0.100	3.0	239	720	553	1660
C_3H_8	.500	22.0	171	3760	530	11660
C_4H_{10}	.100	5.8	159	920	525	3040
C_2H_4	.050	1.4	223	310	506	710
C_3H_6	.250	10.5	169	1770	508	5330
		42.7		7480		22400

$$H_V(500°F, 0\text{–}1 \text{ atm}) - H_L = 22,400 - 7480 = 14,920 \text{ BTU/mole}$$

The change of enthalpy of the vapor at 500°F between 0–1 atm. and 20 atm. is computed by interpolating between C_2H_6 and C_3H_8:

C_2H_6:
$$H_V(500°F, 20 \text{ atm}) - H_V(500°F, 0\text{–}1 \text{ atm}) = 30(546 - 553) = -210 \text{ BTU/mole}$$

C_3H_8:
$$H_V(500°F, 20 \text{ atm}) - H_V(500°F, 0\text{–}1 \text{ atm}) = 44(522 - 530) = -350 \text{ BTU/mole}$$

Mixture:
$$H_V(500°F, 20 \text{ atm}) - H_V(500°F, 0\text{–}1 \text{ atm}) = -210 + \frac{42.7 - 30}{44 - 30}[-350 - (-210)]$$
$$= -340 \text{ BTU/mole}$$

Therefore,
$$H_V(500°F, 20 \text{ atm}) - H_L(100°F) = -340 + 14,920 = 14,580 \text{ BTU/mole}$$

or
$$\frac{14,580}{42.7} = 342 \text{ BTU/lb}$$

The foregoing procedure can be simplified, with a loss of accuracy which does not usually exceed 5%, by interpolating on a basis of molecular weight and total olefin content between the initial and final states:

C_3H_8:

$$H_V(500°F, 20 \text{ atm}) - H_L(100°F) = 44(522 - 171) = 15,440 \text{ BTU/mole}$$

C_2H_4:

$$H_V(500°F, 20 \text{ atm}) - H_L(100°F) = 28(500 - 223) = 7750 \text{ BTU/mole}$$

C_3H_6:

$$H_V(500°F, 20 \text{ atm}) - H_L(100°F) = 42(500 - 169) = 13,900 \text{ BTU/mole}$$

Since the average molecular weight of the paraffin portion of the mixture is 44, the propane values can be used directly, making interpolation unnecessary.

The average molecular weight of the olefin portion is 39.7; hence the enthalpy difference between the initial and final states will be:

$$7750 + \frac{39.7 - 28}{42 - 28} (13,900 - 7750) = 12,880 \text{ BTU/mole}$$

Interpolating between the paraffin and olefin portions,

$$H_V(500°F, 20 \text{ atm}) - H_L(100°F) = 0.70 \times 15,440 + 0.30 \times 12,880$$
$$= 14,670 \text{ BTU/mole}$$

or $\quad \dfrac{14,670}{42.7} = 344 \; BTU/lb$ vs. $342 \; BTU/lb$ by the longer method.

Enthalpy of Petroleum Fractions

The enthalpy[9] of petroleum fractions is given by the charts on pages 114 to 127 for both paraffinic stocks, having a characterization factor of 12.0, and non-paraffinic stocks, having a characterization factor of 11.0 over a mean average boiling point range from 200°F to 800°F. Theoretically, these charts represent pure hydrocarbons of the designated characterization factor and boiling point, but they may be applied to petroleum fractions if the following assumption is made in addition to the three previous ones pertaining to light hydrocarbon mixtures:

4. The average difference between the enthalpy of the vapor at low pressures (0–1 atm) and the enthalpy of the liquid, at constant temperature, is the same for a mixture of chemically similar hydrocarbons as for a single compound of the same molecular weight (or mean average boiling point).

While this assumption is empirical, it is accurate within a few percent except in the region of the pseudo-critical temperature where the enthalpy of the liquid is subject to variation depending upon the true critical temperature of the mixture. Since the dashed line starting at the pseudo-critical point applies only to a pure compound in solution above its critical point, another dashed line was arbitrarily drawn for mixtures, joining the saturated liquid line below the pseudo-critical

[9] Based on an enthalpy of zero for the saturated liquid at 0°F.

point with the pure compound line about 50°F above the pseudo-critical temperature. This is more representative of a mixture and should be used in preference
to the pure compound line.

These charts may be interpolated and extrapolated linearly with both
characterization factor and mean average boiling point. Occasionally, in interpolating between two adjacent boiling point charts the pressure and temperature
of the vapor will be such that they fall inside of the "dome" of the higher boiling
point chart. Since it is impossible to use the charts in this region, it is recommended that the two adjacent lower boiling point charts be extrapolated upward.

Following are two examples illustrating the use of these charts:

Example 4. Determine the difference in enthalpy between the liquid at 500°F
and the vapor at 775°F and 25 psig for the following refined oil fraction:

Crude Assay Distillation	Gravity
I.B.P. 300°F	40°API
50% 440°F	
F.B.P. 580°F	

Vol. Av. B.P. = 440°F

Slope of the distillation curve = $\dfrac{580 - 300}{100}$ = 2.8°F/%

Mean Av. B.P. = 440 − 6 = 434°F

Characterization Factor = 11.65

h_V = Enthalpy of the vapor at 775°F and 2.7 atm (25 psig)

h_L = Enthalpy of the liquid at 500°F

Mean Av. B.P. — 400°F
  Ch. Factor = 12: $h_V - h_L$ = 567 − 286 = 281 BTU/lb
  Ch. Factor = 11: $h_V - h_L$ = 538 − 263 = 275 BTU/lb
  Ch. Factor = 11.65: $h_V - h_L$ = 275 + 0.65(281 − 275) = 279 BTU/lb

Mean Av. B.P. — 500°F
  Ch. Factor = 12: $h_V - h_L$ = 556 − 273 = 283 BTU/lb
  Ch. Factor = 11: $h_V - h_L$ = 534 − 255 = 279 BTU/lb
  Ch. Factor = 11.65: $h_V - h_L$ = 279 + 0.65(283 − 279) = 282 BTU/lb

Mean Av. B.P. — 434°F
  Ch. Factor = 11.65: $h_V - h_L$ = 279 + $\frac{34}{100}$(282 − 279) =.280 BTU/lb

If the charts for 300°F and 400°F Mean Av. B.P.'s had been extrapolated, the
result would have been essentially the same, 281 BTU/lb.

Example 5. Determine the difference in enthalpy between the liquid at 425°F
and the vapor at 925°F and 350 psig for the following gas oil:

<table>
<tr><td>10% Distillation</td><td>Gravity</td></tr>
<tr><td>10% @ 455°F</td><td>15.5°API</td></tr>
<tr><td>50% @ 560°F</td><td></td></tr>
<tr><td>70% @ 620°F</td><td></td></tr>
<tr><td>90% @ 695°F</td><td></td></tr>
</table>

$$\text{Vol. Av. B.P.} = \frac{455 + 2 \times 560 + 695}{4} = 567°F$$

$$\text{Slope of distillation curve} = \frac{620 - 455}{60} = 2.8°F/\%$$

Mean Av. B.P. = $567 - 5 = 562°F$

Characterization Factor = 10.48

h_V = Enthalpy of the vapor at 925°F and 24.8 atm (350 psig)

h_L = Enthalpy of the liquid at 425°F

Mean Av. B.P.—400°F

    Ch. Factor = 12: $h_V - h_L = 662 - 233 = 429$ BTU/lb

    Ch. Factor = 11: $h_V - h_L = 622 - 216 = 406$ BTU/lb

    Ch. Factor = 10.48: $h_V - h_L = 406 - 0.52(429 - 406) = 394$ BTU/lb

Mean Av. B.P.—500°F

    Ch. Factor = 12: $h_V - h_L = 642 - 224 = 418$ BTU/lb

    Ch. Factor = 11: $h_V - h_L = 606 - 208 = 398$ BTU/lb

    Ch. Factor = 10.48: $h_V - h_L = 398 - 0.52(418 - 398) = 388$ BTU/lb

Mean Av. B.P.—562°F

    Ch. Factor = 10.48: $h_V - h_L = 388 - \frac{62}{100}(394 - 388) = 385\ BTU/lb$

Mollier Diagrams

The Mollier diagrams for the individual light hydrocarbons are of essentially the same type as the familiar one for steam. To minimize confusion and to make the charts as easily usable as possible, lines of constant volume are omitted and lines of constant temperature replace lines of constant superheat in the superheated vapor region. These charts will be used principally for adiabatic compressions and expansions.

In applying the Mollier diagrams to hydrocarbon mixtures, the mixture should be treated as a single compound of the average molecular weight. An empirical study of the diagrams indicates that successive charts of the same series (paraffin or olefin) may be interpolated (or extrapolated) by assuming a linear relation exists between molecular weight and (1) isentropic change of *molal* enthalpy with pressure and (2) the product of the square root of the molecular weight and the isentropic change of temperature with pressure.

If both paraffins and olefins are present in the mixture, the charts of each series are interpolated (or extrapolated) to the average molecular weight of the total mixture. These values corresponding, respectively, to a 100% paraffin mixture and a 100% olefin mixture are used for linear interpolation to the actual olefin content of the mixture.

The following example illustrates the application of the Mollier diagrams to a hydrocarbon mixture:

Example 6. Determine the work of compression[10] and final temperature when the following mixture is compressed adiabatically from atmospheric pressure and 60°F to 50 psig:

Component	Mole Fraction	Average Molec. Wt.
CH_4	0.050	0.8
C_2H_4	.100	2.8
C_2H_6	.150	4.5
C_3H_6	.100	4.2
C_3H_8	.200	8.8
C_4H_8	.100	5.6
C_4H_{10}	.200	11.6
C_5H_{12}	.100	7.2
	1.000	45.5

Values corresponding to adiabatic compression from 1 atm and 60°F to 4.4 atm were read from the individual charts and are tabulated below:

Compound	S	BTU/lb		t_2 °F	$\dfrac{\Delta H}{M(h_2 - h_1)}$ BTU/mole	$\Delta t \sqrt{M}$
		h_1	h_2			
C_3H_8	0.763	301.5	338	154	1610	625
C_4H_{10}	.680	295	321	135	1510	570
C_2H_4	.935	300.5	363.5	221	1760	850
C_3H_6	.780	303	342	164	1640	675

By interpolation, $\Delta H = 1600$ BTU/mole and $\Delta t \sqrt{M} = 620$ for a saturated hydrocarbon mixture of 45.5 molec. wt.

By extrapolation, $\Delta H = 1610$ BTU/mole and $\Delta t \sqrt{M} = 632$ for an unsaturated hydrocarbon mixture of 45.5 molec. wt.

By interpolation, $\Delta H = 1603$ BTU/mole and $\Delta t \sqrt{M} = 624$ for a hydrocarbon mixture of 45.5 molec. wt. containing 30% unsaturates.

[10] Change in enthalpy which includes the difference between the work of expulsion and work of admission.

∴ The theoretical work of compression is 35.2 BTU/lb and the final temperature is 152°F.

If other gases (H_2, O_2, H_2O, etc.) are present in a mixture, it is recommended that effective pressures equal to $\pi\sqrt{y_{HC}}$ be used to determine the total work of compression and final temperature of the hydrocarbon portion of the mixture. The inert gases usually may be assumed to be ideal and the work of compression and final temperature for this portion of the mixture calculated by the adiabatic compression formulas for perfect gases. The work of compression for the mixture is then evaluated by combining the change of heat content for the hydrocarbon portion with that for the inert gases on the basis of their mole fractions. In determining the final temperature of the mixture, it is assumed that the change in enthalpy of each portion from its final temperature to that of the mixture is equal and opposite in sign to the other. This method is illustrated by the following example:

Example 7. Determine the work of compression and final temperature when the following mixture is compressed adiabatically from 25 psig and 0°F to 150 psig:

Component	Mole Fraction	Average Molec. Wt.	Hydrocarbon Portion	
			Mole Fraction	Average Molec. Wt.
H_2	0.500	1.0	—	—
CH_4	.100	1.6	0.200	3.2
C_2H_6	.150	4.5	.300	9.0
C_3H_8	.250	11.0	.500	22.0
	1.000	18.1	1.000	34.2

The effective pressures to be used for the hydrocarbon portion of the mixture are:

$$\pi_{e1} = \frac{25 + 14.7}{14.7}\sqrt{0.500} = 1.91 \text{ atm}$$

$$\pi_{e2} = \frac{150 + 14.7}{14.7}\sqrt{0.500} = 7.91 \text{ atm}$$

Values read from the ethane and propane charts are tabulated below:

Compound	S	BTU/lb		t_2 °F	$\frac{\Delta H}{M(h_2 - h_1)}$	$\Delta t\sqrt{M}$
		h_1	h_2			
C_2H_6	0.837	294	340	121	1385	663
C_3H_8	0.686	278	307	92	1280	610

By interpolation, $\Delta H = 1354$ BTU/mole and $\Delta t \sqrt{M} = 647$ for a saturated hydrocarbon mixture of 34.2 molec. wt. The corresponding final temperature for the hydrocarbon portion of the mixture is 111°F.

For the H_2 portion of the mixture, the work of compression and final temperature are calculated as follows:

$$MC_P = 2.016 \times 3.46 = 6.96; \quad K = \frac{6.97}{6.97 - 1.99} = 1.40$$

$$\Delta H = \frac{K}{K-1} RT \left[\left(\frac{\pi_2}{\pi_1} \right)^{\frac{K-1}{1}} - 1 \right]$$

$$= \frac{1.40}{1.40 - 1} \times 1.99 \times 460 \left[\left(\frac{164.7}{39.7} \right)^{\frac{1.40-1}{1.40}} - 1 \right]$$

$$= 3200(1.502 - 1) = 1610 \text{ BTU/mole}$$

$$T_2 = \left(\frac{164.7}{39.7} \right)^{\frac{1.40-1}{1.40}} \times 460 = 691°\text{R} \approx 231°\text{F}$$

For the mixture, the work of compression $= 0.500 \times 1354 + 0.500 \times 1610$
$$= 1482 \text{ BTU/mole} \approx 82 \text{ BTU/lb}$$

The final temperature of the mixture is assumed to be the temperature t, at which

$$0.500[H_{HC}(t, 7.91 \text{ atm}) - H_{HC}(111°\text{F}, 7.91 \text{ atm})]$$
$$= 0.500[H_H(231°\text{F}) - H_H(t)] = 0.500 \times 6.97(231 - t)$$

Since it is necessary to use enthalpy for evaluating ΔH_{HC}, t will be determined by trial and error.

Assume $t = 140°$F.

Interpolating between the charts on pages 99 and 100,
$$0.500 \times 34.2[342 - 328] = 0.500 \times 6.97[231 - 140]$$
$$240 \neq 317$$

Assume $t = 148°$F.
$$0.500 \times 34.2[346 - 328] = 0.500 \times 6.97[231 - 148]$$
$$308 \neq 290$$

By interpolation, the final temperature is *147°F*.

While the foregoing procedure permits the Mollier diagrams to be used for mixtures of hydrocarbons and inert gases, the method of combining the enthalpies and the temperatures of the two portions of the mixture is theoretically incorrect. In this procedure it is assumed that if two gases, having different thermal properies, are compressed individually from the same initial temperature and pressure to the same final pressure and then mixed, the resulting thermodynamic properties of the mixture will be the same as if the gases were mixed initially and then compressed. This assumption is not quite correct and will always lead to small positive errors in the work of compression and temperature rise. The errors usually will not exceed a couple of percent with a maximum of about 5% if the average molecular weight of the hydrocarbons is not greater than 50 and the compression ratio is not greater than 5:1.

As an alternative to this method, the equations for an ideal gas may be applied to the entire mixture, provided the gas law correction factor for the hydrocarbons, μ_{HC}, is not less than 0.95. In arriving at an average molal specific heat at constant pressure for the mixture, the molal specific heats of the individual components at 0–1 atm should be used irrespective of the initial and final pressures of the compression. The following equations apply to this alternative method:

$$\mu_m = (y_{HC}\mu_{HC} + y_a\mu_a + y_b\mu_b + \cdots)$$

$$(MC_P)_m = y_{HC}(MC_P)_{HC} + y_a(MC_P)_a + y_b(MC_P)_b + \cdots$$

$$K = \frac{(MC_P)_m}{(MC_P)_m - 1.99}$$

$$\Delta H = \frac{K}{K - 1}\mu_m R T_1 \left[\left(\frac{\pi_2}{\pi_1}\right)^{\frac{K-1}{K}} - 1\right]$$

$$T_2 = \left(\frac{\pi_2}{\pi_1}\right)^{\frac{K-1}{K}} T_1$$

where μ = correction factor for deviation from the ideal gas law at initial conditions
y = mole fraction of any component
MC_P = molal specific heat at constant pressure (0–1 atm) and at the average temperature
$K = \dfrac{MC_P}{MC_V}$
ΔH = change in enthalpy during an adiabatic compression = work of compression
T_1, T_2 = initial and final temperatures in °R
π_1, π_2 = initial and final pressures
HC = subscript referring to the total hydrocarbons
a, b, etc. = subscripts referring to individual inert gases

Example 7 will be recalculated by the alternative method:

For the hydrocarbon portion:

$$T_r = \frac{460}{575} = 0.800; \quad \pi_{cr} = \frac{1.91}{47.2} = 0.041; \quad \mu_{HC} = 0.966$$

$$MC_P(70°F) = 34.2 \times 0.410 = 14.0$$

For the hydrogen:

$$\mu = 1.000; \quad MC_P = 6.97$$

For the mixture:

$$\mu_m = 0.500 \times 0.966 = 0.500 \times 1.000 = 0.983$$
$$MC_P = 0.500 \times 14.0 + 0.500 \times 6.97 = 10.5$$

$$K = \frac{10.5}{10.5 - 1.99} = 1.235$$

$$\Delta H = \frac{1.235}{0.235} \times 0.983 \times 1.99 \times 460 \left[\left(\frac{164.7}{39.7} \right)^{\frac{0.235}{1.235}} - 1 \right]$$

$= 4740[1.311 - 1] = 1470$ BTU/mole as compared with 1482 BTU/mole previously calculated.

$T_2 = 1.311 \times 460 = 603°R \approx 143°F$ as compared with 147°F by the first method.

If desired, this alternative method may also be applied to hydrocarbon mixtures if μ at the initial conditions *is not less than 0.95.*

GENERAL REFERENCES

Communication from The M. W. Kellogg Co., New York, N.Y.

Gary, Rubin and Ward, *Ind. Eng. Chem.* **25**, 178 (1933).

Gilliland, Unpublished data, Mass. Inst. Tech.

Keenan and Keys, "Thermodynamic Properties of Steam," John Wiley & Sons (1936).

Misc. Publication of Bur. Standards, No. 97 (1929).

Nat. Bur. Standards Circular C461 (1947).

Sage, Webster and Lacey, *Ind. Eng. Chem.* **29**, 1309 (1937).

Weir and Eaton, *Ind. Eng. Chem.* **24**, 211 (1932).

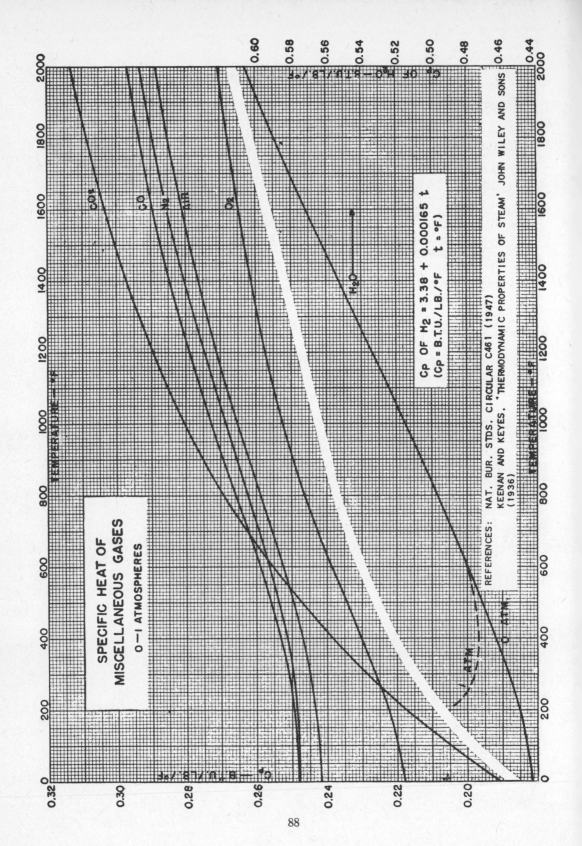

SPECIFIC HEAT OF
MISCELLANEOUS GASES

0—1 ATMOSPHERES

Cp OF H_2 = 3.38 + 0.000165 t
(Cp = B.T.U./LB./°F   t = °F)

REFERENCES: NAT. BUR. STDS. CIRCULAR C461 (1947)
KEENAN AND KEYES, 'THERMODYNAMIC PROPERTIES OF STEAM' JOHN WILEY AND SONS
(1936)

C_p OF H_2O — B.T.U./LB./°F

TEMPERATURE—°F

C_p — B.T.U./LB./°F

CO_2
CO
N_2
AIR
O_2
H_2O

ATM
O ATM

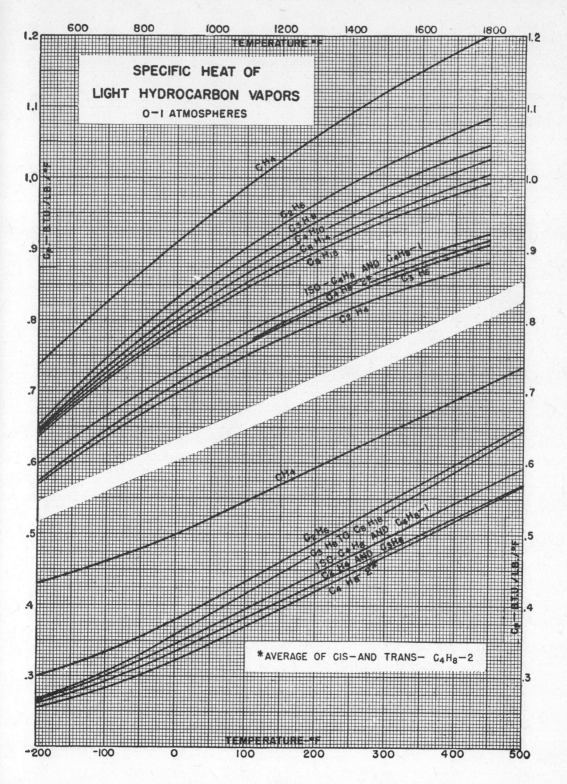

SPECIFIC HEAT OF
LIGHT HYDROCARBON VAPORS
0-1 ATMOSPHERES

TEMPERATURE °F

C_p — B.T.U./LB./°F

*AVERAGE OF CIS-AND TRANS- C_4H_8-2

TEMPERATURE °F

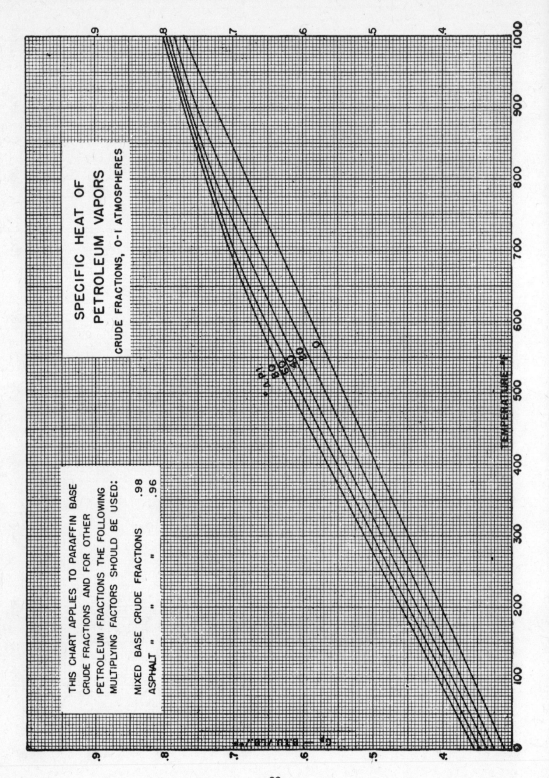

SPECIFIC HEAT OF
PETROLEUM VAPORS
CRUDE FRACTIONS, 0-1 ATMOSPHERES

THIS CHART APPLIES TO PARAFFIN BASE
CRUDE FRACTIONS AND FOR OTHER
PETROLEUM FRACTIONS THE FOLLOWING
MULTIPLYING FACTORS SHOULD BE USED:

MIXED BASE CRUDE FRACTIONS   .98
ASPHALT   "   "   .96

TEMPERATURE-°F

Cp — BTU/LB/°F

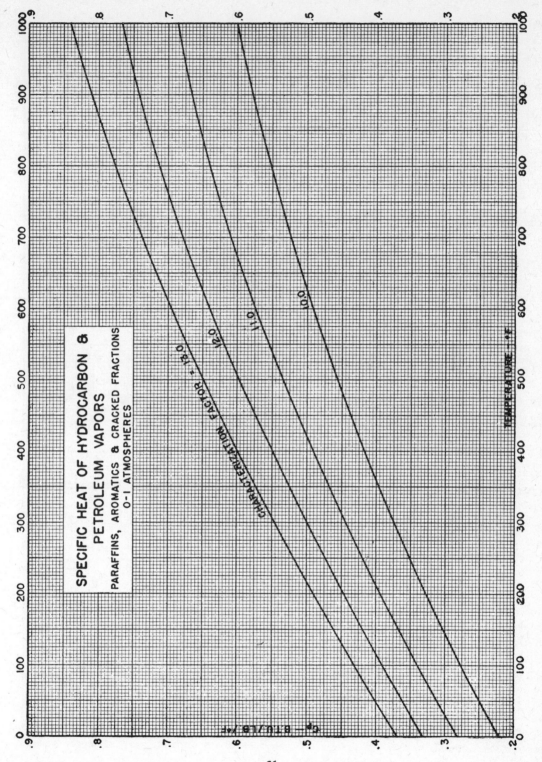

SPECIFIC HEAT OF HYDROCARBON &
PETROLEUM VAPORS
PARAFFINS, AROMATICS & CRACKED FRACTIONS
0-1 ATMOSPHERES

CHARACTERIZATION FACTOR = 13.0
12.0
11.0
10.0

CP — BTU/LB/°F

TEMPERATURE — °F

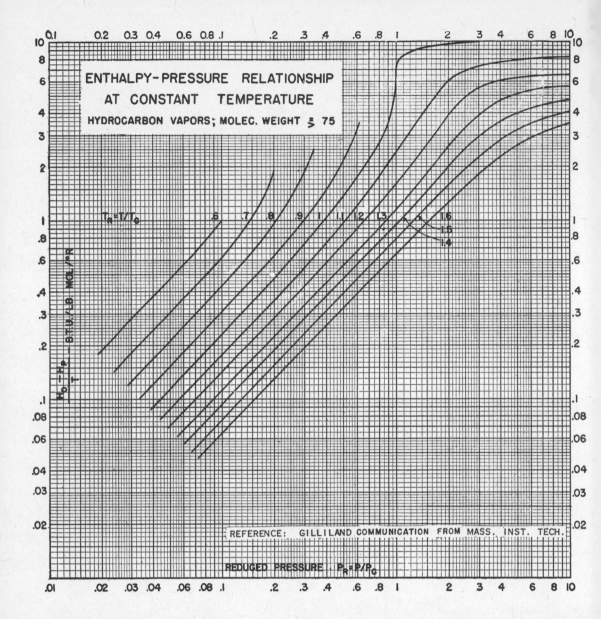

ENTHALPY-PRESSURE RELATIONSHIP
AT CONSTANT TEMPERATURE
HYDROCARBON VAPORS; MOLEC. WEIGHT ≲ 75

$T_R = T/T_C$

$\frac{H_0 - H_p}{T}$ — BTU./LB MOL./°R

REDUCED PRESSURE $P_R = P/P_C$

REFERENCE: GILLILAND COMMUNICATION FROM MASS. INST. TECH.

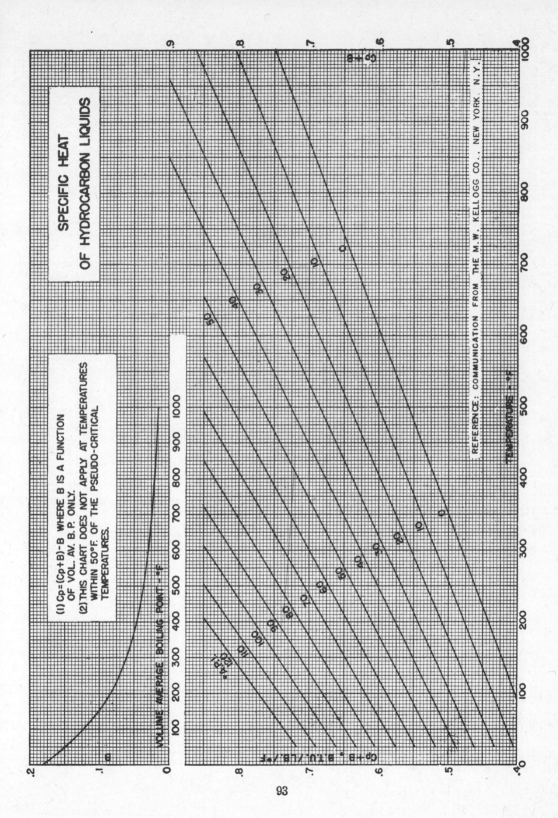

SPECIFIC HEAT OF HYDROCARBON LIQUIDS

(1) $C_p = (C_p + B) - B$ WHERE B IS A FUNCTION OF VOL. AV. B.P. ONLY.

(2) THIS CHART DOES NOT APPLY AT TEMPERATURES WITHIN 50°F. OF THE PSEUDO-CRITICAL TEMPERATURES.

VOLUME AVERAGE BOILING POINT - °F

TEMPERATURE - °F

$C_p + B$, B.T.U./LB./°F

REFERENCE: COMMUNICATION FROM THE M.W. KELLOGG CO., NEW YORK, N.Y.

93

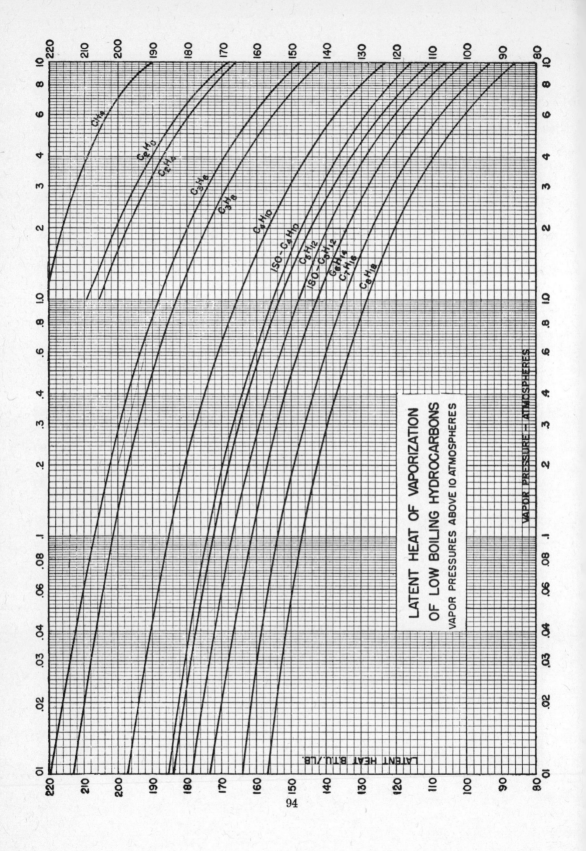

LATENT HEAT OF VAPORIZATION
OF LOW BOILING HYDROCARBONS
VAPOR PRESSURES ABOVE 10 ATMOSPHERES

VAPOR PRESSURE - ATMOSPHERES

LATENT HEAT B.T.U./LB.

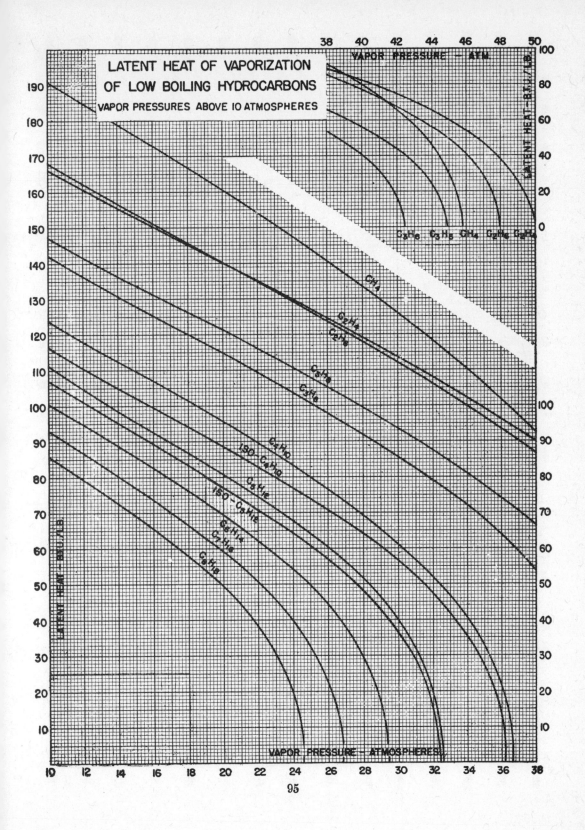

LATENT HEAT OF VAPORIZATION
OF LOW BOILING HYDROCARBONS
VAPOR PRESSURES ABOVE 10 ATMOSPHERES

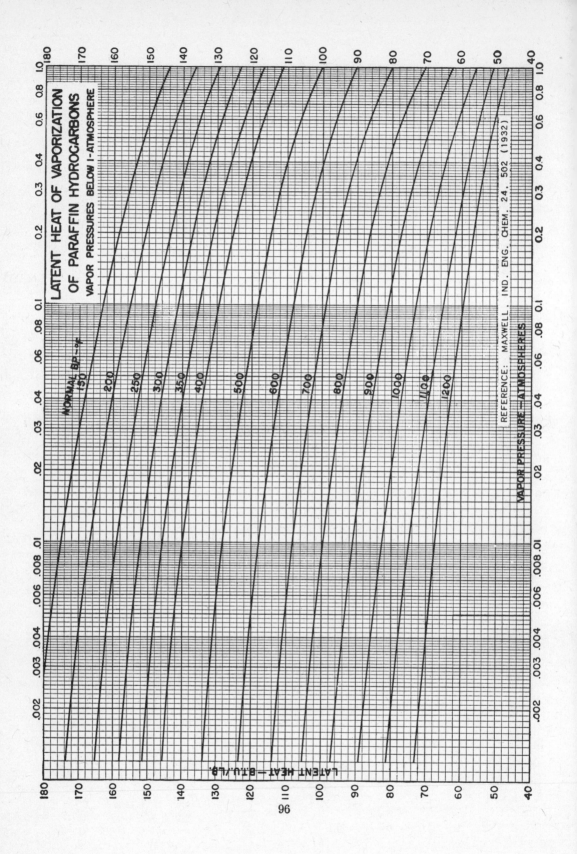

LATENT HEAT OF VAPORIZATION
OF PARAFFIN HYDROCARBONS
VAPOR PRESSURES BELOW 1-ATMOSPHERE

NORMAL BP—°F

150
200
250
300
350
400
500
600
700
800
900
1000
1100
1200

REFERENCE: MAXWELL, IND. ENG. CHEM. 24, 502 (1932)

VAPOR PRESSURE—ATMOSPHERES

LATENT HEAT — BTU./LB.

96

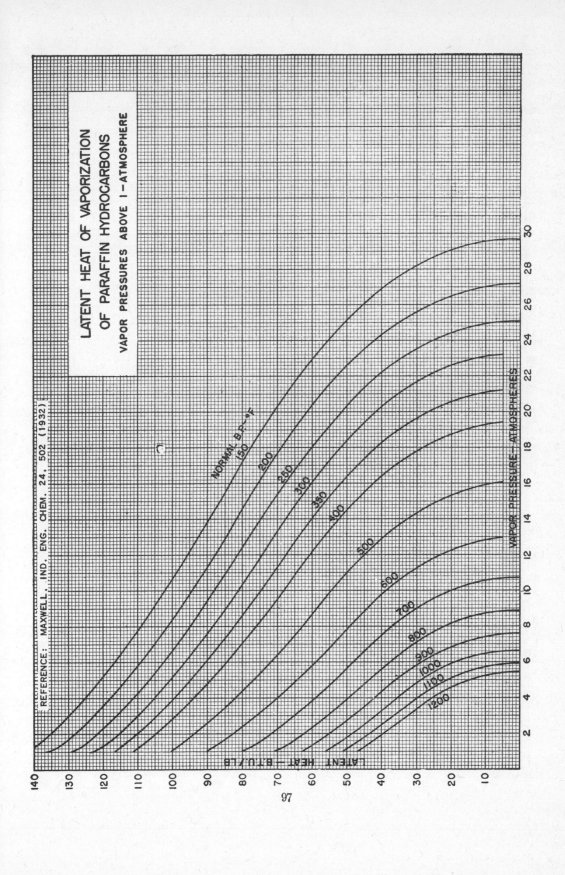

LATENT HEAT OF VAPORIZATION
OF PARAFFIN HYDROCARBONS
VAPOR PRESSURES ABOVE 1—ATMOSPHERE

REFERENCE: MAXWELL, IND. ENG. CHEM. 24, 502 (1932)

NORMAL B.P.-°F
150
200
250
300
350
400
500
600
700
800
900
1000
1100
1200

VAPOR PRESSURE—ATMOSPHERES

LATENT HEAT — B.T.U./LB

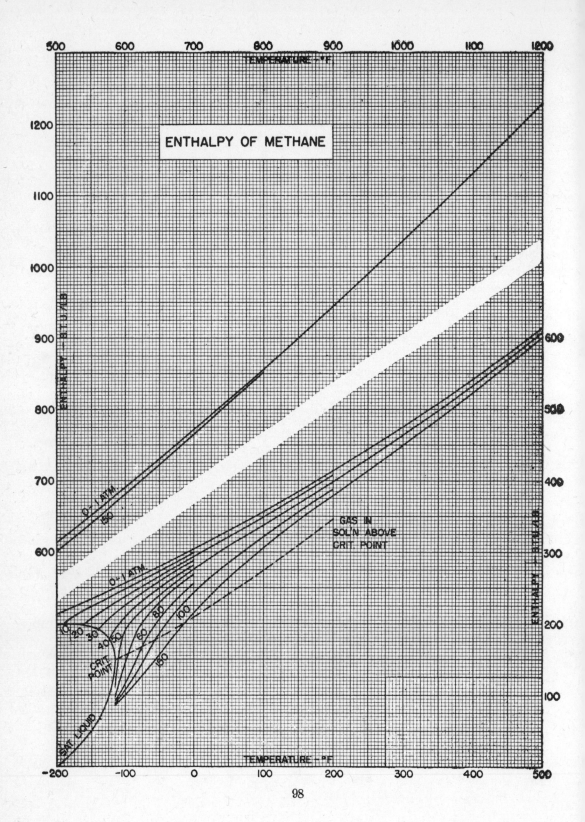

ENTHALPY OF METHANE

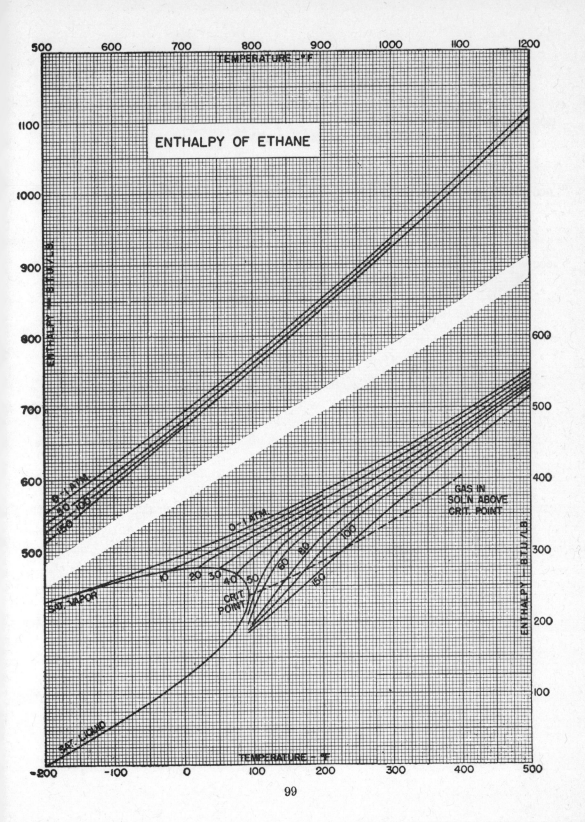

ENTHALPY OF ETHANE

99

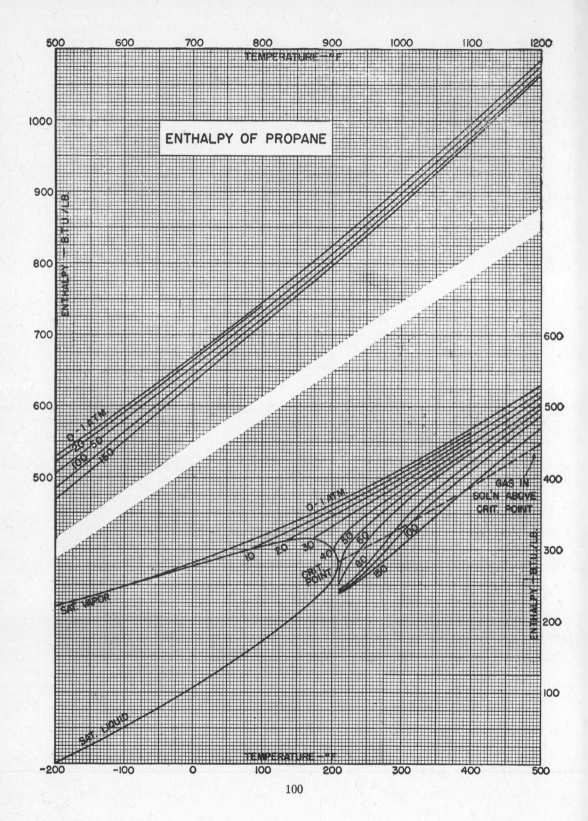

ENTHALPY OF PROPANE

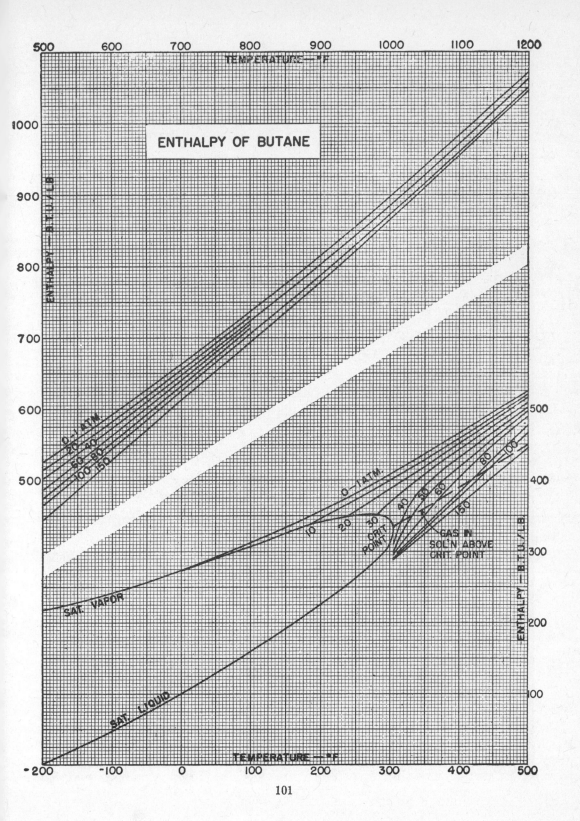

ENTHALPY OF BUTANE

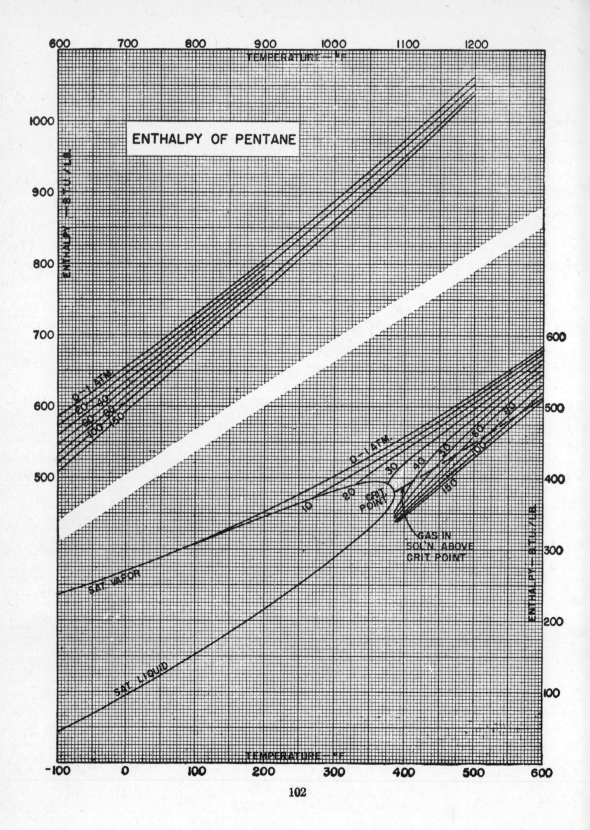

ENTHALPY OF PENTANE

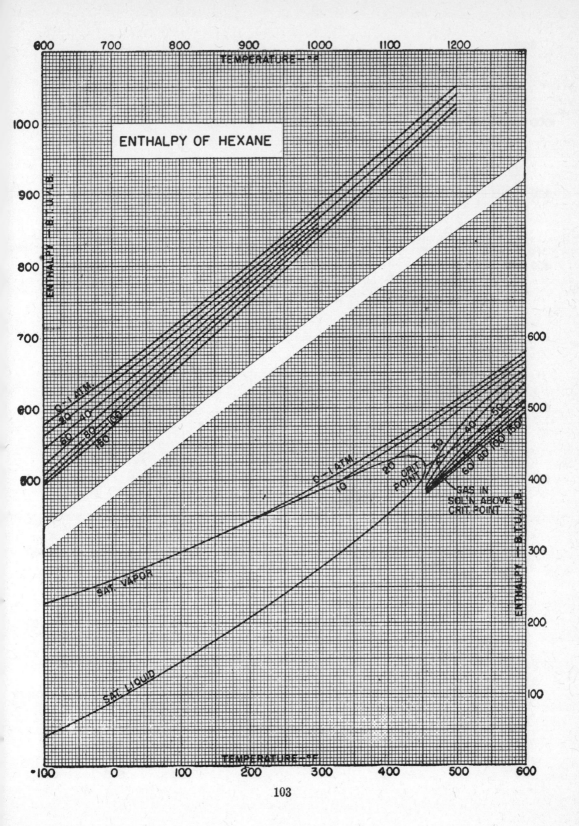

ENTHALPY OF HEXANE

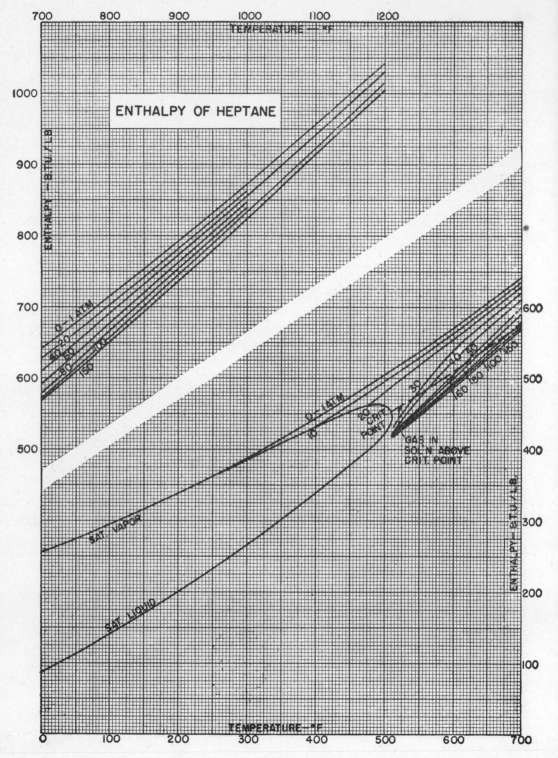

ENTHALPY OF HEPTANE

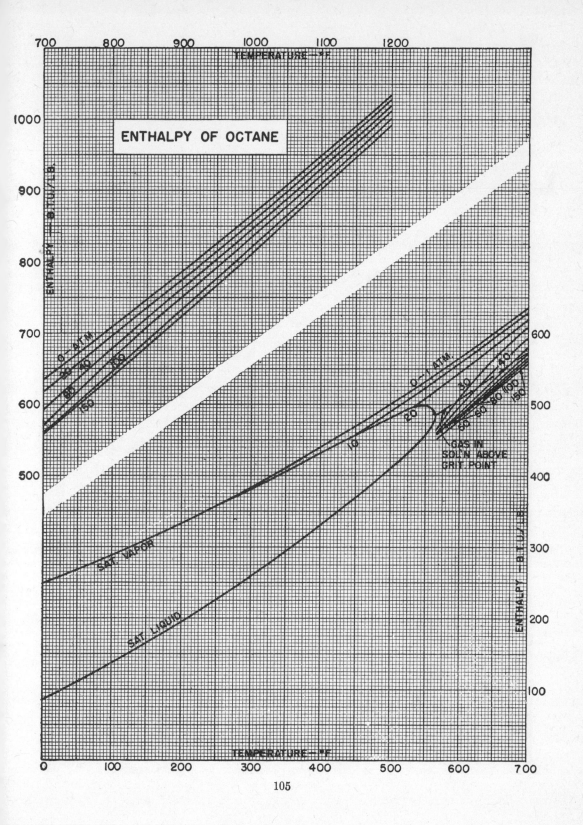

ENTHALPY OF OCTANE

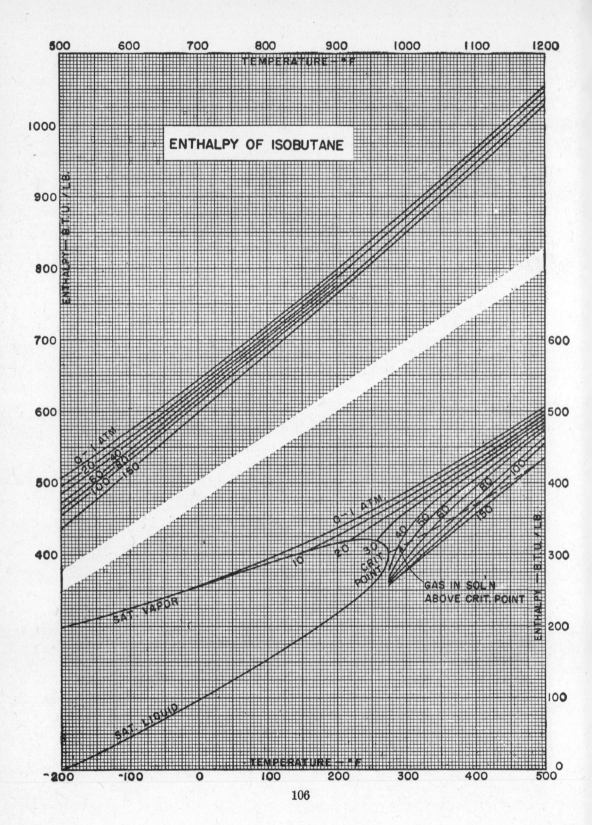

ENTHALPY OF ISOBUTANE

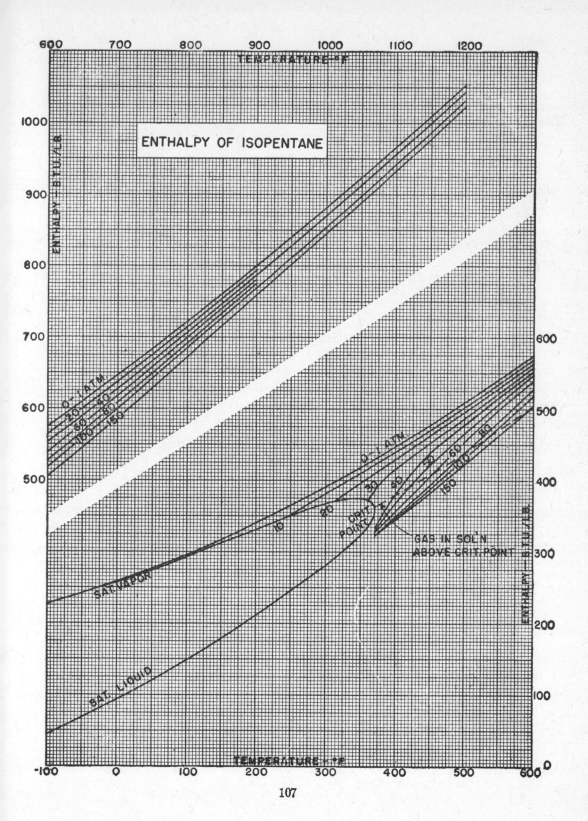

ENTHALPY OF ISOPENTANE

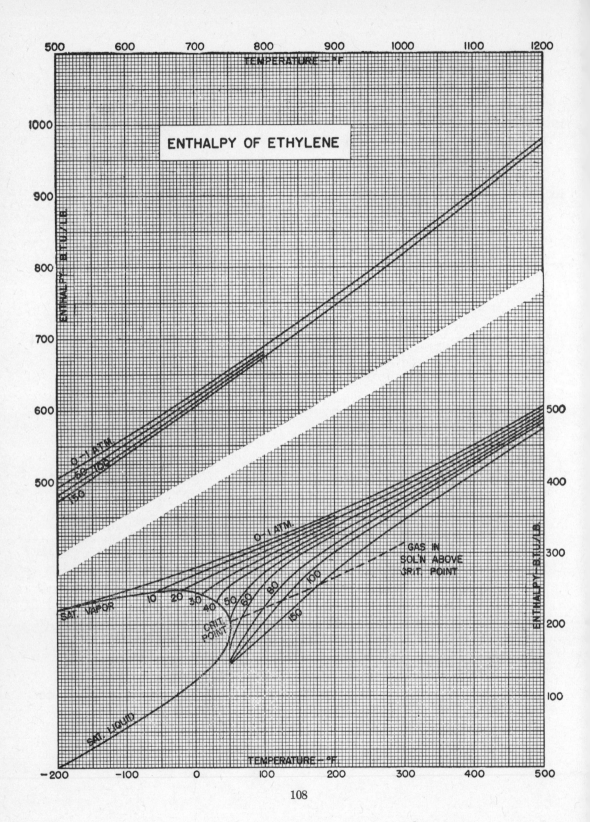

ENTHALPY OF ETHYLENE

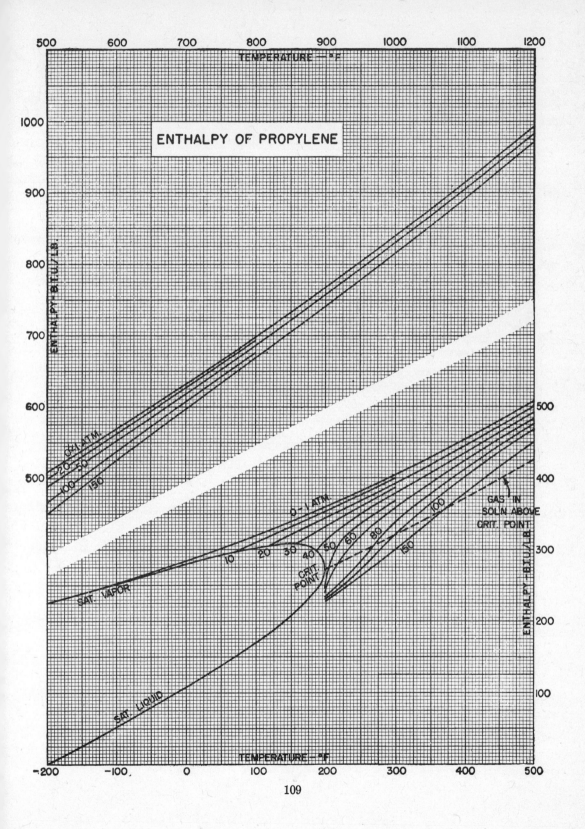

ENTHALPY OF PROPYLENE

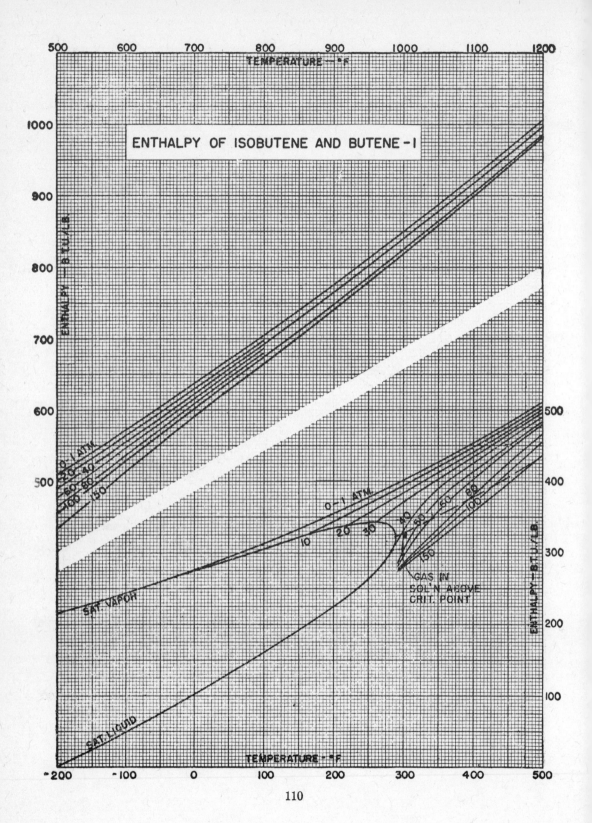

ENTHALPY OF ISOBUTENE AND BUTENE-1

110

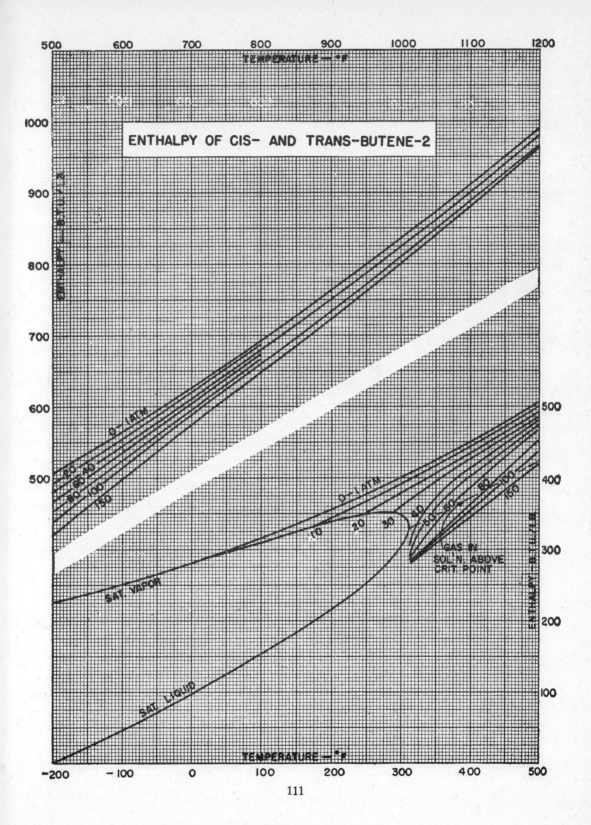

ENTHALPY OF CIS- AND TRANS-BUTENE-2

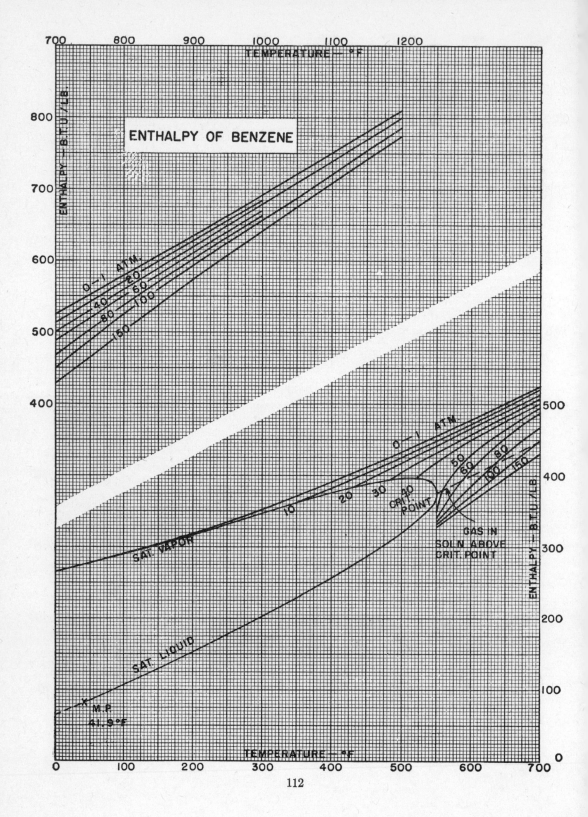

ENTHALPY OF BENZENE

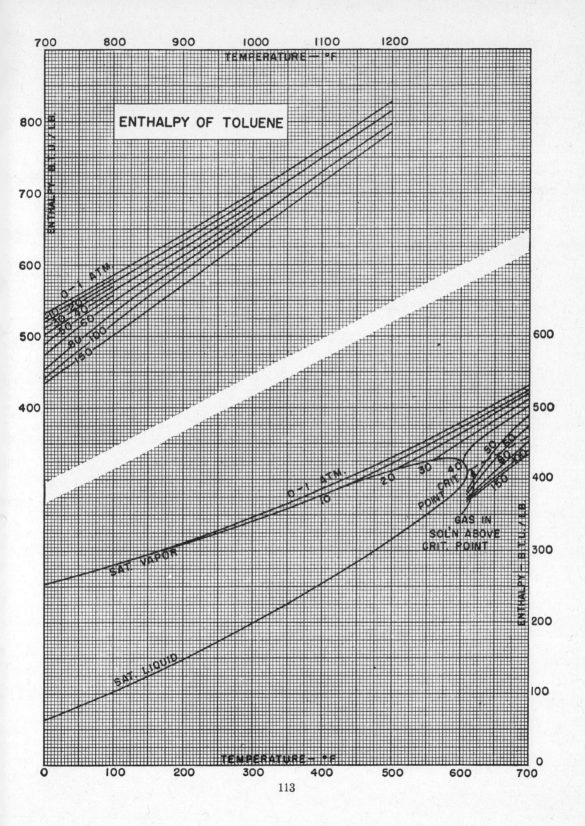

ENTHALPY OF TOLUENE

113

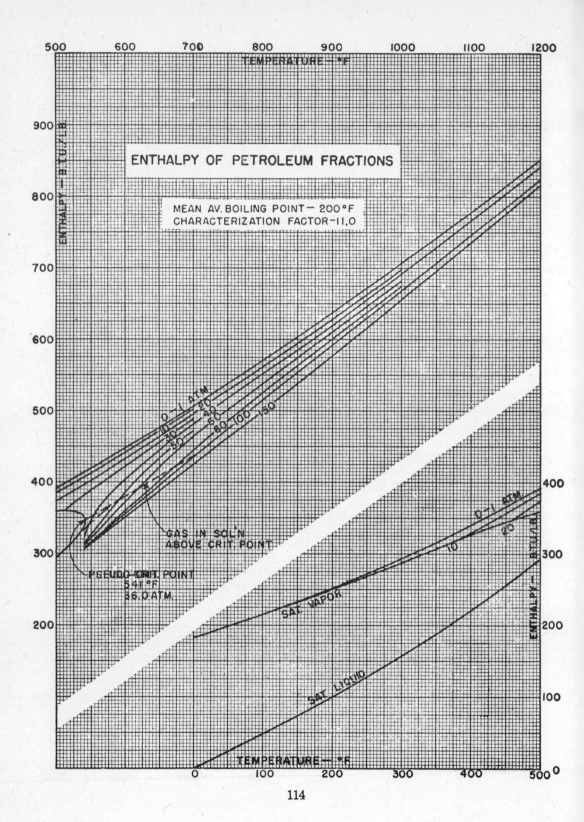

ENTHALPY OF PETROLEUM FRACTIONS

MEAN AV. BOILING POINT — 200°F
CHARACTERIZATION FACTOR — 11.0

114

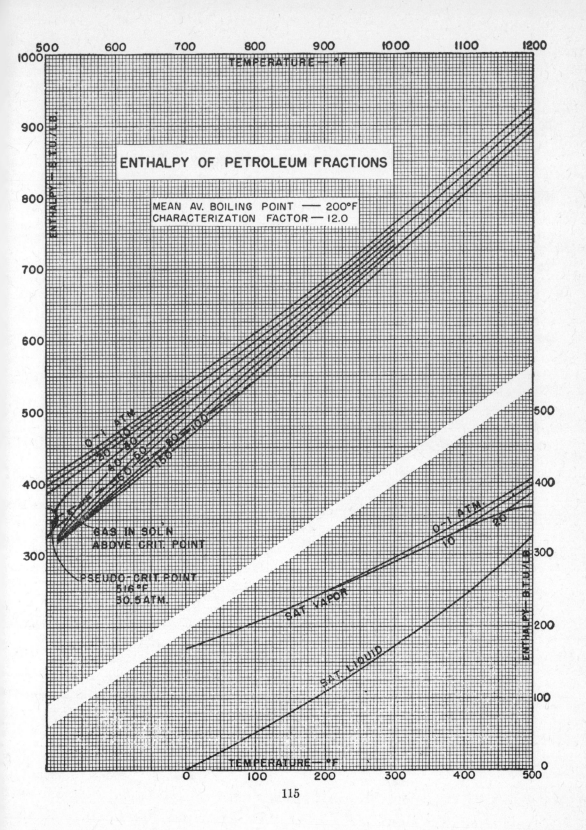

ENTHALPY OF PETROLEUM FRACTIONS

MEAN AV. BOILING POINT — 200°F
CHARACTERIZATION FACTOR — 12.0

115

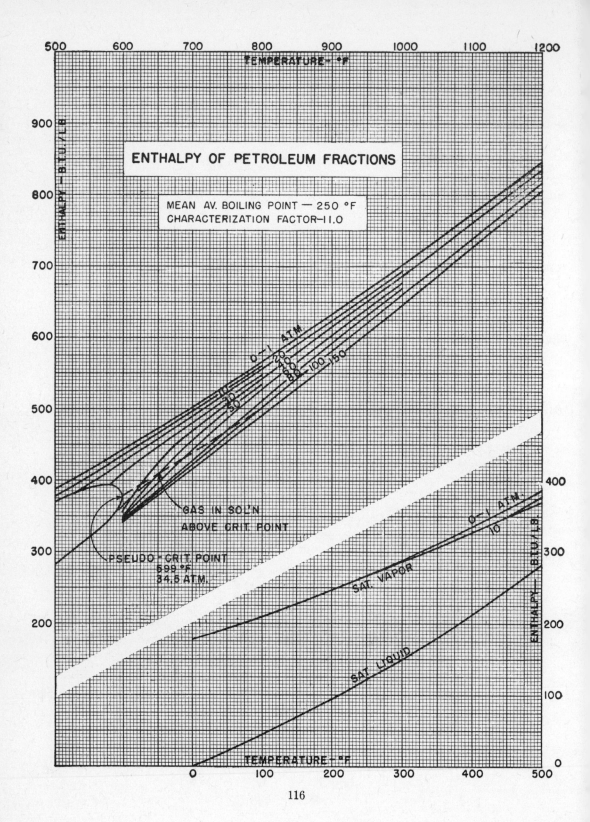

ENTHALPY OF PETROLEUM FRACTIONS

MEAN AV. BOILING POINT — 250 °F
CHARACTERIZATION FACTOR—11.0

GAS IN SOL'N
ABOVE CRIT. POINT

PSEUDO - CRIT. POINT
599 °F.
34.5 ATM.

SAT. VAPOR

SAT. LIQUID

116

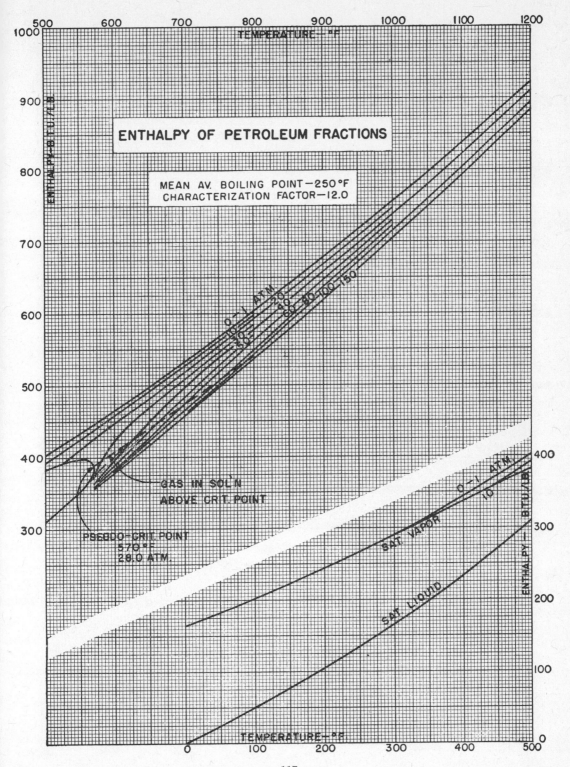

ENTHALPY OF PETROLEUM FRACTIONS

MEAN AV. BOILING POINT—250°F
CHARACTERIZATION FACTOR—12.0

GAS IN SOL'N
ABOVE CRIT. POINT

PSEUDO-CRIT POINT
570°F
28.0 ATM.

SAT. VAPOR

SAT. LIQUID

TEMPERATURE—°F

ENTHALPY—BTU/LB

ENTHALPY—BTU/LB

117

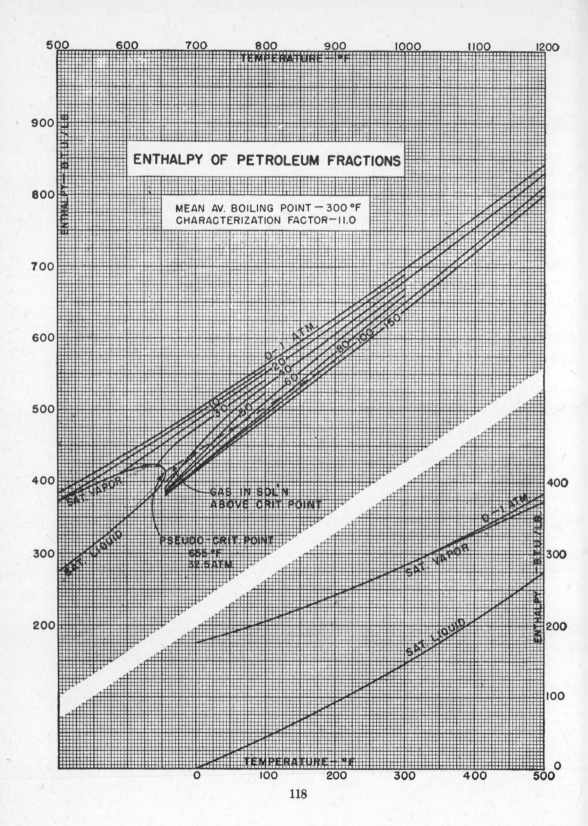

ENTHALPY OF PETROLEUM FRACTIONS

MEAN AV. BOILING POINT — 300 °F
CHARACTERIZATION FACTOR — 11.0

118

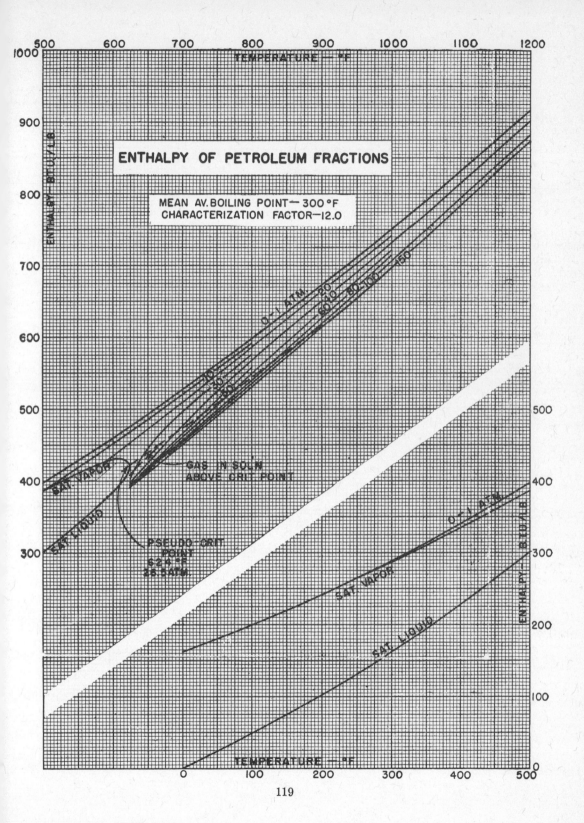

ENTHALPY OF PETROLEUM FRACTIONS

MEAN AV. BOILING POINT— 300°F
CHARACTERIZATION FACTOR—12.0

119

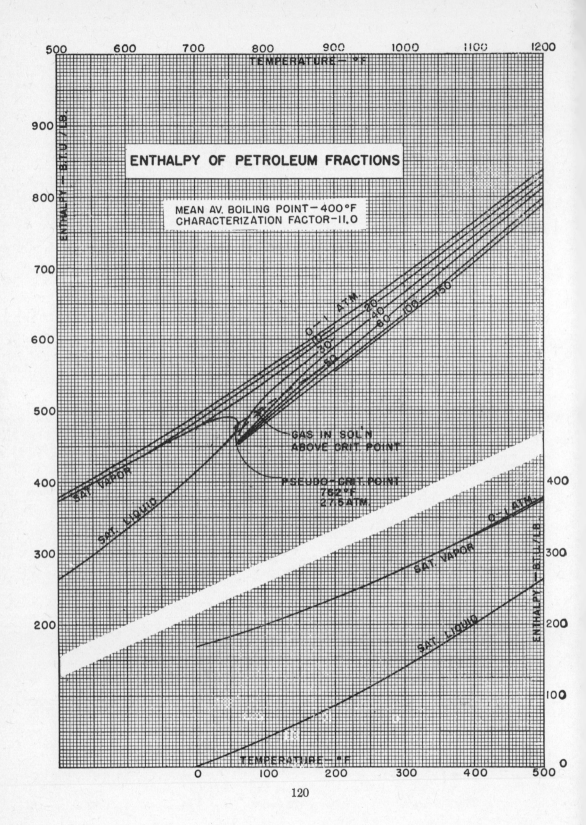

ENTHALPY OF PETROLEUM FRACTIONS

MEAN AV. BOILING POINT—400°F
CHARACTERIZATION FACTOR—11.0

GAS IN SOL'N
ABOVE CRIT POINT

PSEUDO-CRIT. POINT
762°F
27.8 ATM.

120

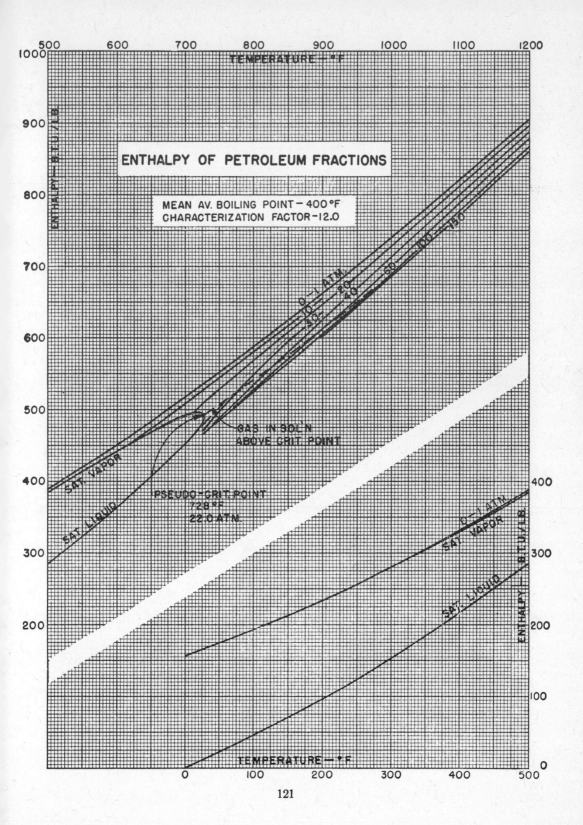

ENTHALPY OF PETROLEUM FRACTIONS

MEAN AV. BOILING POINT – 400°F
CHARACTERIZATION FACTOR – 12.0

121

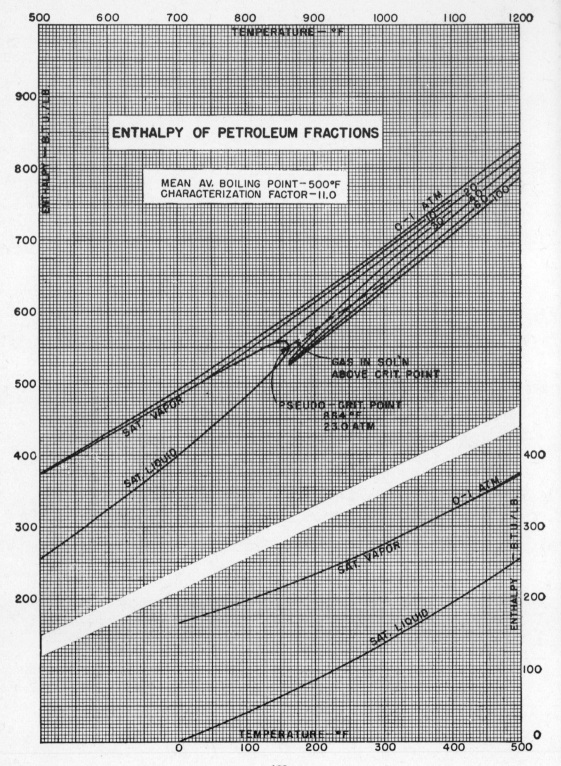

ENTHALPY OF PETROLEUM FRACTIONS

MEAN AV. BOILING POINT—500°F
CHARACTERIZATION FACTOR—11.0

GAS IN SOL'N
ABOVE CRIT. POINT

PSEUDO - CRIT. POINT
864 °F.
23.0 ATM.

SAT. VAPOR

SAT. LIQUID

0-1 ATM.

SAT. VAPOR

SAT. LIQUID

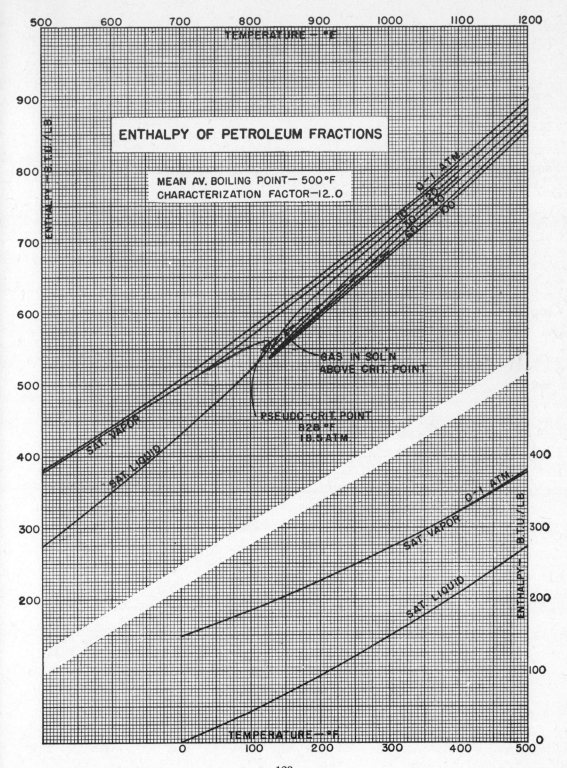

ENTHALPY OF PETROLEUM FRACTIONS

MEAN AV. BOILING POINT— 500°F
CHARACTERIZATION FACTOR—12.0

GAS IN SOL'N
ABOVE CRIT. POINT

PSEUDO-CRIT. POINT
828 °F
18.5 ATM

SAT. VAPOR

SAT. LIQUID

0~1 ATM
10
25
50
100

SAT. VAPOR

SAT. LIQUID

0~1 ATM

TEMPERATURE — °F

ENTHALPY — B.T.U./LB.

ENTHALPY — B.T.U./LB.

TEMPERATURE — °F

123

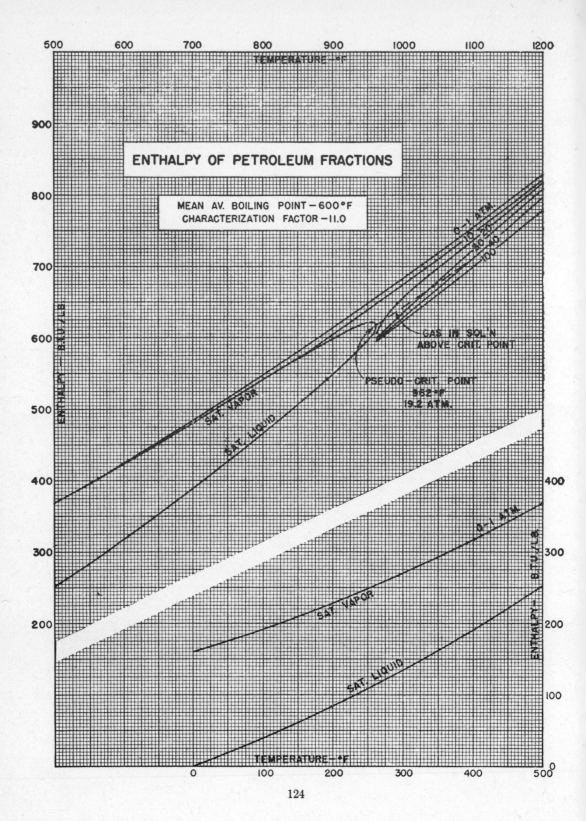

ENTHALPY OF PETROLEUM FRACTIONS

MEAN AV. BOILING POINT — 600°F
CHARACTERIZATION FACTOR — 11.0

124

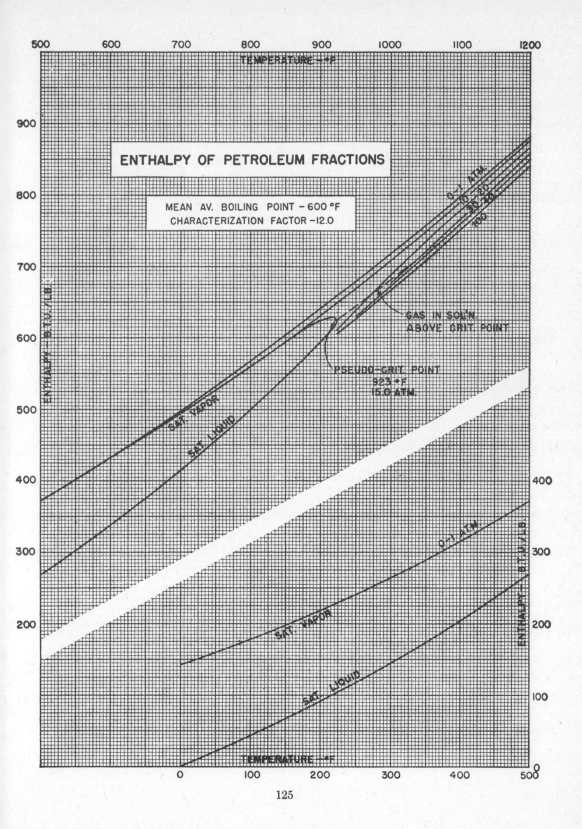

ENTHALPY OF PETROLEUM FRACTIONS

MEAN AV. BOILING POINT – 600 °F
CHARACTERIZATION FACTOR –12.0

0–1 ATM.
10 20
100 50

GAS IN SOL'N.
ABOVE CRIT. POINT

PSEUDO-CRIT. POINT
923 °F
15.0 ATM.

SAT. VAPOR
SAT. LIQUID

TEMPERATURE – °F

ENTHALPY – B.T.U./LB.

0–1 ATM

SAT. VAPOR

SAT. LIQUID

TEMPERATURE – °F

ENTHALPY – B.T.U./LB

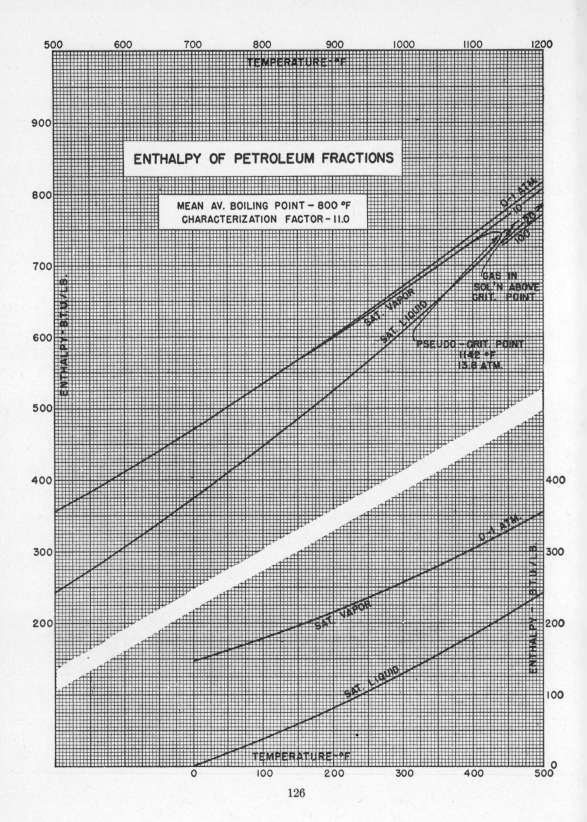

ENTHALPY OF PETROLEUM FRACTIONS

MEAN AV. BOILING POINT – 800 °F
CHARACTERIZATION FACTOR – 11.0

SAT. VAPOR
SAT. LIQUID

0-1 ATM.
10
20
50
100 200

GAS IN
SOL'N ABOVE
CRIT. POINT

PSEUDO - CRIT. POINT
1142 °F
13.8 ATM.

ENTHALPY – B.T.U./LB.

TEMPERATURE – °F

0-1 ATM.

SAT. VAPOR

SAT. LIQUID

ENTHALPY – B.T.U./LB.

TEMPERATURE – °F

126

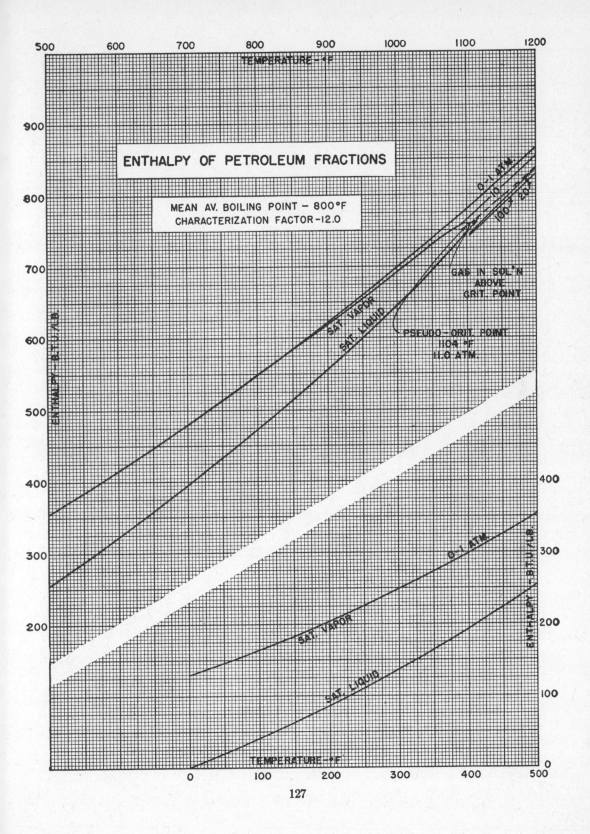

ENTHALPY OF PETROLEUM FRACTIONS

MEAN AV. BOILING POINT – 800°F
CHARACTERIZATION FACTOR –12.0

127

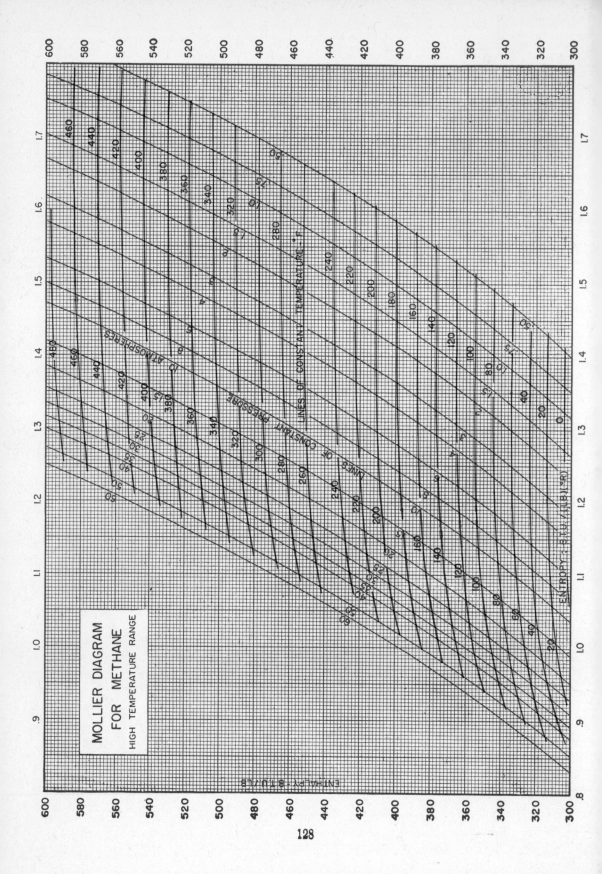

MOLLIER DIAGRAM
FOR METHANE
HIGH TEMPERATURE RANGE

ENTHALPY - B.T.U./LB.

ENTROPY - B.T.U./(LB.)(°R)

LINES OF CONSTANT TEMPERATURE - °F

LINES OF CONSTANT PRESSURE

ATMOSPHERES

128

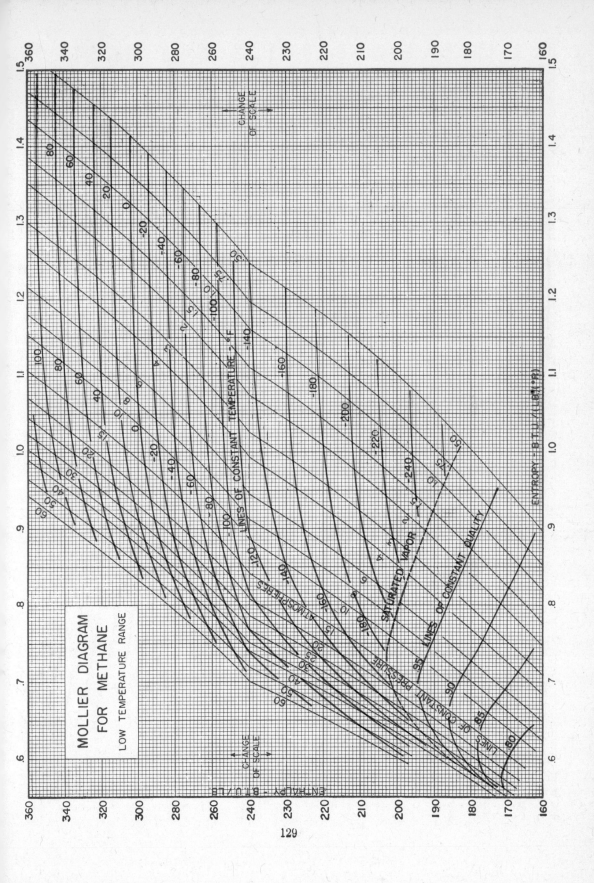

MOLLIER DIAGRAM
FOR METHANE
LOW TEMPERATURE RANGE

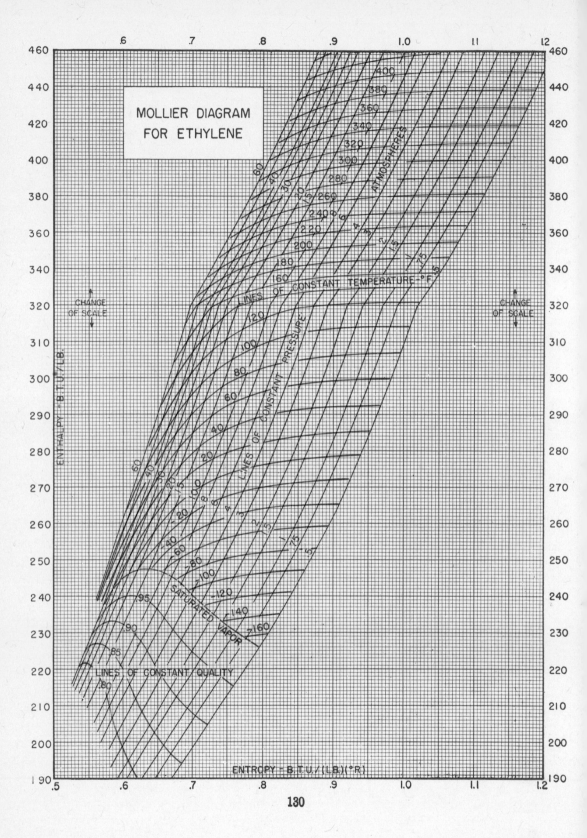

MOLLIER DIAGRAM
FOR ETHYLENE

CHANGE OF SCALE

CHANGE OF SCALE

ATMOSPHERES

LINES OF CONSTANT TEMPERATURE °F.

LINES OF CONSTANT PRESSURE

SATURATED VAPOR

LINES OF CONSTANT QUALITY

ENTHALPY - B.T.U./LB.

ENTROPY - B.T.U./(LB.)(°R)

130

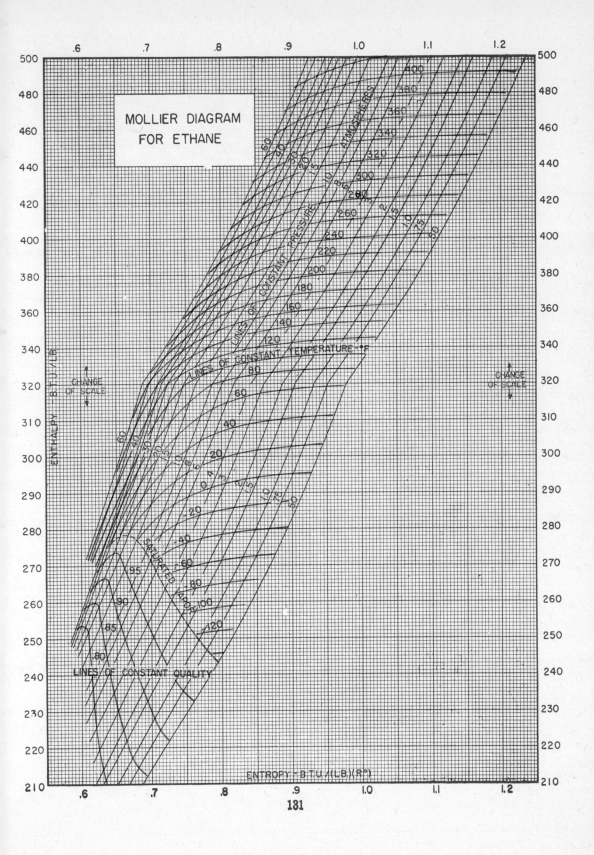

MOLLIER DIAGRAM FOR ETHANE

131

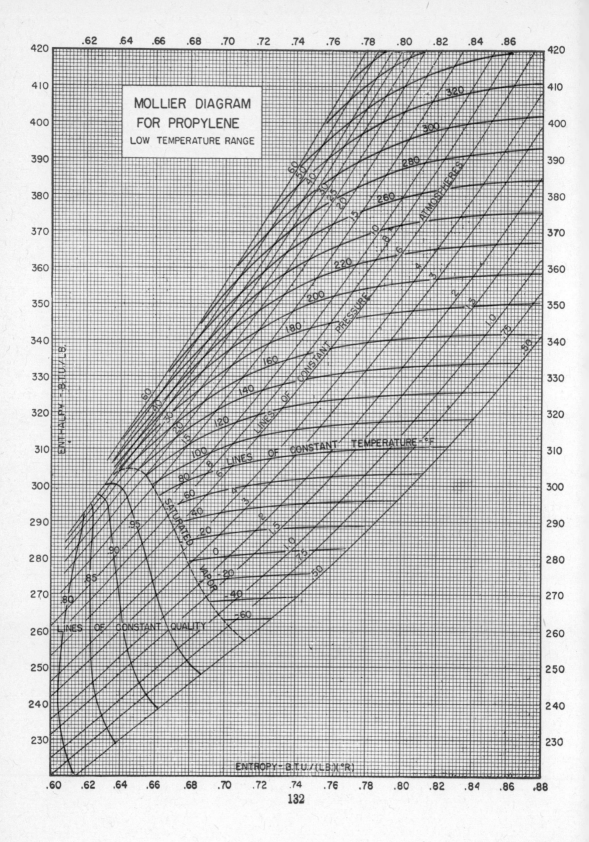

MOLLIER DIAGRAM
FOR PROPYLENE
LOW TEMPERATURE RANGE

ENTHALPY - B.T.U./LB.

LINES OF CONSTANT PRESSURE

ATMOSPHERES

LINES OF CONSTANT TEMPERATURE °F

SATURATED VAPOR

LINES OF CONSTANT QUALITY

ENTROPY - B.T.U./(LB.)(°R)

132

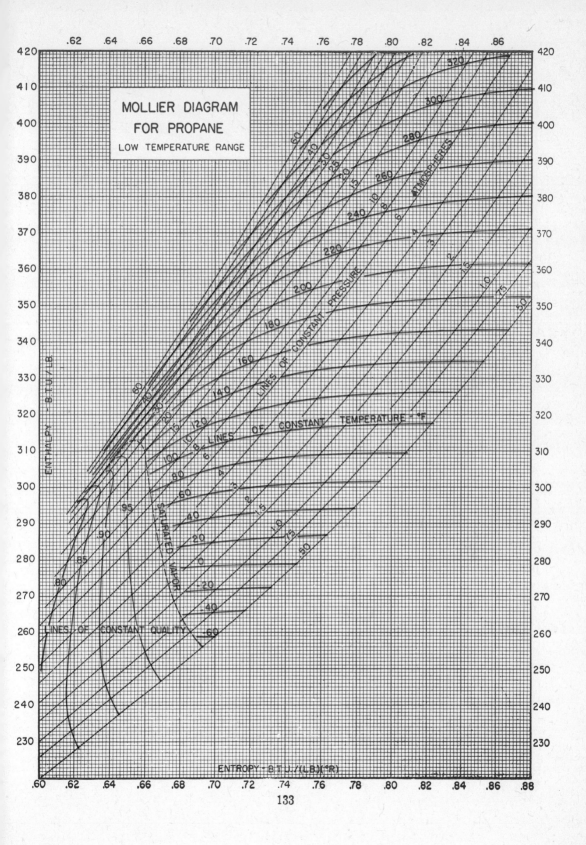

MOLLIER DIAGRAM
FOR PROPANE
LOW TEMPERATURE RANGE

133

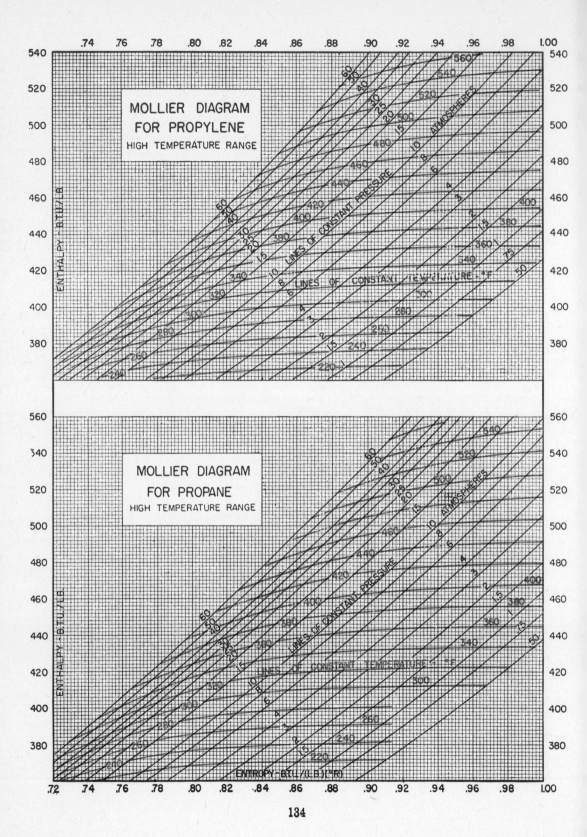

MOLLIER DIAGRAM
FOR PROPYLENE
HIGH TEMPERATURE RANGE

MOLLIER DIAGRAM
FOR PROPANE
HIGH TEMPERATURE RANGE

ENTROPY - B.T.U./(LB.)(°R)

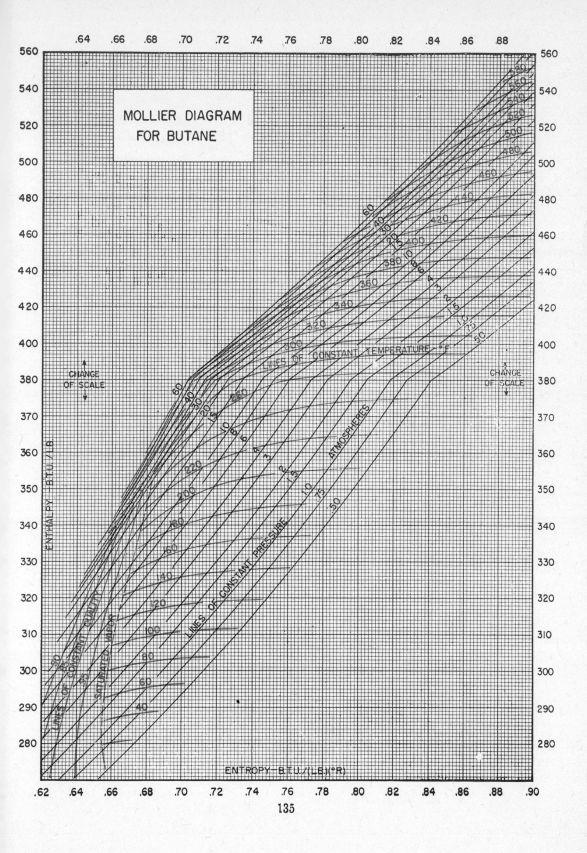

MOLLIER DIAGRAM FOR BUTANE

ENTHALPY - B.T.U./LB.

ENTROPY - B.T.U./(LB.)(°R)

LINES OF CONSTANT TEMPERATURE °F

LINES OF CONSTANT PRESSURE

LINES OF CONSTANT QUALITY

SATURATED VAPOR

ATMOSPHERES

CHANGE OF SCALE

CHANGE OF SCALE

135

Section 8
DENSITY

Low-Boiling Hydrocarbons

The specific gravity of the saturated liquid, from low temperatures to the critical point, is given on pages 140 to 142 for a number of low-boiling hydrocarbons. A hydrocarbon mixture is assumed to be an ideal solution, and its specific gravity can be calculated by adding the products of the specific gravities of individual components times their volume fractions. This assumption is essentially true for members of a homologous series and is a good approximation for mixtures composed of hydrocarbons from different series as long as no component is in the region of its critical temperature.

Thermal Expansion of Liquid Petroleum Fractions

The thermal expansions of liquid petroleum fractions at pressures up to 1500 psig were derived from the thermal expansion and compressibility correlations of Watson, Nelson and Murphy.[1] As in the case of many physical properties of petroleum fractions, thermal expansion is more sensitive to average boiling point than it is to gravity, although both independent variables are necessary to correlate the data properly. Up to 1.25 multiples of the volume at 60°F and 1 atm, it was found that gravity could be neglected and that the thermal expansion could be represented by the molal average boiling point alone. Above this expansion of 1.25 volumes, gravity is introduced into the correlation in the form of characterization factor. For each average boiling point two lines are shown, one corresponding to a characterization factor of 12.0 and the other to 11.0. Interpolation and extrapolation may be made on the basis of characterization factor or, if preferred, gravity, which is also given for each curve.

P-V-T Relations of Hydrocarbon Vapors

A series of charts on pages 148 to 153 give $\mu = PV/RT$, the correction factor to be applied to the ideal gas law for hydrocarbon and petroleum vapors. The correction factor is plotted as a function of reduced temperature, T/T_c, and reduced pressure, P/P_c, where T and P are the temperature and pressure of the vapor and T_c and P_c, its critical temperature and pressure. As explained in the section on Critical Properties, the pseudo-critical, not the true critical, temperature and pressure should always be used for hydrocarbon mixtures. This method of using the pseudo-critical properties of the entire hydrocarbon mixture is not only more accurate but more readily used than the application of either Amagat's Law or Dalton's Law to the individual components.

[1] *Oil and Gas Journal* **35**, 85 (1936).

Since there is evidence of some trend in μ with increase in molecular weight for $T_r \lessgtr 1.00$, there are three sets of charts for the region where T_r is greater than 1.0, covering different ranges of molecular weight. Below $T_r = 1.0$, the data are insufficient to take into account a similar trend, so a single chart[2] covers the entire molecular weight range.

If other gases (H_2, O_2, H_2O, etc.) are present in a mixture of hydrocarbon vapors, an effective pressure equal to $\pi \sqrt{y_{HC}}$ should be used to obtain the reduced pressure of the hydrocarbon portion. Likewise, if it is necessary to take into account gas law deviations for any of the other gases, μ should be determined for each of these gases at an effective pressure equal to the total pressure multiplied by the square root of its mole fraction. The molal volume is then calculated by Amagat's Law,

$$V_m = \frac{RT}{\pi} \left(y_{HC}\mu_{HC} + y_a\mu_a + y_b\mu_b + \cdots \right)$$

where V_m is the molal volume of the mixture, the subscript HC refers to the total hydrocarbon fraction, and the subscripts a, b, etc., refer to other gases. Usually μ_a, μ_b, etc., may be taken as 1.00 with very little error, since most of these gases approximate a perfect gas at the effective pressures encountered. In the absence of other data, the hydrocarbon charts may be used for these gases.

VALUES OF GAS CONSTANT—R

Pressure			Temp.	R
Lb/sq in. abs	Cu ft/lb-mole	....	°R	10.73
Lb/sq ft abs	Cu ft/lb-mole	....	°R	1545
Atm	Cu ft/lb-mole	....	°R	0.7302
Atm	Liters/g-mole	....	°K	0.08205
Atm	Cu ft/lb-mole	....	°K	1.314
Mm of Hg	Liters/g-mole	....	°K	62.36
Lb/sq ft abs	Cu ft/lb-mole	....	°K	2781

GENERAL REFERENCES

Beattie, Hadlock and Poffenberger, *J. Chem. Phys.* **3**, 93 (1935).
Beattie, Kay and Kaminsky, *J. Am. Chem. Soc.* **59**, 1589 (1937).
Beattie, Simard and Su, *J. Am. Chem. Soc.* **61**, 26 (1939).
International Critical Tables, Vol. III.
Kay, *Ind. Eng. Chem.* **28**, 1014 (1936); **30**, 459 (1938); **32**, 358 (1940).
Kelso and Felsing, *J. Am. Chem. Soc.* **62**, 3132 (1940).
Lewis, *Ind. Eng. Chem.* **28**, 257 (1936).
Sage and Lacey, *Ind. Eng. Chem.* **30**, 673 (1938).
Sage, Schaafsma and Lacey, *Ind. Eng. Chem.* **26**, 1218 (1934).
Sage, Webster and Lacey, *Ind. Eng. Chem.* **29**, 658, 1188 (1937).
Smith, Beattie and Kay, *J. Am. Chem. Soc.* **59**, 1587 (1937).

[2] Cope, Lewis and Weber, *Ind. Eng. Chem.* **23**, 887 (1931).

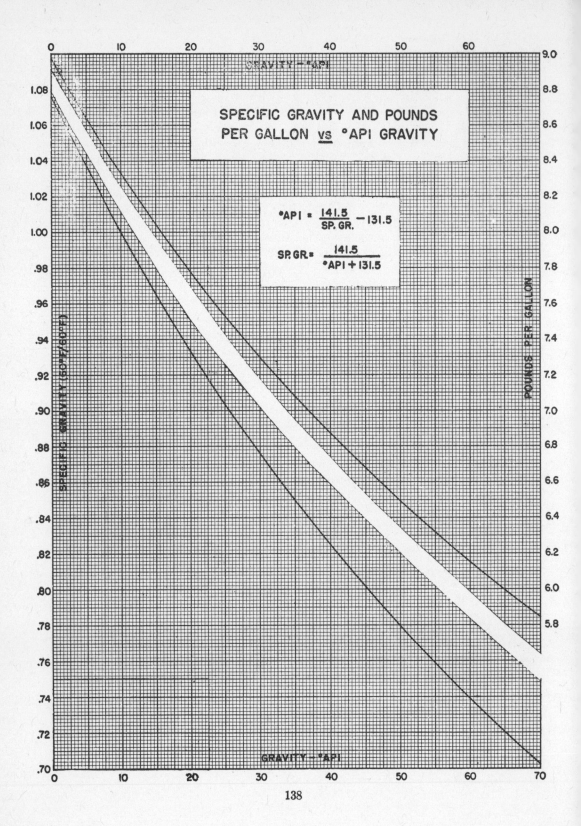

SPECIFIC GRAVITY AND POUNDS
PER GALLON vs °API GRAVITY

$$°API = \frac{141.5}{SP.\ GR.} - 131.5$$

$$SP.\ GR. = \frac{141.5}{°API + 131.5}$$

138

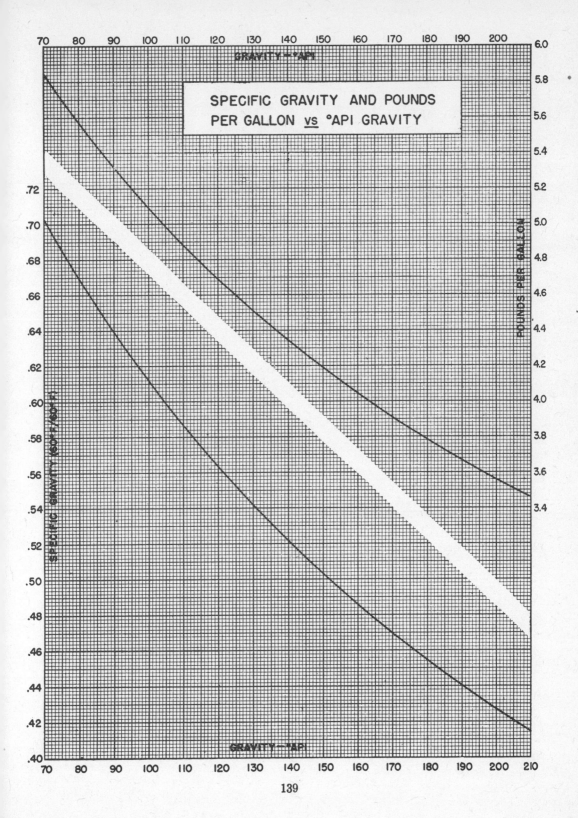

SPECIFIC GRAVITY AND POUNDS
PER GALLON vs °API GRAVITY

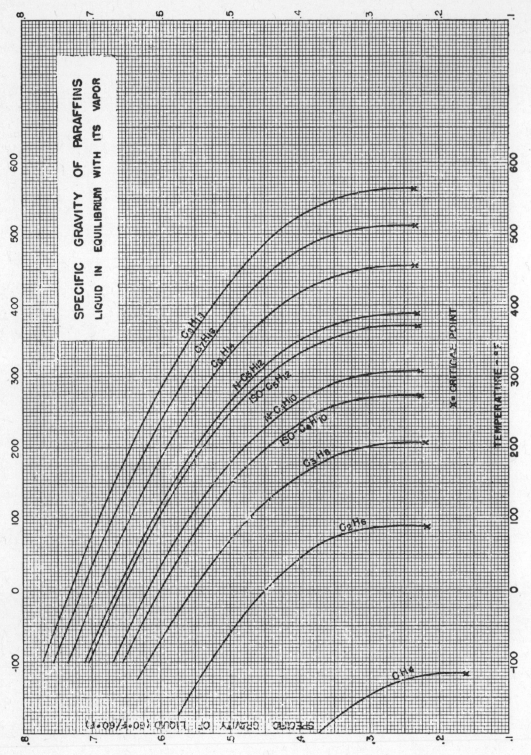

SPECIFIC GRAVITY OF PARAFFINS
LIQUID IN EQUILIBRIUM WITH ITS VAPOR

140

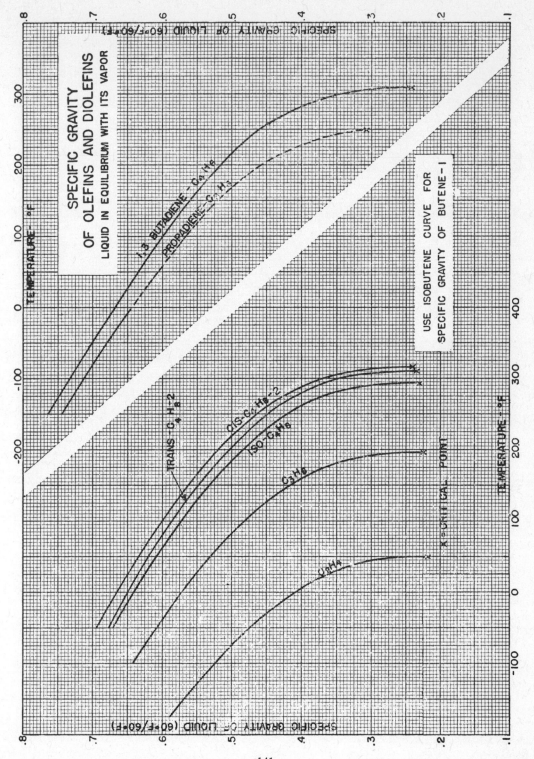

SPECIFIC GRAVITY
OF OLEFINS AND DIOLEFINS
LIQUID IN EQUILIBRIUM WITH ITS VAPOR

SPECIFIC GRAVITY OF LIQUID (60°F/60°F)

TEMPERATURE—°F

1,3-BUTADIENE — C_4H_6

PROPADIENE — C_3H_4

USE ISOBUTENE CURVE FOR
SPECIFIC GRAVITY OF BUTENE-1

TRANS-C_4H_8-2

CIS-C_4H_8-2

ISO-C_4H_8

C_3H_6

C_2H_4

X = CRITICAL POINT

TEMPERATURE—°F

SPECIFIC GRAVITY OF LIQUID (60°F/60°F)

141

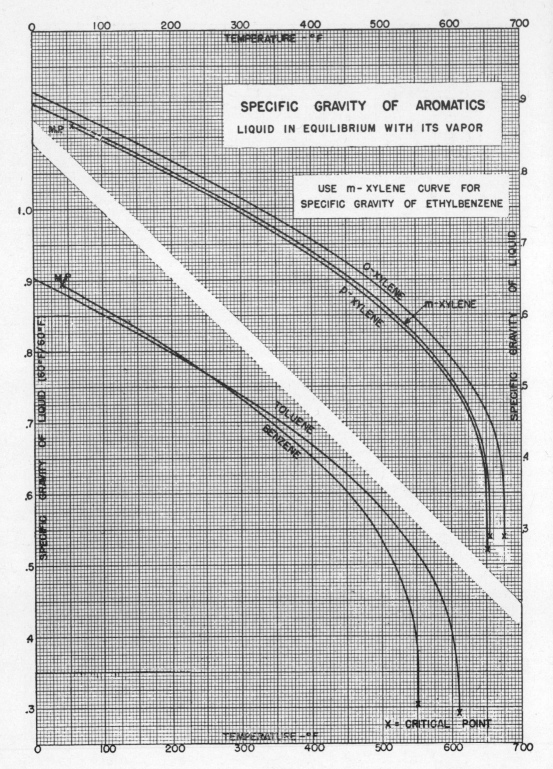

SPECIFIC GRAVITY OF AROMATICS
LIQUID IN EQUILIBRIUM WITH ITS VAPOR

USE m-XYLENE CURVE FOR
SPECIFIC GRAVITY OF ETHYLBENZENE

o-XYLENE

p-XYLENE

m-XYLENE

TOLUENE

BENZENE

TEMPERATURE - °F

SPECIFIC GRAVITY OF LIQUID (60°F/60°F)

SPECIFIC GRAVITY OF LIQUID

X = CRITICAL POINT

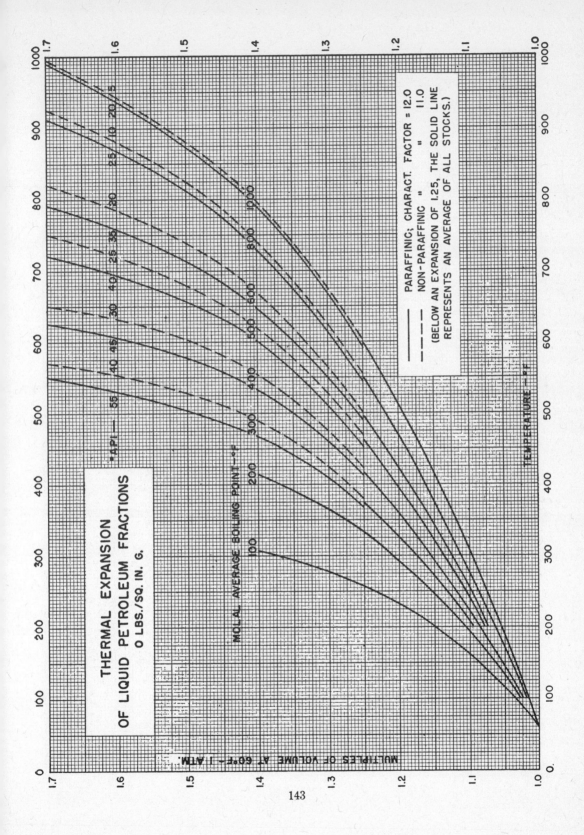

THERMAL EXPANSION
OF LIQUID PETROLEUM FRACTIONS
0 LBS./SQ. IN. G.

PARAFFINIC; CHARACT. FACTOR = 12.0
NON-PARAFFINIC " " = 11.0

(BELOW AN EXPANSION OF 1.25, THE SOLID LINE
REPRESENTS AN AVERAGE OF ALL STOCKS.)

TEMPERATURE —°F.

MOLAL AVERAGE BOILING POINT —°F

MULTIPLES OF VOLUME AT 60°F.— 1 ATM.

°API—

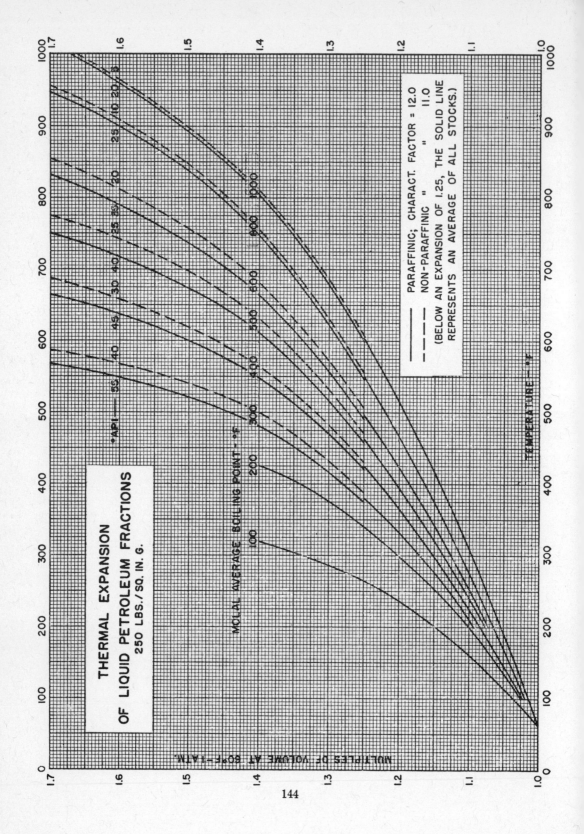

THERMAL EXPANSION
OF LIQUID PETROLEUM FRACTIONS
250 LBS./SQ. IN. G.

PARAFFINIC; CHARACT. FACTOR = 12.0
NON-PARAFFINIC   "   "   = 11.0
(BELOW AN EXPANSION OF 1.25, THE SOLID LINE
REPRESENTS AN AVERAGE OF ALL STOCKS.)

TEMPERATURE—°F

MOLAL AVERAGE BOILING POINT—°F

MULTIPLES OF VOLUME AT 60°F.-1 ATM.

°API—— 55   40   45   40   30   35 35 40   20   25 /10 20 15

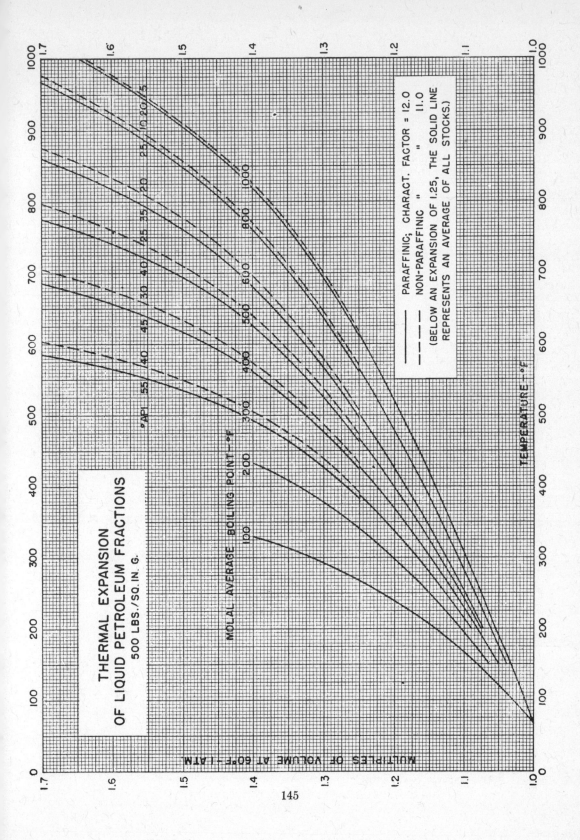

THERMAL EXPANSION
OF LIQUID PETROLEUM FRACTIONS
500 LBS./SQ. IN. G.

PARAFFINIC; CHARACT. FACTOR = 12.0
NON-PARAFFINIC " " 11.0
(BELOW AN EXPANSION OF 1.25, THE SOLID LINE
REPRESENTS AN AVERAGE OF ALL STOCKS.)

MOLAL AVERAGE BOILING POINT—°F

MULTIPLES OF VOLUME AT 60°F-1 ATM.

TEMPERATURE—°F

°API 55 40 45 30 40 35 35 20 25 10 20 5

145

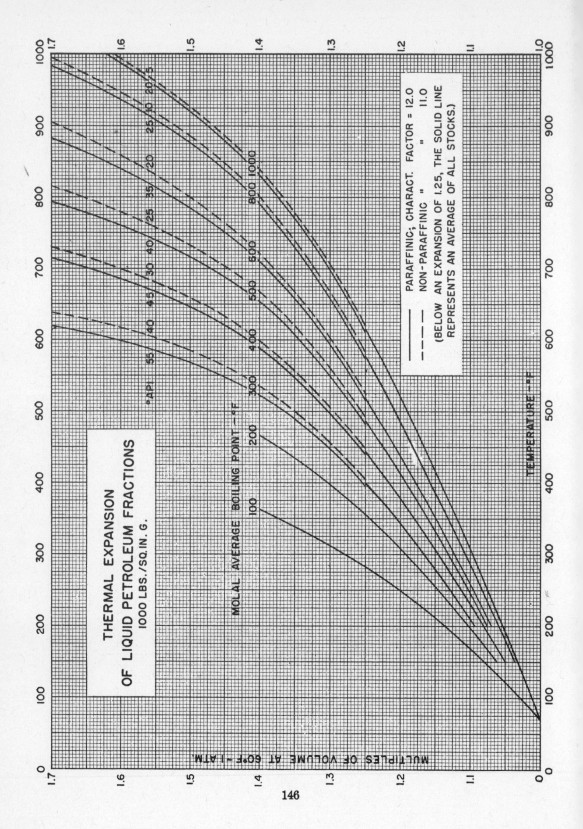

THERMAL EXPANSION
OF LIQUID PETROLEUM FRACTIONS
1000 LBS./SQ.IN. G.

PARAFFINIC; CHARACT. FACTOR = 12.0
NON-PARAFFINIC   "   "   = 11.0
(BELOW AN EXPANSION OF 1.25, THE SOLID LINE
REPRESENTS AN AVERAGE OF ALL STOCKS.)

MULTIPLES OF VOLUME AT 60°F - 1 ATM.

MOLAL AVERAGE BOILING POINT — °F

TEMPERATURE —°F

°API

146

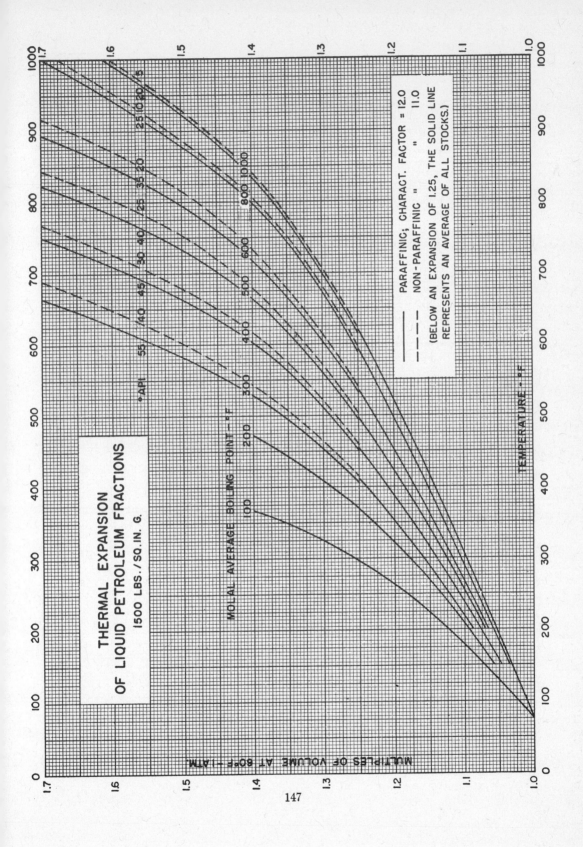

THERMAL EXPANSION
OF LIQUID PETROLEUM FRACTIONS
1500 LBS./SQ. IN. G.

PARAFFINIC; CHARACT. FACTOR = 12.0
NON-PARAFFINIC " " = 11.0

(BELOW AN EXPANSION OF 1.25, THE SOLID LINE
REPRESENTS AN AVERAGE OF ALL STOCKS.)

TEMPERATURE - °F

MOLAL AVERAGE BOILING POINT - °F

MULTIPLES OF VOLUME AT 60°F - 1 ATM

°API

147

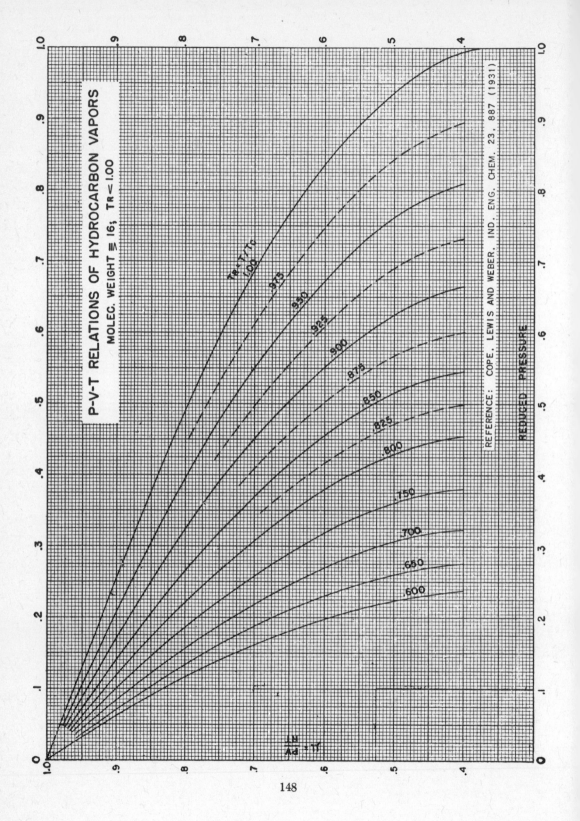

P–V–T RELATIONS OF HYDROCARBON VAPORS

MOLEC. WEIGHT ≅ 16; Tr < 1.00

$Tr = T/T_C$

1.00
.975
.950
.925
.900
.875
.850
.825
.800
.750
.700
.650
.600

$\mu = \dfrac{PV}{RT}$

REDUCED PRESSURE

REFERENCE: COPE, LEWIS AND WEBER, IND. ENG. CHEM. 23, 887 (1931)

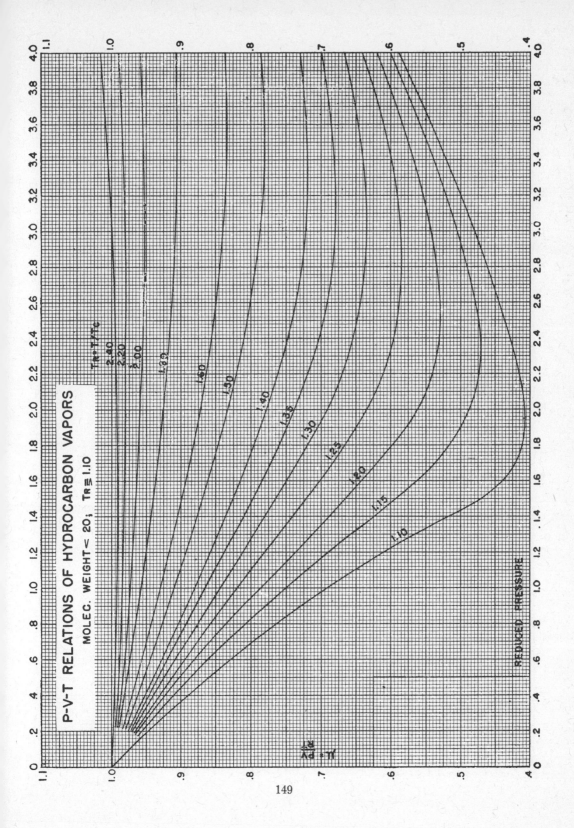

P-V-T RELATIONS OF HYDROCARBON VAPORS

MOLEC. WEIGHT < 20; $T_R \leqq 1.10$

$T_R = T/T_C$

2.40
2.20
2.00
1.80
1.60
1.50
1.40
1.35
1.30
1.25
1.20
1.15
1.10

$\mu = \dfrac{PV}{RT}$

REDUCED PRESSURE

149

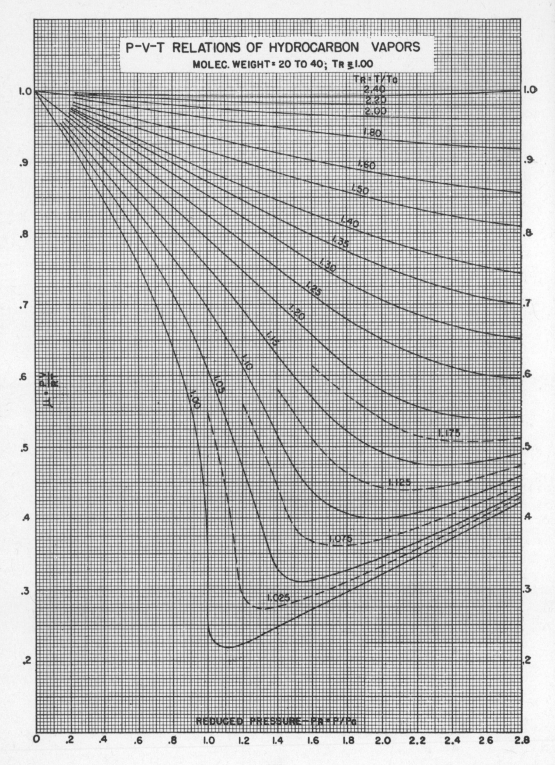

P-V-T RELATIONS OF HYDROCARBON VAPORS

MOLEC. WEIGHT = 20 TO 40; TR ≧ 1.00

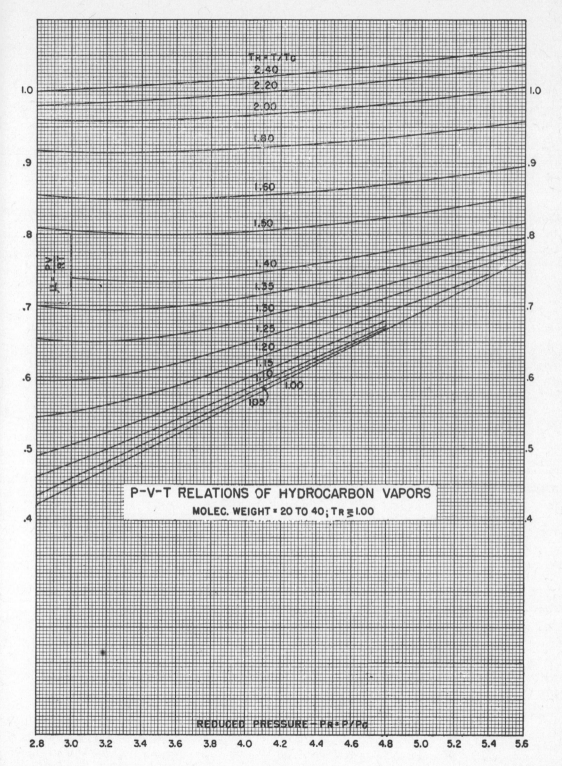

P-V-T RELATIONS OF HYDROCARBON VAPORS

MOLEC. WEIGHT = 20 TO 40; $T_R \gtrless 1.00$

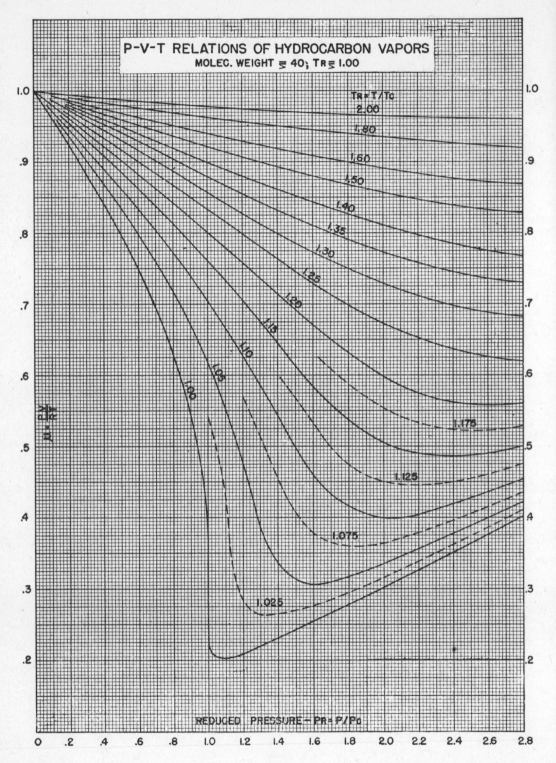

P-V-T RELATIONS OF HYDROCARBON VAPORS
MOLEC. WEIGHT ≅ 40; Tʀ ≅ 1.00

Tʀ = T/Tᴄ
2.00
1.80
1.60
1.50
1.40
1.35
1.30
1.25
1.20
1.15
1.10
1.05
1.00
1.175
1.125
1.075
1.025

REDUCED PRESSURE – Pʀ = P/Pᴄ

152

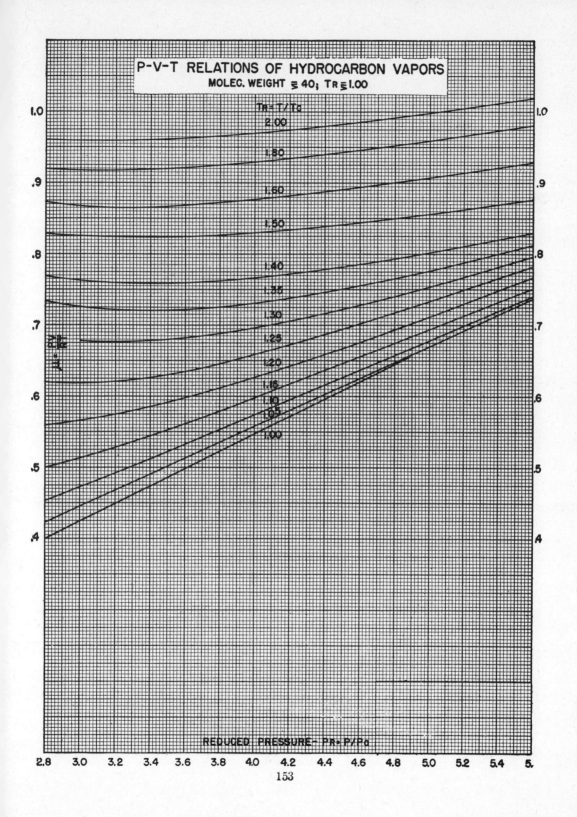

P-V-T RELATIONS OF HYDROCARBON VAPORS
MOLEC. WEIGHT ≦ 40; Tr ≦ 1.00

$T_R = T/T_C$

REDUCED PRESSURE - $P_R = P/P_C$

153

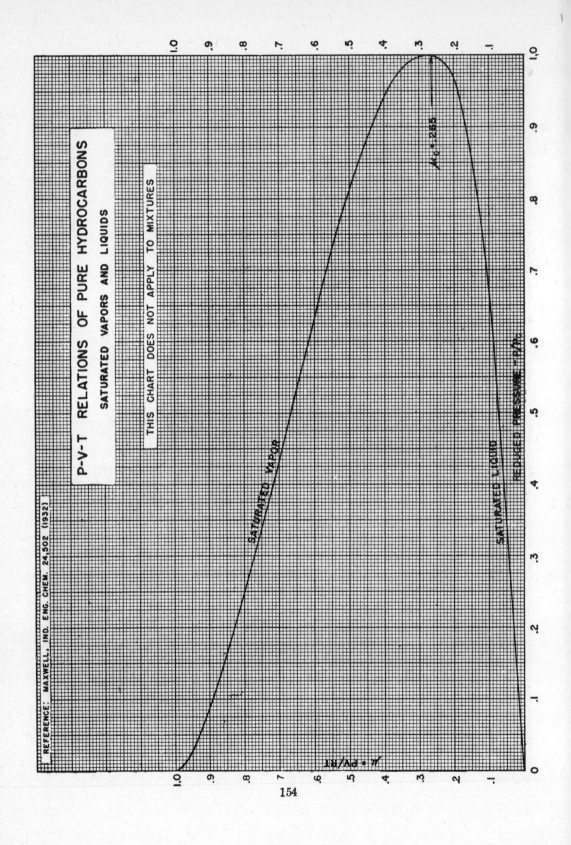

P-V-T RELATIONS OF PURE HYDROCARBONS
SATURATED VAPORS AND LIQUIDS

THIS CHART DOES NOT APPLY TO MIXTURES

REFERENCE: MAXWELL, IND. ENG. CHEM. 24,502 (1932)

SATURATED VAPOR

SATURATED LIQUID

$\mu_c = .265$

$\mu = PV/RT$

REDUCED PRESSURE $= P/P_c$

Section 9

VISCOSITY

Absolute Viscosity

In the metric system the unit of viscosity is the poise which is equivalent to a force of 1 dyne per sq cm shearing a liquid at the rate of 1 cm per sec per cm. By reduction to minimum dimensionality, the poise becomes $1 \ g/(cm)(sec)$. The corresponding English unit is $1 \ lb/(ft)(sec)$, or $(poundal)(sec)/(ft)^2$, which is equal to 14.88 poises.

However, the unit of viscosity most commonly used is the centipoise (0.01 poise), which happens to be the viscosity of water at almost exactly 68°F. Therefore, the absolute viscosity of any fluid in centipoises may be considered to be numerically equal to its viscosity relative to water at 68°F.

Kinematic Viscosity

Since the density of the liquid involved in the measurement of viscosity by the standard industrial viscometers, it is necessary to introduce kinematic viscosity, which is the absolute viscosity of a fluid divided by its density at the temperature under consideration. The metric units of kinematic viscosity corresponding to poises and centipoises are stokes and centistokes, of which the latter is more commonly used. The kinematic viscosity of water is 1 centistoke at just about 68°F.

Industrial Viscometers

The industrial viscometers which are widely used throughout the petroleum industry in this country are the Saybolt Thermo for refined oils, the Saybolt Universal for lubricating and gas oils, and the Saybolt Furol for crude residua and heavy fuel oils. The Redwood Standard and Engler viscometers are used mostly abroad. Curves for the conversion of these standard viscometer measurements to kinematic viscosity are given on pages 158 to 160.

Except for the Engler instrument, these conversions are slightly affected by the temperature at which the viscosity is measured, but this effect has been neglected in the present conversion charts. While Saybolt Universal viscosity may be measured at any one of several temperatures, 100°F, 130°F, or 210°F, the maximum variation between the temperature extremes in the conversion to kinematic viscosity is only 3% and, above kinematic viscosities of 5 centistokes, it is less than 2%. The variation between the extremes of the Redwood Standard instrument (70°F to 200°F) is appreciable at low viscosities but does not exceed 3% above 10 centistokes. Saybolt Thermo viscosity is normally measured at room

155

temperature and Saybolt Furol at 122°F so that it is usually unnecessary to consider conversions at any other temperatures for these instruments.

Change of Viscosity with Temperature

Viscosity-temperature curves are given for pure hydrocarbons and crude fractions on pages 161 to 165. In the absence of other data, these curves may be used to approximate viscosity-temperature relations for other hydrocarbons and petroleum fractions if the viscosity is known at only one temperature. However, if the viscosity is known at two or more temperatures, the charts on pages 166 and 167 should be used for linear interpolation and extrapolation.

Viscosity Index

Viscosity index is a generally accepted criterion for evaluating lubricating oils with respect to change of viscosity with temperature. The viscosity index of any oil may be read directly from the charts on pages 168 to 172 if its viscosities at 100°F and 210°F are known. If these particular viscosities are not available, but viscosities are known for two other temperatures, the viscosity-temperature charts on pages 166 and 167 may be used to find the values at 100°F and 210°F.

Viscosity Blending

To predict the viscosity of a blend of two or more fractions at any given temperature, the blending index for each fraction is determined from its viscosity at this temperature, using the chart on page 173. The blending indexes of the individual fractions are additive by volume fraction and the resulting sum may be converted to the viscosity of the mixture by referring to the blending chart again. If the viscosity of one or more of the components is not available at the desired temperature, it must be converted to this temperature, since blending indexes are additive only at constant temperature.

The viscosity of a blend of two stocks may also be obtained graphically by using the viscosity-temperature charts. A straight line connecting the viscosity of the less viscous stock on the 0°F abscissa and the more viscous stock on the 100°F abscissa represents the locus of the viscosity of all blends of these stocks. The ordinate corresponding to the percentage of the more viscous stock—whereby the temperatures between 0°F and 100°F are considered percentages—represents the viscosity of the blend. While the blending index chart was derived from the ordinate scales of the viscosity-temperature charts, the two methods will differ slightly since the temperature divisions vary between 0°F and 100°F.

Viscosity of Gases

While pressure has very little effect on the viscosity of liquids except near the critical temperature, its effect on gases may be considerable, especially above the critical pressure. The change in viscosity of a gas or vapor with pressure may be predicted from the chart on page 177. By the use of reduced temperature and pressure, this chart provides a generalized correlation of the ratio of viscosity at any temperature and pressure to the viscosity at the same temperature and atmospheric pressure.

The viscosity of a mixture of two or more gases at atmospheric pressure may be computed by the following formula:

$$Z_m = \frac{N_1 Z_1 \sqrt{M_1} + N_2 Z_2 \sqrt{M_2} + \cdots + N_n Z_n \sqrt{M_n}}{N_1 \sqrt{M_1} + N_2 \sqrt{M_2} + \cdots + N_n \sqrt{M_n}}$$

where Z_m = the viscosity of the mixture

N_1, N_2, etc. = the mole fractions or moles of individual components

Z_1, Z_2, etc. = the viscosities of the individual components

M_1, M_2, etc. = the molecular weights of the individual components

The chart for change in viscosity with pressure may be applied to mixtures by using the pseudo-critical properties of the mixture to determine reduced temperature and pressure.

GENERAL REFERENCES

ASTM Standard Viscosity-Temperature Charts for Liquid Petroleum Products (D341–39), Charts C and D.

Beale, "The Science of Petroleum," Vol. II, 1080, Oxford University Press, New York, N.Y. (1938).

Comings and Egly, *Ind. Eng. Chem.* **32**, 714 (1940).

Davis, Lapeyrouse and Dean, *Oil Gas J.* **30**, No. 46, 92 (1932).

Dean and Davis, *Chem & Met. Eng.* **36**, 618 (1929).

Edwards and Bonilla, *Ind. Eng. Chem.* **36**, 1038 (1944).

Etherington, Sc. D. Thesis, Mass. Inst. Tech. (1948).

Evans, *J. Inst. Petroleum Tech.* **24**, 321 (1938).

Fortch and Wilson, *Ind. Eng. Chem.* **16**, 789 (1924).

Lane and Dean, *Ind. Eng. Chem.* **16**, 905 (1924).

Lipkin, Davison and Kurtz, *Ind. Eng. Chem.* **34**, 976 (1942).

Nat. Bur. Standards Circular C461 (1947).

Sage and Lacey, *Ind. Eng. Chem.* **30**, 829 (1938).

Sage, Yale and Lacey, *Ind. Eng. Chem.* **31**, 223 (1939).

Watson, Wien and Murphy, *Ind. Eng. Chem.* **28**, 605 (1936).

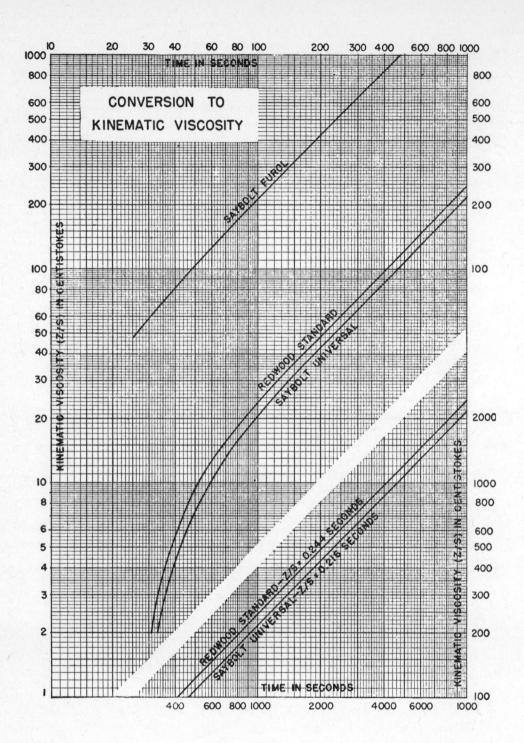

CONVERSION TO KINEMATIC VISCOSITY

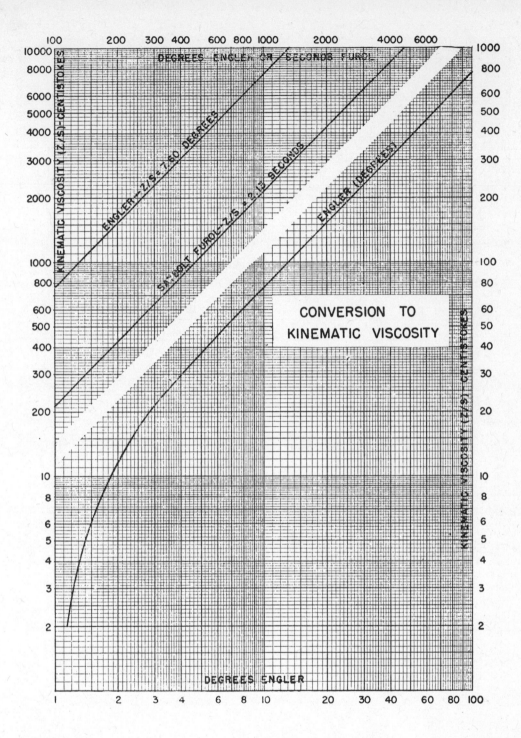

CONVERSION TO KINEMATIC VISCOSITY

DEGREES ENGLER OR SECONDS FUROL

KINEMATIC VISCOSITY (Z/S)-CENTISTOKES

ENGLER = Z/S = 7.60 DEGREES

SAYBOLT FUROL = Z/S = 2.15 SECONDS

ENGLER (DEGREES)

KINEMATIC VISCOSITY (Z/S) CENTISTOKES

DEGREES ENGLER

159

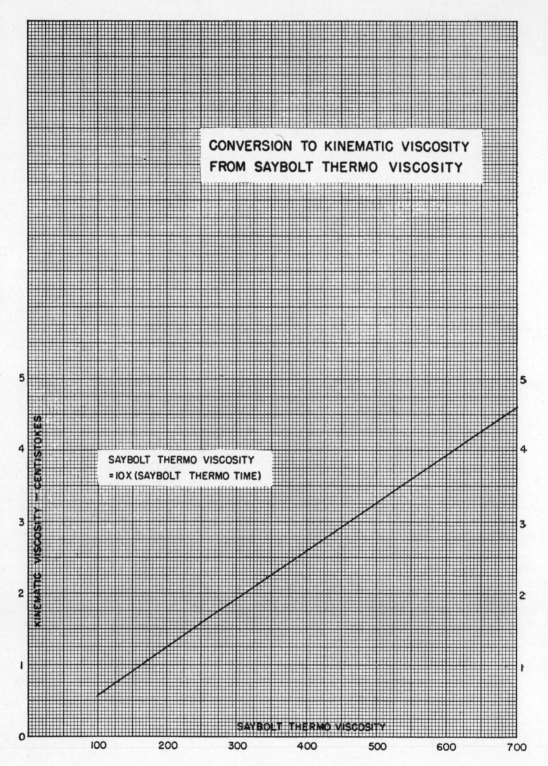

CONVERSION TO KINEMATIC VISCOSITY
FROM SAYBOLT THERMO VISCOSITY

SAYBOLT THERMO VISCOSITY
= 10 X (SAYBOLT THERMO TIME)

KINEMATIC VISCOSITY — CENTISTOKES

SAYBOLT THERMO VISCOSITY

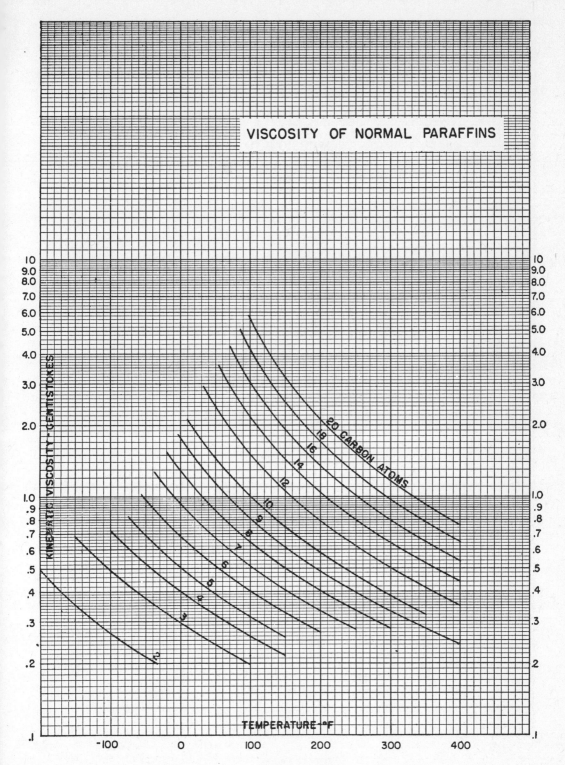

VISCOSITY OF NORMAL PARAFFINS

KINEMATIC VISCOSITY - CENTISTOKES

TEMPERATURE-°F

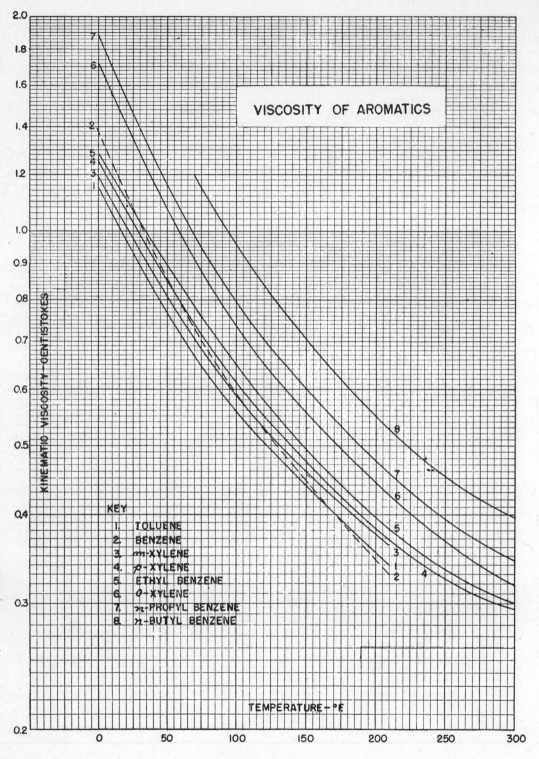

VISCOSITY OF AROMATICS

KINEMATIC VISCOSITY-CENTISTOKES

KEY

1. TOLUENE
2. BENZENE
3. m-XYLENE
4. p-XYLENE
5. ETHYL BENZENE
6. o-XYLENE
7. n-PROPYL BENZENE
8. n-BUTYL BENZENE

TEMPERATURE-°F

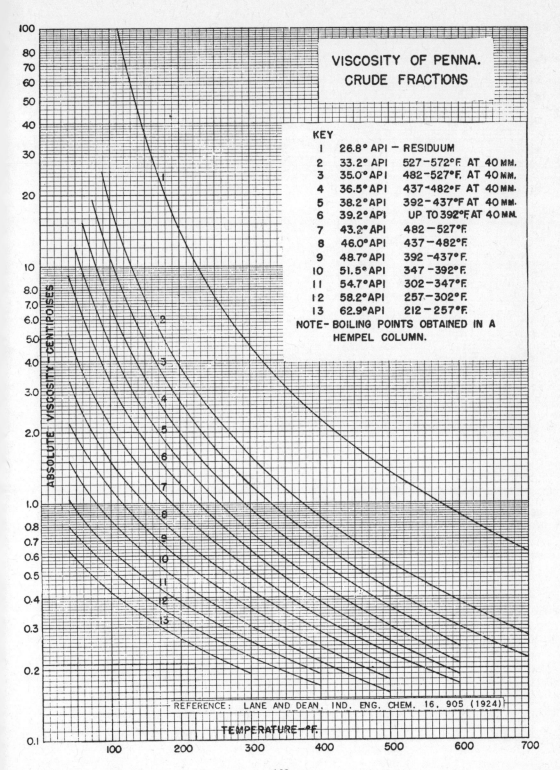

VISCOSITY OF PENNA.
CRUDE FRACTIONS

KEY
1   26.8° API – RESIDUUM
2   33.2° API   527–572°F. AT 40 MM.
3   35.0° API   482–527°F. AT 40 MM.
4   36.5° API   437–482°F. AT 40 MM.
5   38.2° API   392–437°F. AT 40 MM.
6   39.2° API   UP TO 392°F. AT 40 MM.
7   43.2° API   482–527°F.
8   46.0° API   437–482°F.
9   48.7° API   392–437°F.
10 51.5° API   347–392°F.
11 54.7° API   302–347°F.
12 58.2° API   257–302°F.
13 62.9° API   212–257°F.
NOTE– BOILING POINTS OBTAINED IN A
      HEMPEL COLUMN.

ABSOLUTE VISCOSITY-CENTIPOISES

REFERENCE: LANE AND DEAN, IND. ENG. CHEM. 16, 905 (1924)

TEMPERATURE—°F.

163

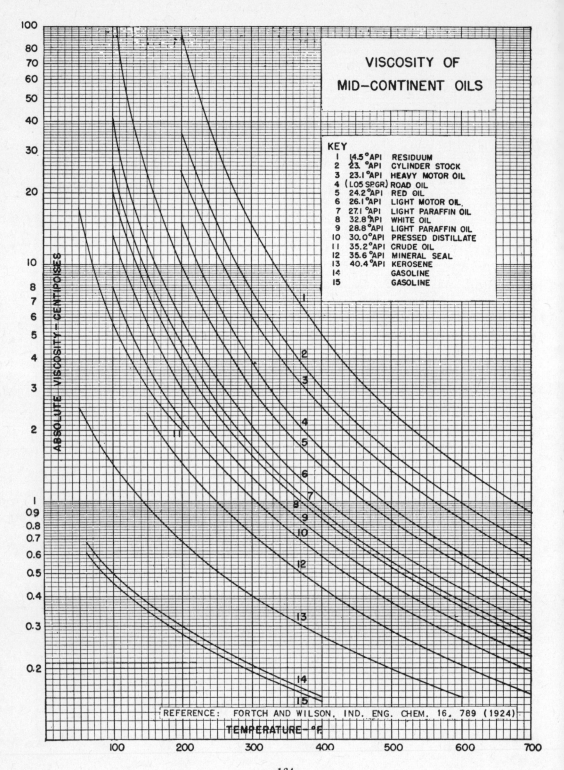

VISCOSITY OF
MID-CONTINENT OILS

KEY

1	14.5°API	RESIDUUM
2	23.°API	CYLINDER STOCK
3	23.1°API	HEAVY MOTOR OIL
4	(1.05 SP.GR.)	ROAD OIL
5	24.2°API	RED OIL
6	26.1°API	LIGHT MOTOR OIL
7	27.1°API	LIGHT PARAFFIN OIL
8	32.8°API	WHITE OIL
9	28.8°API	LIGHT PARAFFIN OIL
10	30.0°API	PRESSED DISTILLATE
11	35.2°API	CRUDE OIL
12	35.6°API	MINERAL SEAL
13	40.4°API	KEROSENE
14		GASOLINE
15		GASOLINE

ABSOLUTE VISCOSITY—CENTIPOISES

TEMPERATURE—°F.

REFERENCE: FORTCH AND WILSON, IND. ENG. CHEM. 16, 789 (1924)

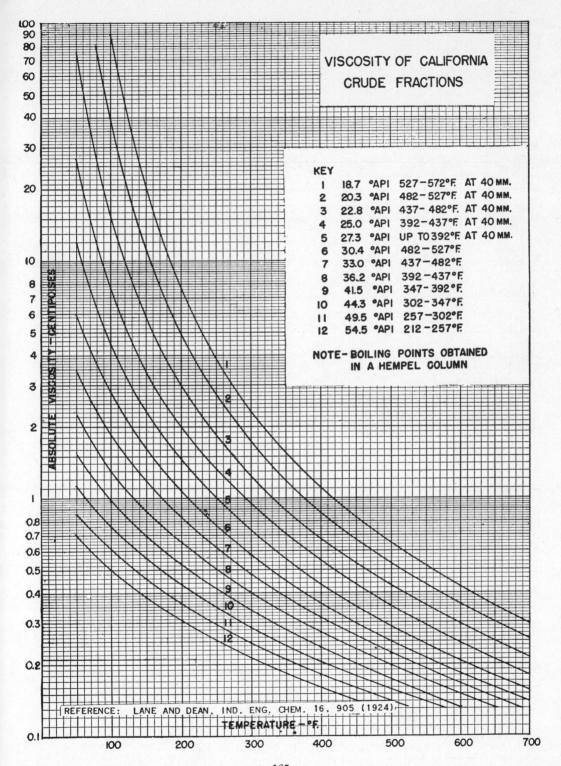

VISCOSITY OF CALIFORNIA CRUDE FRACTIONS

KEY

1	18.7 °API	527−572°F. AT 40 MM.
2	20.3 °API	482−527°F. AT 40 MM.
3	22.8 °API	437−482°F. AT 40 MM.
4	25.0 °API	392−437°F. AT 40 MM.
5	27.3 °API	UP TO 392°F. AT 40 MM.
6	30.4 °API	482−527°F.
7	33.0 °API	437−482°F.
8	36.2 °API	392−437°F.
9	41.5 °API	347−392°F.
10	44.3 °API	302−347°F.
11	49.5 °API	257−302°F.
12	54.5 °API	212−257°F.

NOTE- BOILING POINTS OBTAINED IN A HEMPEL COLUMN

ABSOLUTE VISCOSITY – CENTIPOISES

REFERENCE: LANE AND DEAN, IND. ENG. CHEM. 16, 905 (1924)

TEMPERATURE – °F.

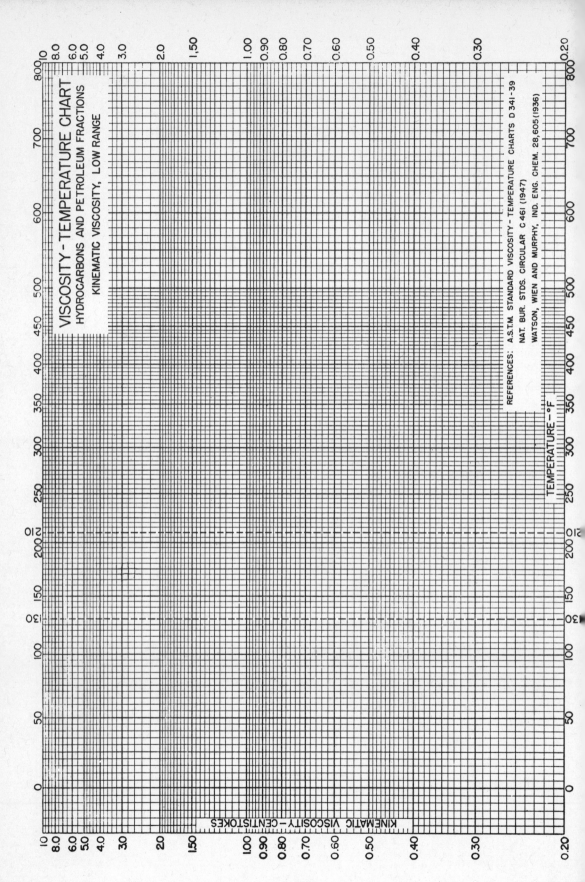

VISCOSITY-TEMPERATURE CHART
HYDROCARBONS AND PETROLEUM FRACTIONS
KINEMATIC VISCOSITY, LOW RANGE

REFERENCES: A.S.T.M. STANDARD VISCOSITY-TEMPERATURE CHARTS D 341-39
NAT. BUR. STDS. CIRCULAR C 461 (1947)
WATSON, WIEN AND MURPHY, IND. ENG. CHEM. 28,605 (1936)

TEMPERATURE—°F

KINEMATIC VISCOSITY—CENTISTOKES

166

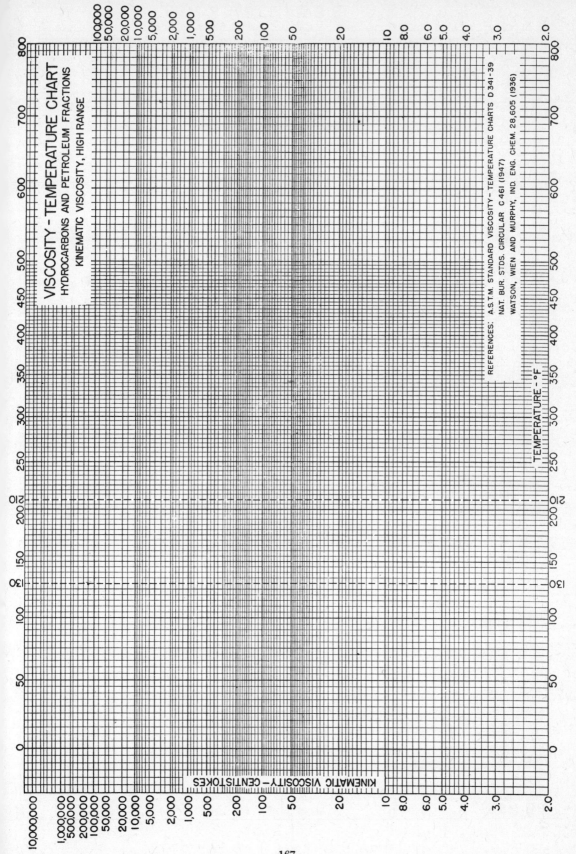

VISCOSITY - TEMPERATURE CHART
HYDROCARBONS AND PETROLEUM FRACTIONS
KINEMATIC VISCOSITY, HIGH RANGE

REFERENCES: A.S.T.M. STANDARD VISCOSITY - TEMPERATURE CHARTS D 341-39
NAT. BUR. STDS. CIRCULAR C 461 (1947)
WATSON, WIEN AND MURPHY, IND. ENG. CHEM. 28,605 (1936)

TEMPERATURE - °F

KINEMATIC VISCOSITY - CENTISTOKES

167

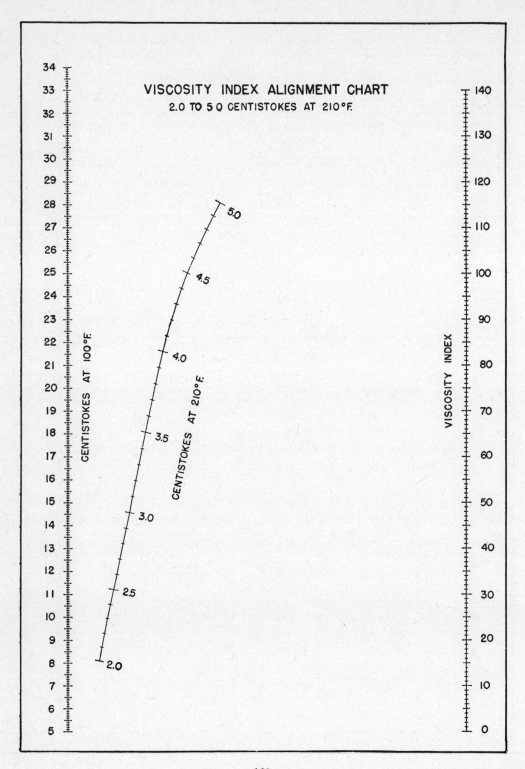

VISCOSITY INDEX ALIGNMENT CHART

2.0 TO 5.0 CENTISTOKES AT 210°F.

CENTISTOKES AT 100°F.

CENTISTOKES AT 210°F.

VISCOSITY INDEX

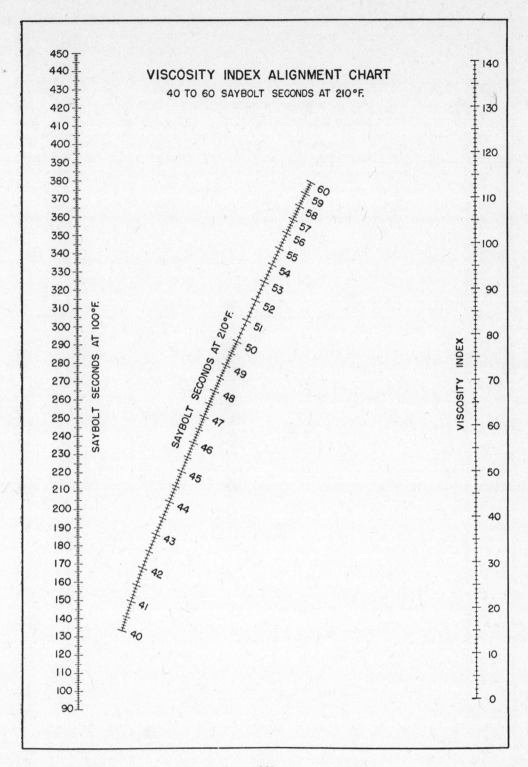

VISCOSITY INDEX ALIGNMENT CHART
40 TO 60 SAYBOLT SECONDS AT 210°F.

SAYBOLT SECONDS AT 100°F.

SAYBOLT SECONDS AT 210°F.

VISCOSITY INDEX

169

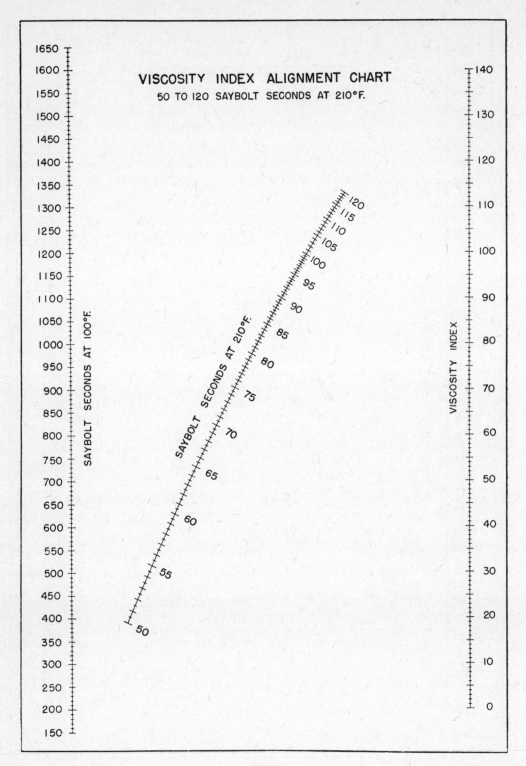

VISCOSITY INDEX ALIGNMENT CHART

50 TO 120 SAYBOLT SECONDS AT 210°F.

SAYBOLT SECONDS AT 100°F.

SAYBOLT SECONDS AT 210°F.

VISCOSITY INDEX

170

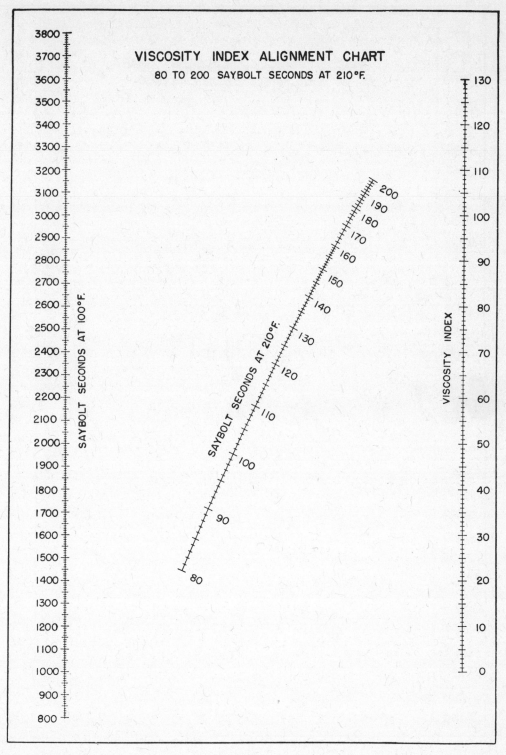

VISCOSITY INDEX ALIGNMENT CHART
80 TO 200 SAYBOLT SECONDS AT 210°F.

SAYBOLT SECONDS AT 100°F.

SAYBOLT SECONDS AT 210°F.

VISCOSITY INDEX

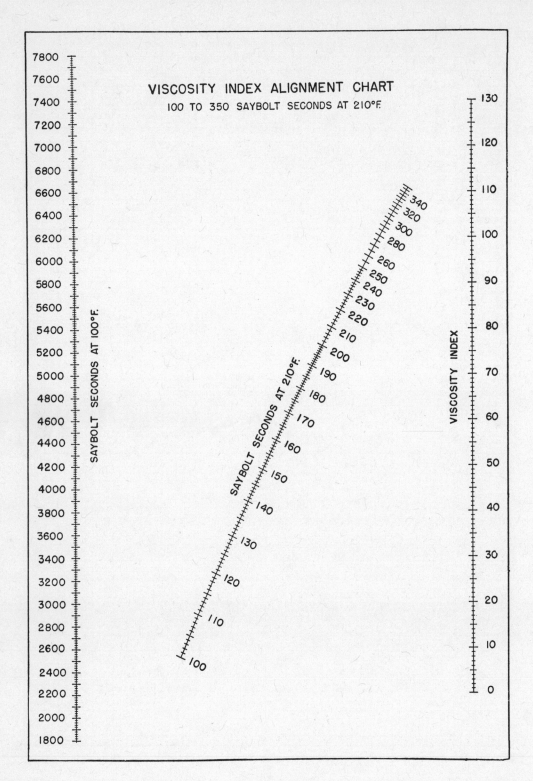

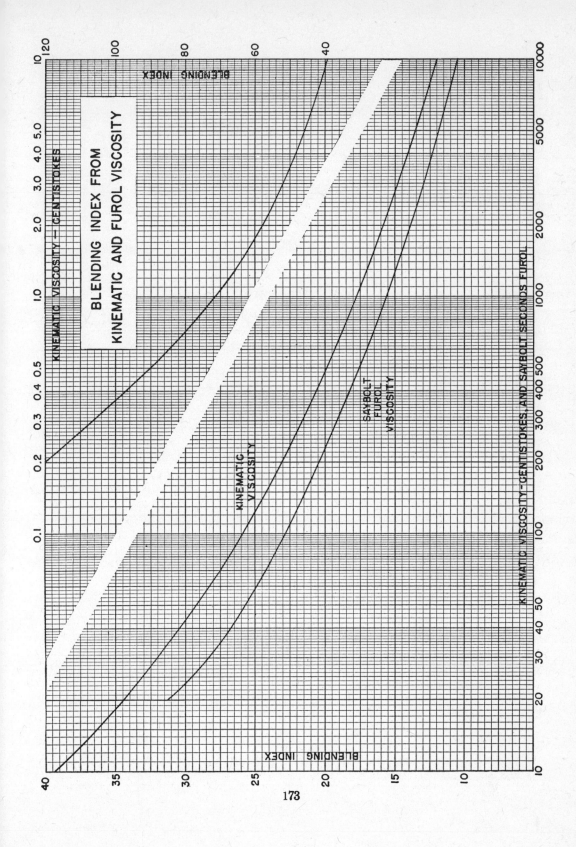

BLENDING INDEX FROM
KINEMATIC AND FUROL VISCOSITY

KINEMATIC VISCOSITY — CENTISTOKES

BLENDING INDEX

KINEMATIC
VISCOSITY

SAYBOLT
FUROL
VISCOSITY

KINEMATIC VISCOSITY–CENTISTOKES, AND SAYBOLT SECONDS FUROL

BLENDING INDEX

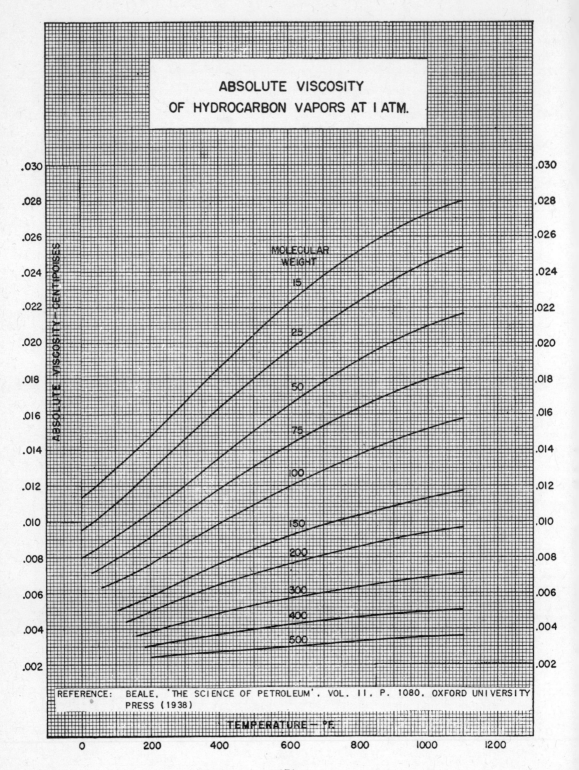

ABSOLUTE VISCOSITY
OF HYDROCARBON VAPORS AT I ATM.

MOLECULAR WEIGHT

15

25

50

75

100

150

200

300

400

500

ABSOLUTE VISCOSITY – CENTIPOISES

TEMPERATURE – °F.

REFERENCE: BEALE, 'THE SCIENCE OF PETROLEUM', VOL. II, P. 1080, OXFORD UNIVERSITY PRESS (1938)

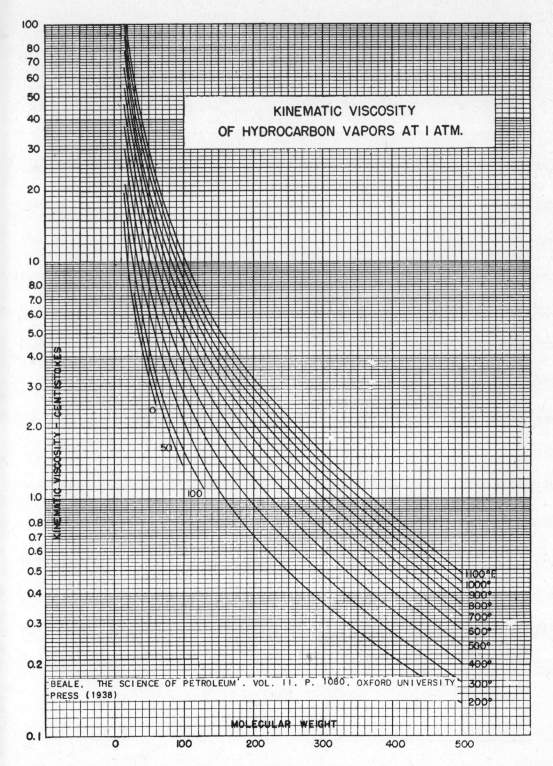

KINEMATIC VISCOSITY
OF HYDROCARBON VAPORS AT I ATM.

KINEMATIC VISCOSITY - CENTISTOKES

MOLECULAR WEIGHT

BEALE. THE SCIENCE OF PETROLEUM'. VOL. II. P. 1080. OXFORD UNIVERSITY PRESS (1938)

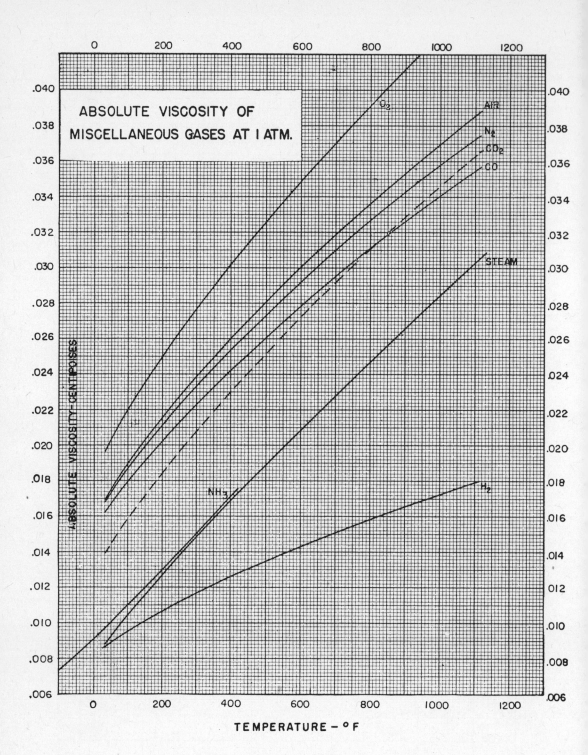

ABSOLUTE VISCOSITY OF MISCELLANEOUS GASES AT 1 ATM.

TEMPERATURE – °F

ABSOLUTE VISCOSITY–CENTIPOISES

176

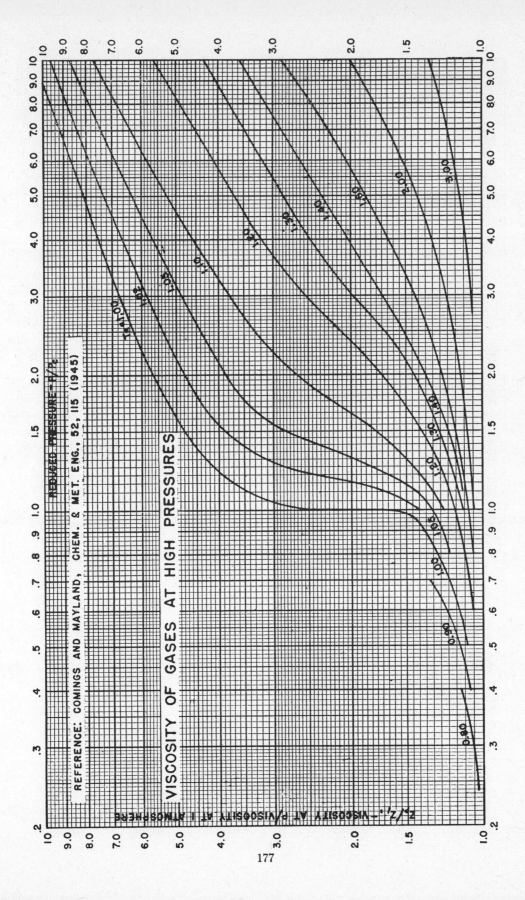

REDUCED PRESSURE—P_r/P_c

REFERENCE: COMINGS AND MAYLAND, CHEM. & MET. ENG., 52, 115 (1945)

VISCOSITY OF GASES AT HIGH PRESSURES

$Z\bar{z}/Z_1$.—VISCOSITY AT P/VISCOSITY AT 1 ATMOSPHERE

177

Section 10

COMBUSTION

Liquid Fuels

The heats of combustion of fuel oils and petroleum fractions are expressed as a function of gravity by the chart on page 180. Both the high and low heating values have been corrected for the average impurities other than water which are usually present in oils of various gravities. These average impurities, tabulated on the chart, are fairly representative, although there may be appreciable deviations for a given stock. In general, the heating values of average fuel oils are within 1% of the curves.

The heat available from the combustion at 60°F of liquid fuels is given on pages 186 to 188 for fuel oils of 5°, 10° and 15°API. Because of the small variation between these charts, interpolation is unnecessary and the available heat at any temperature and percent excess air may be read from the chart which most nearly corresponds to the gravity of the fuel oil. If the impurities are known to be appreciably different from the average values tabulated on page 180, the available heat may be corrected in direct proportion to the hydrocarbon portion of the fuel with sulfur considered as inert material.

Gaseous Fuels

Heats of combustion of paraffin and olefin gases are given as a function of molecular weight by the chart on page 181. The paraffin curves on this chart were used as a basis for deriving the charts on pages 184 and 185 for the heat available from the combustion at 60°F of dry refinery gases having high heating values of 1000 and 1600 BTU/S.C.F. Allowance was made for average impurities of 2.5% H_2S and 2.5% inerts (equal parts CO_2 and air) by volume. As in the case of liquid fuels, the chart more nearly corresponding to the high heating value of the fuel gas may be used without interpolation with very little error. However, in correcting for variation in impurities, the available heat must be adjusted in proportion to the *weight percentage* of the hydrocarbon portion of the fuel gas. In making an adjustment for the H_2S content of the gas, its volume percent may be distributed equally between the inerts and hydrocarbon portion as a good approximation. The following table gives relevant information for refinery fuel gases of average impurities:

178

Nominal HHV, BTU/S.C.F.[1]	1000	1200	1400	1600	1800	2000
Wt. Percent Impurities	10.1	8.3	7.1	6.2	5.4	4.90
Sp Gr of Fuel Gas (Air = 1.0)	0.60	0.73	0.86	0.99	1.12	1.25
M.W. of Hydrocarbon Portion	16.5	20.4	24.3	28.2	32.1	36.1
Actual HHV of HC Portion-BTU/S.C.F.[1]	1037	1248	1458	1669	1879	2090

[1] Calculated by the perfect gas law at 60°F and 1 atm.

Properties of Flue Gas

The CO_2 content of flue gas and the weight ratio of flue gas to fuel are given both for liquid and gaseous fuels as a function of excess air on pages 189 and 190. Since the effect of percent excess of air is almost imperceptible on the viscosity and thermal conductivity of flue gas, it has been neglected entirely and each of these properties is expressed as a function of temperature alone.

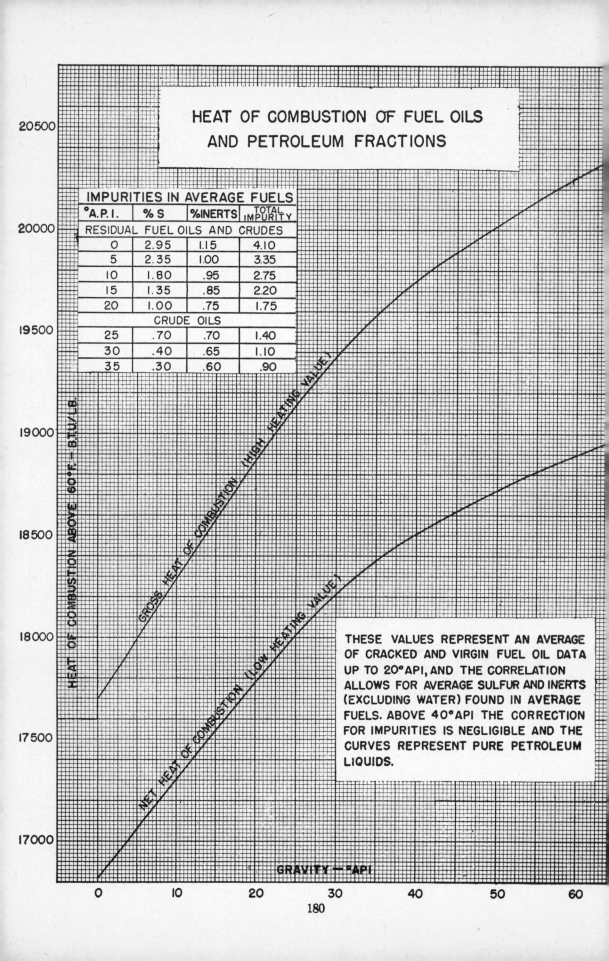

HEAT OF COMBUSTION OF FUEL OILS
AND PETROLEUM FRACTIONS

IMPURITIES IN AVERAGE FUELS

°A.P.I.	% S	%INERTS	TOTAL IMPURITY
RESIDUAL FUEL OILS AND CRUDES			
0	2.95	1.15	4.10
5	2.35	1.00	3.35
10	1.80	.95	2.75
15	1.35	.85	2.20
20	1.00	.75	1.75
CRUDE OILS			
25	.70	.70	1.40
30	.40	.65	1.10
35	.30	.60	.90

GROSS HEAT OF COMBUSTION (HIGH HEATING VALUE)

NET HEAT OF COMBUSTION (LOW HEATING VALUE)

HEAT OF COMBUSTION ABOVE 60°F. — B.T.U./LB.

THESE VALUES REPRESENT AN AVERAGE
OF CRACKED AND VIRGIN FUEL OIL DATA
UP TO 20° API, AND THE CORRELATION
ALLOWS FOR AVERAGE SULFUR AND INERTS
(EXCLUDING WATER) FOUND IN AVERAGE
FUELS. ABOVE 40° API THE CORRECTION
FOR IMPURITIES IS NEGLIGIBLE AND THE
CURVES REPRESENT PURE PETROLEUM
LIQUIDS.

GRAVITY — °API

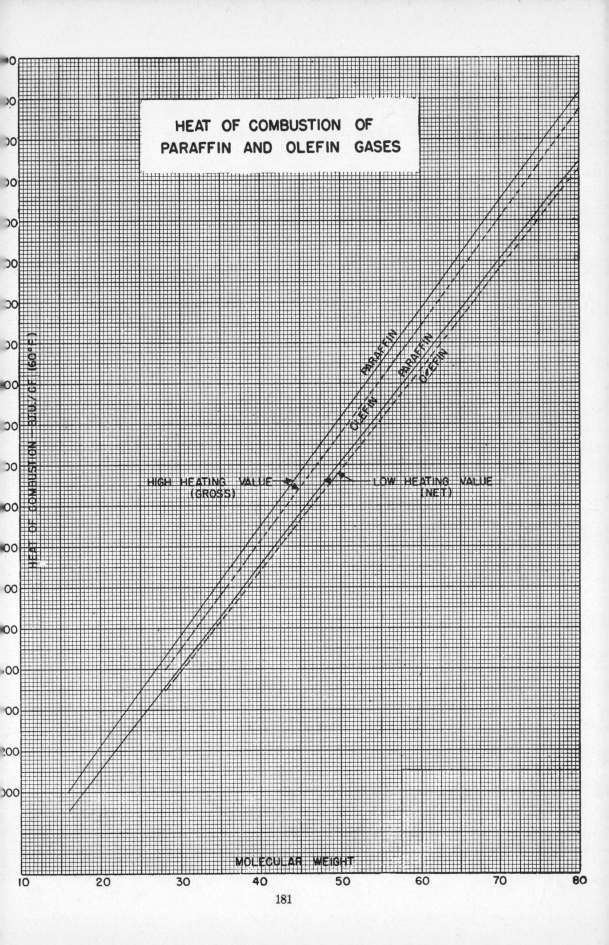

HEAT OF COMBUSTION OF
PARAFFIN AND OLEFIN GASES

HEAT OF COMBUSTION — BTU/ CF (60° F.)

PARAFFIN

OLEFIN

PARAFFIN

OLEFIN

HIGH HEATING VALUE
(GROSS)

LOW HEATING VALUE
(NET)

MOLECULAR WEIGHT

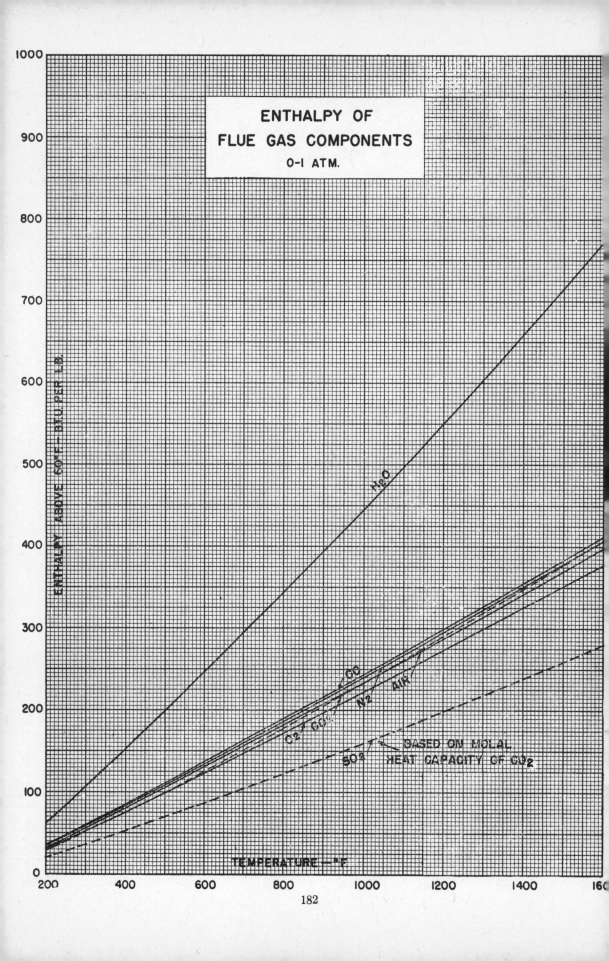

ENTHALPY OF
FLUE GAS COMPONENTS
0-1 ATM.

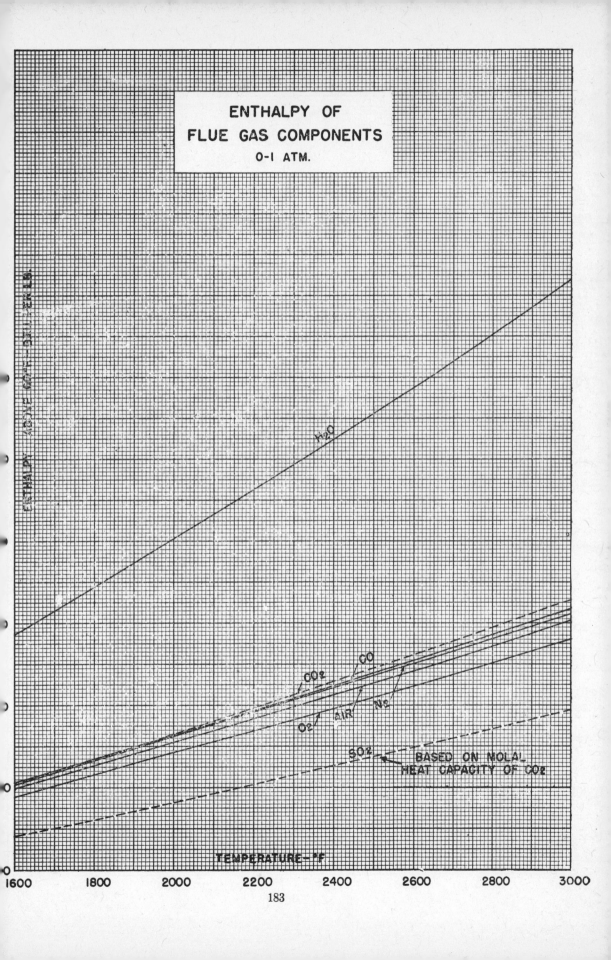

ENTHALPY OF
FLUE GAS COMPONENTS
0-1 ATM.

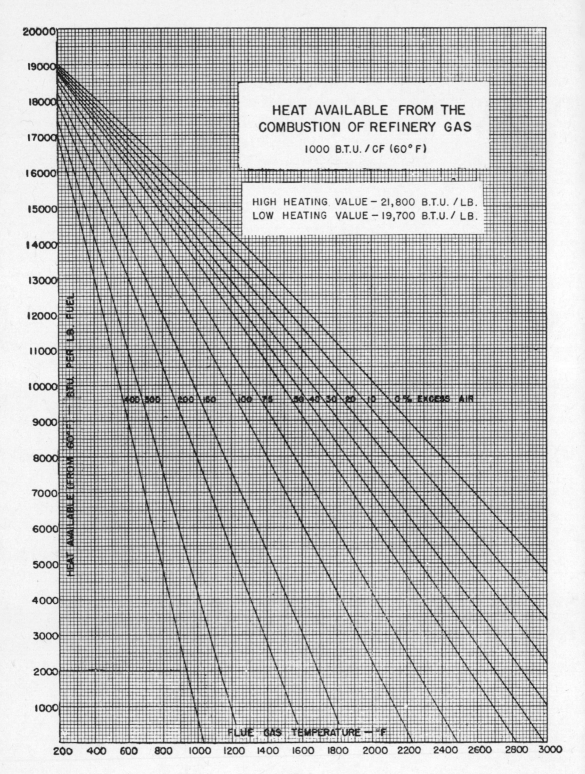

HEAT AVAILABLE FROM THE
COMBUSTION OF REFINERY GAS

1000 B.T.U. / CF (60° F)

HIGH HEATING VALUE – 21,800 B.T.U. / LB.
LOW HEATING VALUE – 19,700 B.T.U. / LB.

HEAT AVAILABLE (FROM 60°F) — BTU PER LB. FUEL

FLUE GAS TEMPERATURE — °F

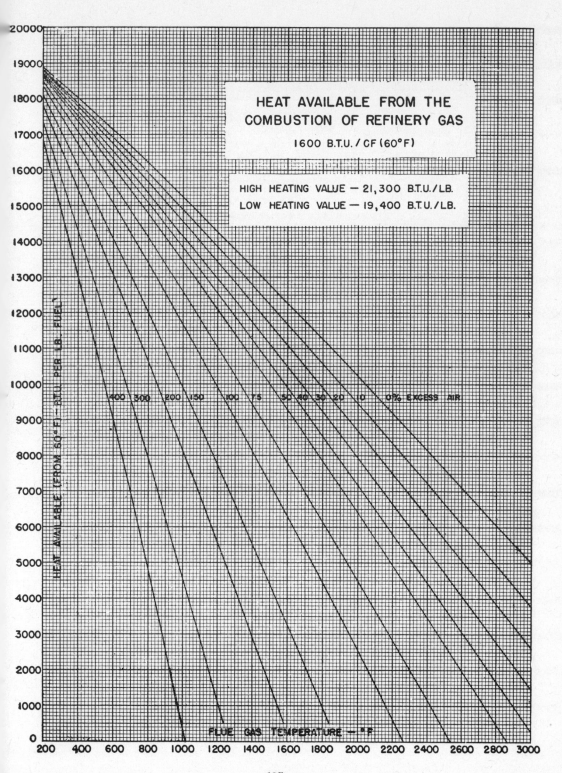

HEAT AVAILABLE FROM THE
COMBUSTION OF REFINERY GAS

1600 B.T.U. / CF (60°F)

HIGH HEATING VALUE — 21,300 B.T.U./LB.
LOW HEATING VALUE — 19,400 B.T.U./LB.

400 300 200 150 100 75 50 40 30 20 10 0% EXCESS AIR

HEAT AVAILABLE (FROM 60°F) BTU PER LB. FUEL

FLUE GAS TEMPERATURE — °F

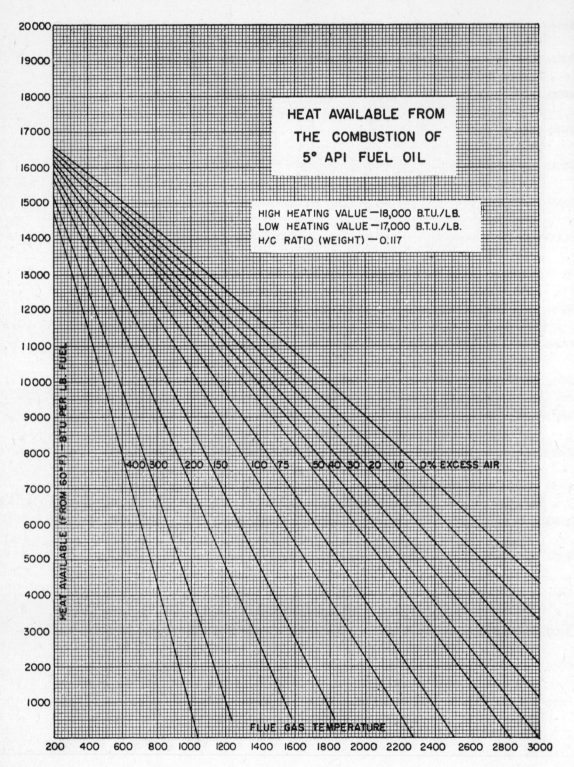

HEAT AVAILABLE FROM
THE COMBUSTION OF
5° API FUEL OIL

HIGH HEATING VALUE —18,000 B.T.U./LB.
LOW HEATING VALUE —17,000 B.T.U./LB.
H/C RATIO (WEIGHT) —0.117

HEAT AVAILABLE (FROM 60°F) —BTU PER LB. FUEL

400 300   200 150   100 75   50 40 30 20   10   0% EXCESS AIR

FLUE GAS TEMPERATURE

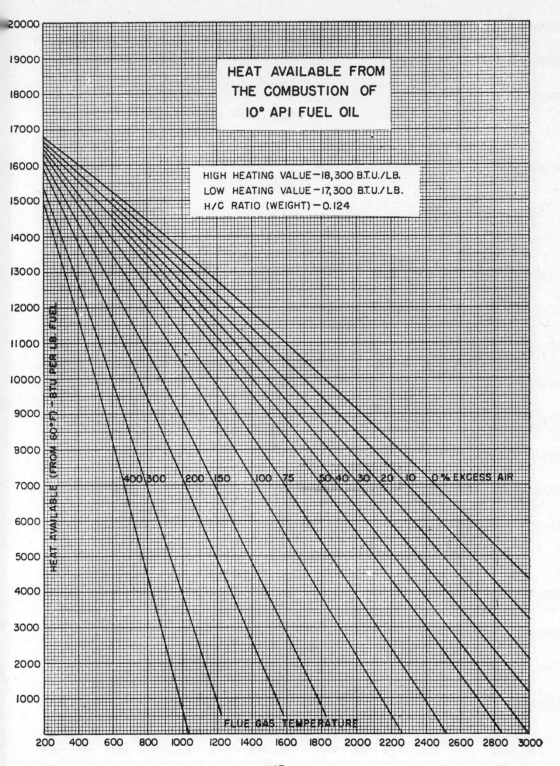

HEAT AVAILABLE FROM
THE COMBUSTION OF
10° API FUEL OIL

HIGH HEATING VALUE — 18,300 B.T.U./LB.
LOW HEATING VALUE — 17,300 B.T.U./LB.
H/C RATIO (WEIGHT) — 0.124

HEAT AVAILABLE (FROM 60°F) — BTU PER LB. FUEL

400 300   200 150   100 75   50 40 30 20   10   0 % EXCESS AIR

FLUE GAS TEMPERATURE

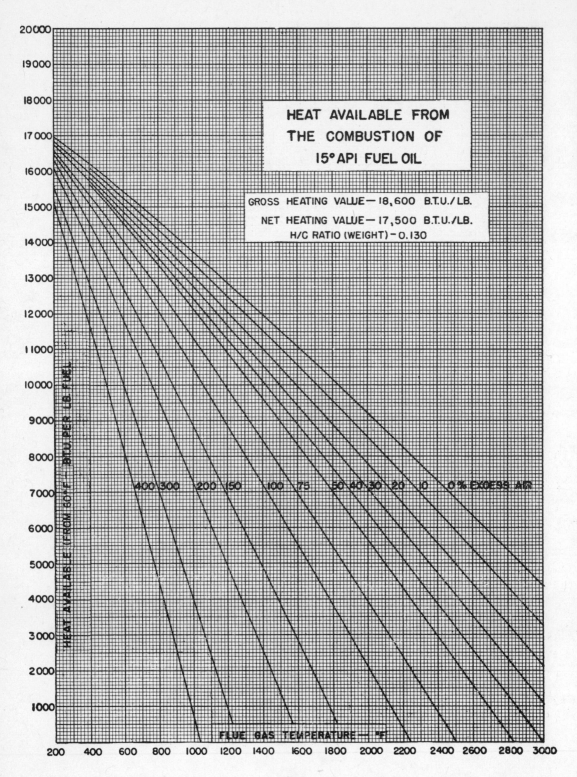

HEAT AVAILABLE FROM
THE COMBUSTION OF
15° API FUEL OIL

GROSS HEATING VALUE — 18,600 B.T.U./LB.

NET HEATING VALUE — 17,500 B.T.U./LB.

H/C RATIO (WEIGHT) — 0.130

FLUE GAS TEMPERATURE — °F

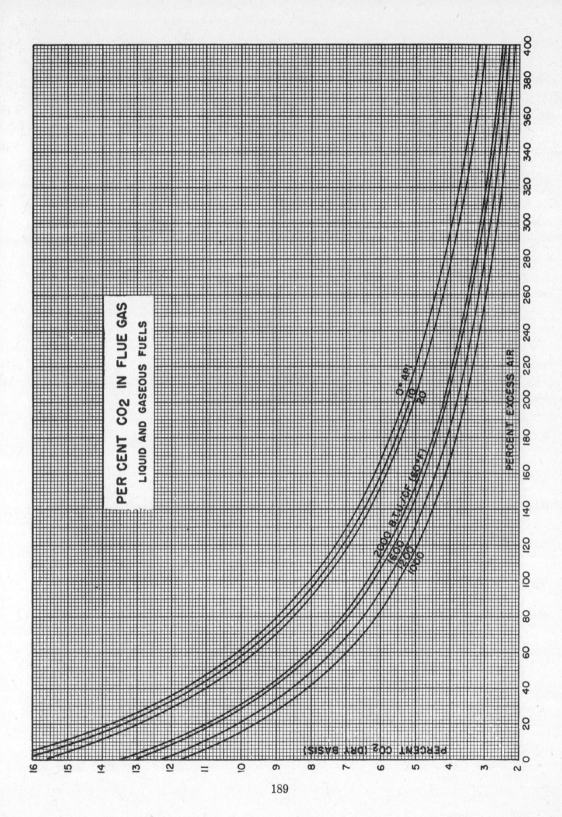

PER CENT CO2 IN FLUE GAS
LIQUID AND GASEOUS FUELS

PERCENT EXCESS AIR

PERCENT CO2 (DRY BASIS)

0° API
10
20

2000 BTU/CF (60°F)
1600
1300
1000

189

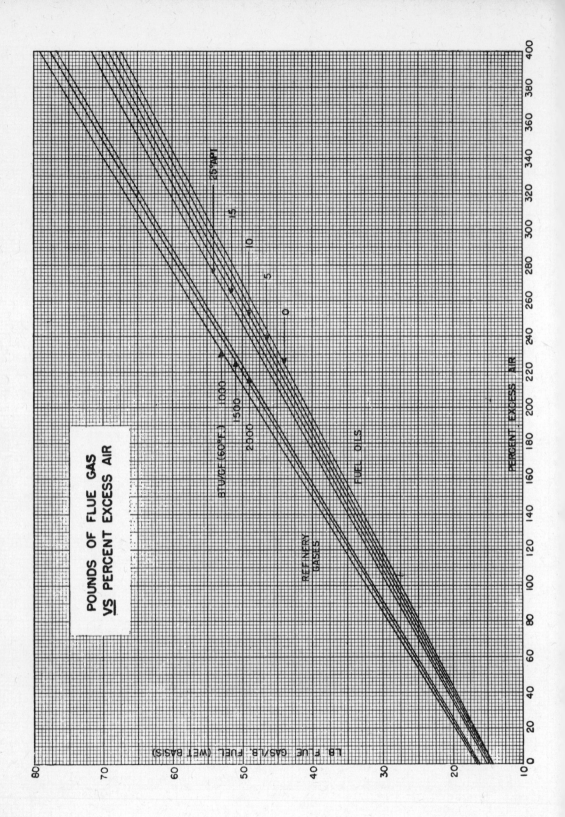

POUNDS OF FLUE GAS
VS PERCENT EXCESS AIR

LB FLUE GAS/LB. FUEL (WET BASIS)

PERCENT EXCESS AIR

BTU/CF (60°F.)

REFINERY GASES

FUEL OILS

25°API

190

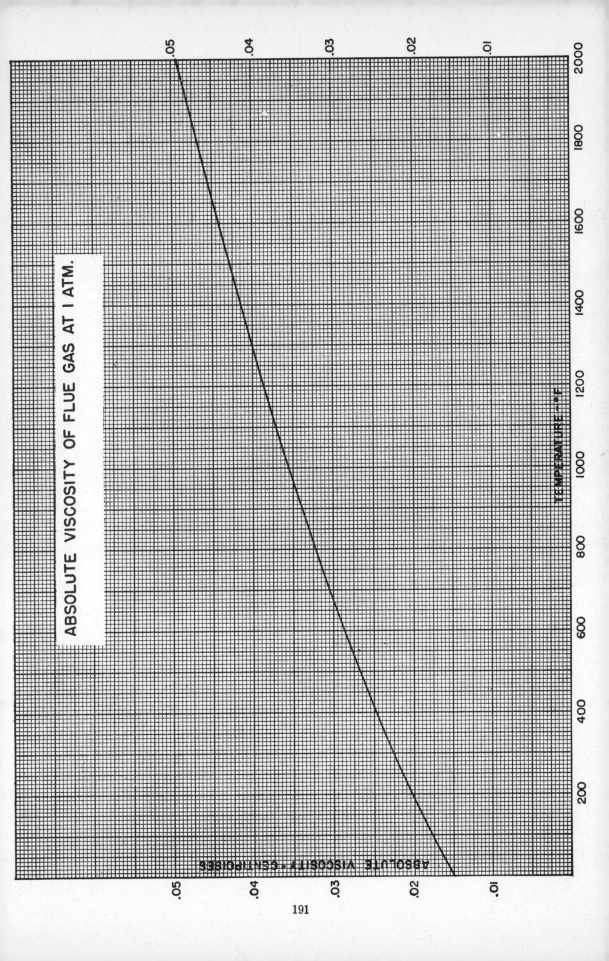

ABSOLUTE VISCOSITY OF FLUE GAS AT 1 ATM.

TEMPERATURE—°F

ABSOLUTE VISCOSITY—CENTIPOISES

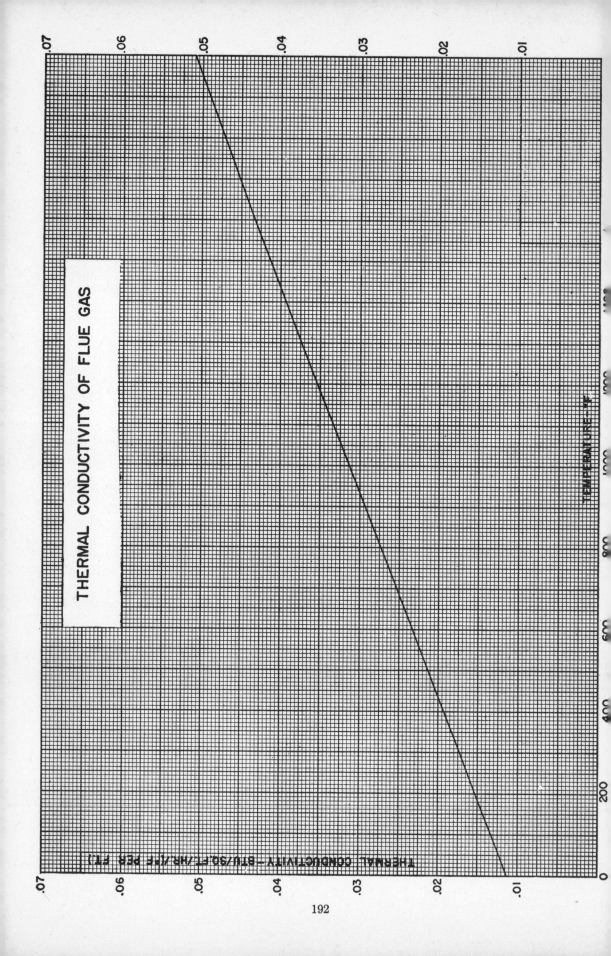

THERMAL CONDUCTIVITY OF FLUE GAS

TEMPERATURE-°F

THERMAL CONDUCTIVITY - BTU/SQ.FT./HR./(°F PER FT.)

Section 11

FLOW OF FLUIDS

Friction Factor

The friction factor for turbulent flow of all fluids (liquids and vapors) is expressed as a function of a modified Reynolds number (DUS/Z) by the chart on page 198 for both commercial pipes and smooth tubes. In the unstable flow region between values of DUS/Z of 0.135 and 0.390 (or approximately 1000 and 3000 in consistent units for $DU\rho/\mu$) the turbulent flow curves have been extended to the stable streamline flow region. These extrapolated curves for turbulent flow give maximum values of the friction factor in the unstable region and are representative of the flow usually found in commercial pipes. For streamline flow the pressure drop may be computed directly from either of the formulas given on the chart, since the friction factor is incorporated in these formulas.

Pressure Drop in Commercial Pipes

To facilitate the determination of pressure drop for liquids in commercial pipes, the charts on pages 199 to 201 were derived from the friction factor curve and the formula for turbulent flow. The following example illustrates the application of these charts:

Example 1. Determine the pressure drop for 21,800 gal/hr of gasoline flowing through 800 ft of standard 6-in. pipe. The kinematic viscosity of the gasoline is 0.60 cs and its specific gravity is 0.750 at 100°F, which is the average temperature of the gasoline in the pipe.

$$Q/D = \frac{21,800}{6.065} = 3600 \text{ gal/hr/in.}$$

By following the dotted lines on the chart on page 200 as indicated for $Q/D = 3600$ gal/hr/in. to a kinematic viscosity of 0.60 cs, then over to the inside pipe diameter of 6.065 in., the value of $\Delta P/S = .38$ lb/sq in. per 100 ft.

The pressure drop for 800 ft of pipe will be:

$$\Delta P = 0.38 \times 0.750 \times \frac{800}{100} = 2.3 \text{ lb/sq in.}$$

Equivalent Lengths of Fittings

Data on the frictional resistance of fittings are usually correlated by the equation $\Delta h = Ku^2/2g$, where K is a constant for each type of fitting. However,

193

in problems of fluid flow it is more convenient to express these resistances as equivalent lengths of straight pipe for use in the general friction factor equation. Since the latter is a function of Reynolds number while K is an independent constant, it is necessary to correct the equivalent lengths for variation in Reynolds number in inverse proportion to the friction factor. In the table on page 202 the equivalent lengths correspond to a Reynolds number of 10 and, for appreciably different values of the latter, should be multiplied by the correction factor on page 203.

Example (Liquid Flow). Kerosene at 100°F is being pumped at a rate of 18,000 gal/hr (gal/hr at 60°F) through 500 ft of standard steel 4 in. pipe in which there are eight standard elbows, one tee (side out) and two gate valves. Calculate the pressure drop through this line using the friction factor curve for the flow through the pipe and the "K" factors for the fittings; check the result using the pressure drop charts and equivalent lengths for the fittings. The kerosene has an absolute viscosity of 1.5 cp at 100°F, a specific gravity of 0.825 at 60°F, and a volume expansion ratio of 1.025 at 100°F relative to 60°F.

$$Q = 18,000 \times 1.025 = 18,500 \text{ gal/hr at } 100°F$$

$$U = \frac{0.00680 \times 18,500}{(4.026)^2} = 7.8 \text{ ft/sec}$$

$$\text{Specific Gravity at } 100°F = \frac{0.825}{1.025} = 0.805$$

$$\frac{DUS}{Z} = \frac{4.026 \times 7.8 \times 0.805}{1.5} = 16.8; \quad f = 0.0052$$

$$\Delta P \text{ (pipe)} = \frac{0.323 \times 0.0052 \times 0.805(7.8)^2 \times 500}{4.026} = 10.2 \text{ lb/sq in.}$$

$$\Delta P \text{ (fittings)} = (8 \times 0.45 + 1 \times 0.90 + 2 \times 0.19)\frac{(7.8)^2 \times 0.805}{148.2}$$

$$= \frac{4.88 \times (7.8)^2 \times 0.805}{148.2} = 1.6 \text{ lb/sq in.}$$

Total pressure drop = 10.2 + 1.6 = *11.8 lb/sq in.*

    Check

Uncorrected equiv. length of fittings = $8 \times 6.6 + 13.2 + 2 \times 2.8 = 71.6$ ft

Correction factor $\left(\dfrac{DUS}{Z} = 16.8\right) = 1.1$

Corrected equiv. length of fittings = $1.1 \times 71.6 = 79$ ft

Total equiv. length $= 500 + 79 = 579$ ft

$$\frac{Q}{D} = \frac{18,500}{4.026} = 4600; \quad \frac{Z}{S} = \frac{1.5}{0.805} = 1.9$$

$$\frac{\Delta P}{S} = 2.5 \text{ lb/sq in./100 ft}$$

Total pressure drop $= 2.5 \times 0.805 \times \dfrac{579}{100} = 11.7 \; lb/sq \; in.$

Example (Vapor Flow). Propane vapor at 90°F and an upstream pressure of 20 psig is flowing through 800 ft of 6 in. standard steel pipe at a rate of 25,000 lb/hr. Determine the pressure drop through this line assuming the ideal gas law applies to propane under these conditions. At 90°F the viscosity of propane vapor is 0.0095 cp.

The following equation for isothermal flow of ideal gases and vapors can be derived by applying Bernoulli's theorem to a differential length of pipe and integrating the resulting equation between the limits, 0 and L:

$$U_1 = \sqrt{\frac{gRT(P_1{}^2 - P_2{}^2)}{2MP_1{}^2 \left[\dfrac{fL}{2m} + \ln \dfrac{P_1}{P_2}\right]}}$$

where U_1 = upstream velocity in ft/sec

P_1 = upstream pressure in lb/sq ft abs

P_2 = downstream pressure in lb/sq ft abs

T = absolute temperature—°F $+ 460$

L = length of pipe in ft

m = hydraulic radius in ft = $d/4$ for pipes

f = friction factor

g = gravitational constant = 32.2 ft/sec/sec

R = ideal gas law constant = 1545

M = molecular weight

By substitution and rearrangement the above equation can be converted to a modified form of the equation for liquids, or

$$\Delta P = P_1 - P_2 = \frac{2P_1}{P_1 + P_2}\left[0.323\left(\frac{fL}{D} + \frac{\ln P_1/P_2}{24}\cdot\right)S_1 U_1{}^2\right]$$

where P_1, P_2 = upstream and downstream pressures in lb/sq in. abs

S_1 = specific gravity of vapor relative to water = $0.00150 \dfrac{MP_1}{T}$

D = pipe diameter in inches

Trial and error must be used in the solution of the above equation since P_2 is unknown. The friction factor, f, is independent of the variation of pressure since the mass velocity term, US, in the Reynolds number remains constant, U varying inversely and S directly with the pressure.

$$D = 6.065 \text{ in.}$$

$$S = \frac{0.00150 \times 44 \times (20 + 14.7)}{90 + 460} = 0.00416$$

Density $= 0.00416 \times 62.4 = 0.259 \text{ lb/cu ft}$

$$U_1 = \frac{25{,}000 \times 144 \times 4}{0.259 \times 3600 \times \pi (6.065)^2} = 134 \text{ ft/sec}$$

$$\frac{D U_1 S_1}{Z} = \frac{6.065 \times 134 \times 0.00416}{0.0095} = 355; \quad f = 0.0031$$

For the first trial assume $P_2 = P_1$

$$\Delta P = \frac{0.323 \times 0.0031 \times 800 \times 0.00416(134)^2}{6.065} = 9.9 \text{ lb/sq in.}$$

For the second trial assume $P_2 = 24$ lb sq in.

$$\Delta P = \frac{2 \times 34.7}{34.7 + 24}\left[0.323 \times \left(\frac{0.0031 \times 800}{6.065} + \frac{0.37}{24} \right) \times 0.00416 \times (134)^2 \right]$$

$$= 1.18[0.323 \times (0.409 + 0.015) \times 74.5] = 12.1 \text{ lb/sq in.}$$

A third trial would give a ΔP of 12.4 lb/sq in.

In this example neither the initial velocity nor a contraction loss from a larger vessel into the line was taken into account. If the propane vapor were flowing from a drum into the 6 in. line, it would be necessary to calculate an initial pressure drop as follows assuming isothermal flow:

$$\frac{RT}{M} \ln P_0/P_1 = \frac{U_1{}^2}{2g} + \frac{0.5 U_1{}^2}{2g}$$

The first term on the right-hand side is the velocity head, and the second term is the actual contraction loss due to friction.

If the available head in the drum, P_0, is 34.7 psia, P_1 is determined by trial and error and for the first trial U_1 is assumed to be 134 ft/sec.

$$\ln P_0/P_1 = \frac{1.5M}{2RTg} U_1{}^2 = 1.2 \times 10^{-6} U_1{}^2$$

$$\ln P_0/P_1 = 1.2 \times 10^{-6}(134)^2 = 0.0216$$

$$P_0/P_1 = 1.022$$

$$P_1 = 34.0 \text{ psia}$$

Since the differential is so small, 0.7 lb/sq in., a second trial is unnecessary. If this loss had been considered at the beginning of the example, the latter would then have been based on an upstream pressure of 34.0 instead of 34.7 psia.

GENERAL REFERENCES

Beij, *J. Research Nat. Bur Standards* **21,** 1 (1938).

Chilton and Colburn, *Ind. Eng. Chem.* **26,** 1183 (1934).

Crane Company, "Flow of Fluids Through Valves, Fittings, and Pipe" (1942).

Drew and Genereaux, *Trans. Am. Inst. Chem. Eng.* **32,** 17 (1936).

Foster, *Trans. Am. Soc. Mech. Engrs.* **42,** 647 (1920).

Gourley, *Proc. Inst. Civil Eng.*, p. 297 (1910, Part 2).

Karr and Schultz, *J. Am. Soc. Naval Engrs.* **52,** 239 (1940).

Schoder and Vanderlip, *Cornell Univ. Eng. Exp. Sta. Bull. No. 20* (1935).

Walker, Lewis, McAdams and Gilliland, "Principles of Chemical Engineering," pp. 71, 87–89, McGraw-Hill Book Co., New York, N.Y. (1937).

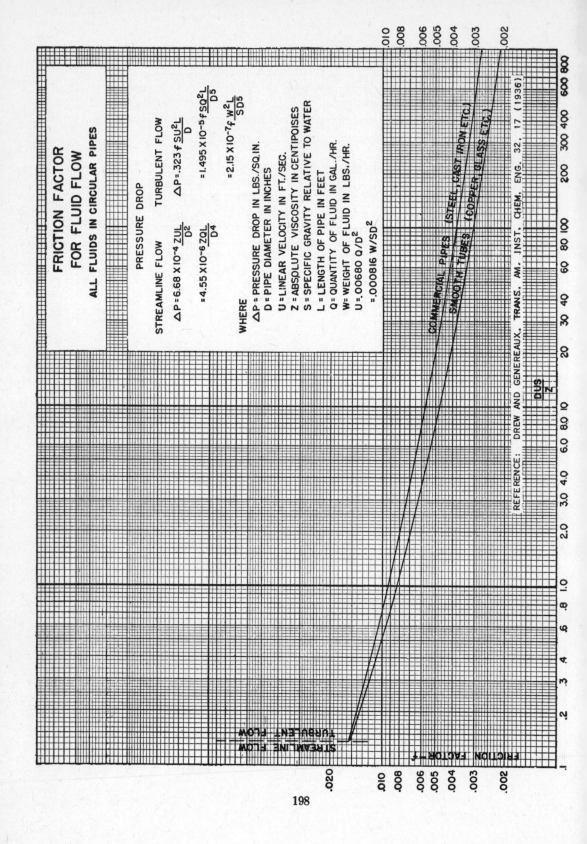

FRICTION FACTOR
FOR FLUID FLOW
ALL FLUIDS IN CIRCULAR PIPES

PRESSURE DROP

STREAMLINE FLOW   TURBULENT FLOW

$\Delta P = 6.68 \times 10^{-4} \dfrac{ZUL}{D^2}$ $\Delta P = .323 f \dfrac{SU^2L}{D}$

$= 4.55 \times 10^{-6} \dfrac{ZQL}{D^4}$ $= 1.495 \times 10^{-5} f \dfrac{SQ^2L}{D^5}$

$= 2.15 \times 10^{-7} f \dfrac{W^2L}{SD^5}$

WHERE

ΔP = PRESSURE DROP IN LBS./SQ.IN.
D = PIPE DIAMETER IN INCHES
U = LINEAR VELOCITY IN FT./SEC.
Z = ABSOLUTE VISCOSITY IN CENTIPOISES
S = SPECIFIC GRAVITY RELATIVE TO WATER
L = LENGTH OF PIPE IN FEET
Q = QUANTITY OF FLUID IN GAL./HR.
W = WEIGHT OF FLUID IN LBS./HR.
$U = .00680 \, Q/D^2$
$= .000816 \, W/SD^2$

COMMERCIAL PIPES (STEEL, CAST IRON ETC.)
SMOOTH TUBES (COPPER, GLASS ETC.)

$\dfrac{DUS}{Z}$

STREAMLINE FLOW
TURBULENT FLOW

FRICTION FACTOR—f

REFERENCE: DREW AND GENEREAUX., TRANS., AM. INST., CHEM., ENG., 32, 17 (1936)

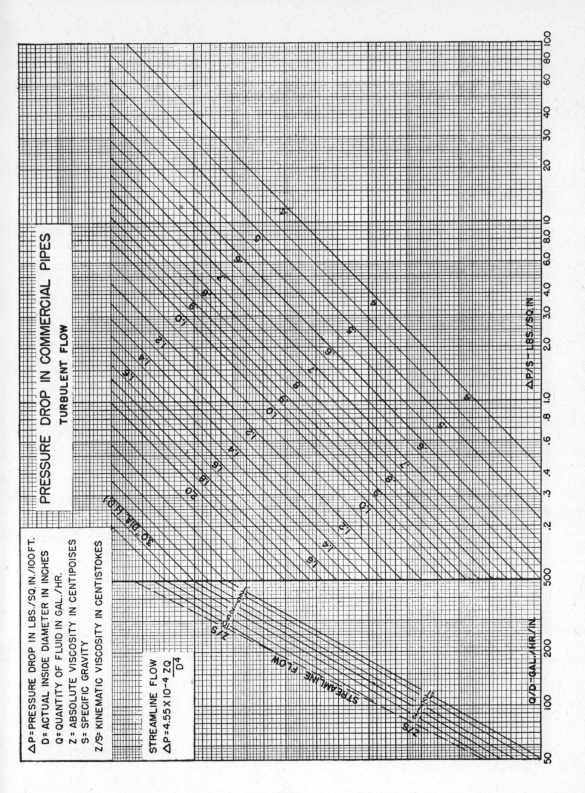

PRESSURE DROP IN COMMERCIAL PIPES

TURBULENT FLOW

ΔP= PRESSURE DROP IN LBS./SQ.IN./100 FT.
D= ACTUAL INSIDE DIAMETER IN INCHES
Q= QUANTITY OF FLUID IN GAL./HR.
Z = ABSOLUTE VISCOSITY IN CENTIPOISES
S = SPECIFIC GRAVITY
Z/S= KINEMATIC VISCOSITY IN CENTISTOKES

STREAMLINE FLOW
$$\Delta P = 4.55 \times 10^{-4} \frac{ZQ}{D^4}$$

30˝ DIA.(I.D.)

STREAMLINE FLOW

Z/S

Z/S

ΔP/S – LBS./SQ.IN.

Q/D – GAL./HR./IN.

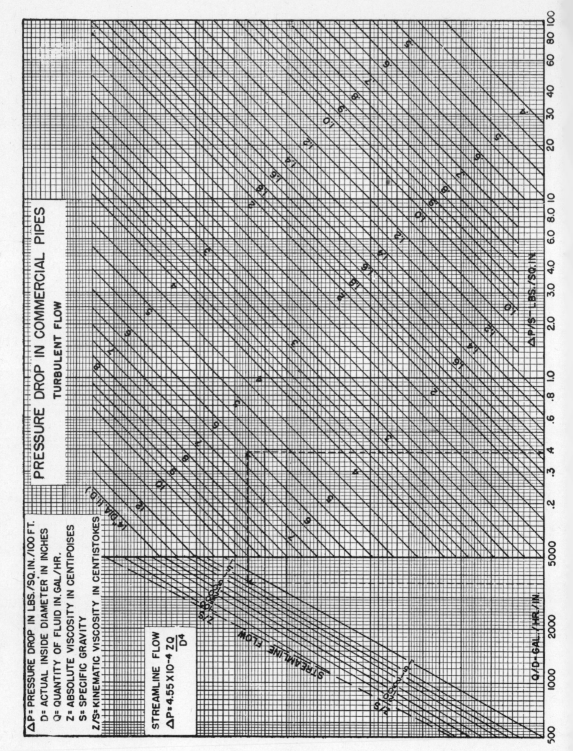

PRESSURE DROP IN COMMERCIAL PIPES
TURBULENT FLOW

ΔP = PRESSURE DROP IN LBS./SQ.IN./100 FT.
D = ACTUAL INSIDE DIAMETER IN INCHES
Q = QUANTITY OF FLUID IN GAL./HR.
Z = ABSOLUTE VISCOSITY IN CENTIPOISES
S = SPECIFIC GRAVITY
Z/S = KINEMATIC VISCOSITY IN CENTISTOKES

STREAMLINE FLOW
$$\Delta P = 4.55 \times 10^{-4} \frac{ZQ}{D^4}$$

ΔP/S – LBS./SQ./IN.

Q/D – GAL./HR./IN.

STREAMLINE FLOW

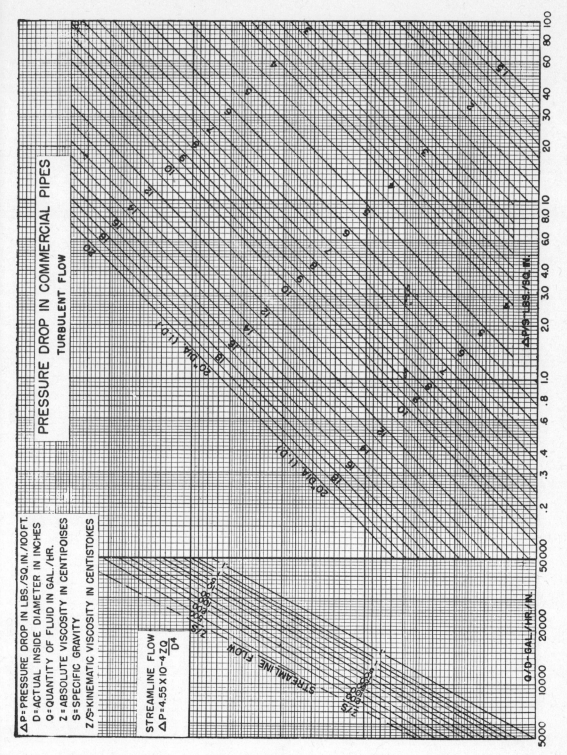

PRESSURE DROP IN COMMERCIAL PIPES
TURBULENT FLOW

ΔP = PRESSURE DROP IN LBS./SQ.IN./100 FT.
D = ACTUAL INSIDE DIAMETER IN INCHES
Q = QUANTITY OF FLUID IN GAL./HR.
Z = ABSOLUTE VISCOSITY IN CENTIPOISES
S = SPECIFIC GRAVITY
Z/S = KINEMATIC VISCOSITY IN CENTISTOKES

STREAMLINE FLOW
$$\Delta P = 4.55 \times 10^{-4} \frac{ZQ}{D^4}$$

STREAMLINE FLOW

ΔP/S~LBS./SQ.IN.

Q/D~GAL./HR./IN.

EQUIVALENT LENGTHS OF FITTINGS

Pipe size — Inches				Equivalent Lengths* — Feet										
		I.D.		Valves			Elbows		Bends			Tees		
Nominal Inside Diam.	O.D.	Standard	Extra Strong	Globe‡	Gate	Angle	Standard	Long Sweep	90° R/D = 6	45° = 1.5	Close Return = 1	Side Out	End Out	Run of Standard
				K†10	.19	3	.45	.30	.25	.21	.75	.90	1.3	.30
¼	0.540	0.364	0.302	13.3	0.3	4.0	0.6	0.4	0.3	0.3	1.0	1.2	1.7	0.4
½	0.840	0.622	0.546	23.	0.4	6.8	1.0	0.7	0.6	0.5	1.7	2.0	3.0	0.7
¾	1.050	0.824	0.742	30.	0.6	9.0	1.3	0.9	0.7	0.6	2.3	2.7	3.9	0.9
1	1.315	1.049	0.957	38.	0.7	11.5	1.7	1.1	1.0	0.8	3.9	3.4	5.0	1.1
1½	1.900	1.610	1.500	59.	1.1	17.6	2.6	1.8	1.5	1.2	4.4	5.3	7.7	1.8
2	2.375	2.067	1.939	75.	1.4	23.	3.4	2.3	1.9	1.6	5.7	6.8	9.8	2.3
3	3.500	3.068	2.900	112.	2.1	34.	5.0	3.4	2.8	2.4	8.4	10.1	14.6	3.4
4	4.500	4.026	3.826	147.	2.8	44.	6.6	4.4	3.7	3.1	11.1	13.2	19.1	4.4
6	6.625	6.065	5.761	220.	4.2	66.	10.0	6.6	5.5	4.7	16.6	19.9	29.	6.6
8	8.625	7.981	7.625	290.	5.5	87.	13.1	8.7	7.3	6.1	22.	26.	38.	8.7
10	10.75	10.020	9.750	360.	7.0	110.	16.5	11.0	9.1	7.7	27.	33.	48.	11.0
12	12.75	12.000	11.750	440.	8.3	131.	19.7	13.1	10.9	9.2	33.	40.	57.	13.1
14	14.00	13.25	—	480.	9.2	145.	22.	14.5	12.0	10.2	36.	44.	63.	14.5
16	16.00	15.25	—	560.	10.6	167.	25.	16.7	13.9	11.7	42.	50.	72.	16.7
18	18.00	17.18	—	630.	11.9	188.	28.	18.8	15.6	13.2	47.	56.	82.	18.8
20	20.00	19.18	—	700.	13.3	210.	32.	21.	17.5	14.7	53.	63.	91.	21.

* The equivalent lengths tabulated correspond to a value of $\frac{DUS}{Z} = 10$. For other values of $\frac{DUS}{Z}$, apply correction factor from the chart on the opposite page.

† $\Delta P = \frac{KU^2}{2g} \times \frac{S}{2.31} = \frac{KU^2 S}{148.2}$

‡ For swing check valve, use ¼ of globe valve equivalent lengths.

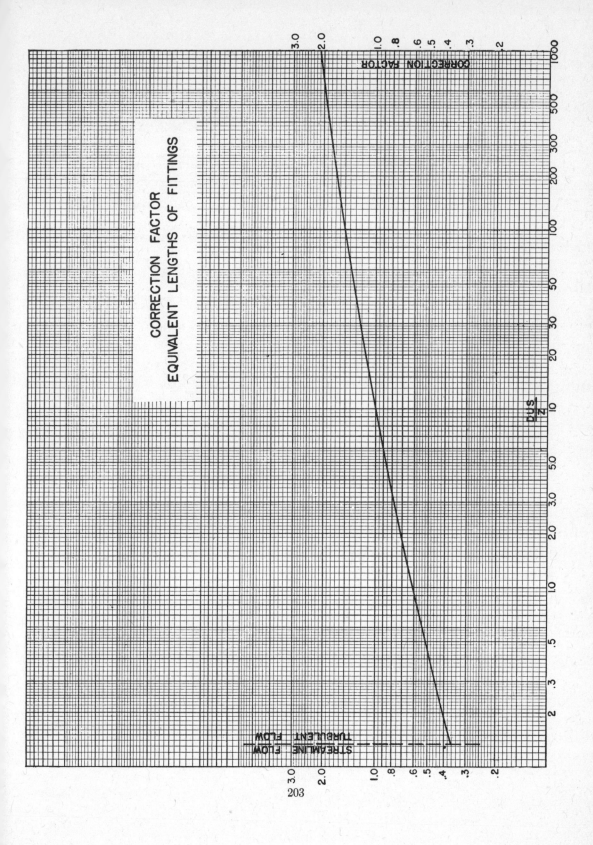

CORRECTION FACTOR
EQUIVALENT LENGTHS OF FITTINGS

CORRECTION FACTOR

$\frac{D U S}{Z}$

STREAMLINE FLOW ———— TURBULENT FLOW

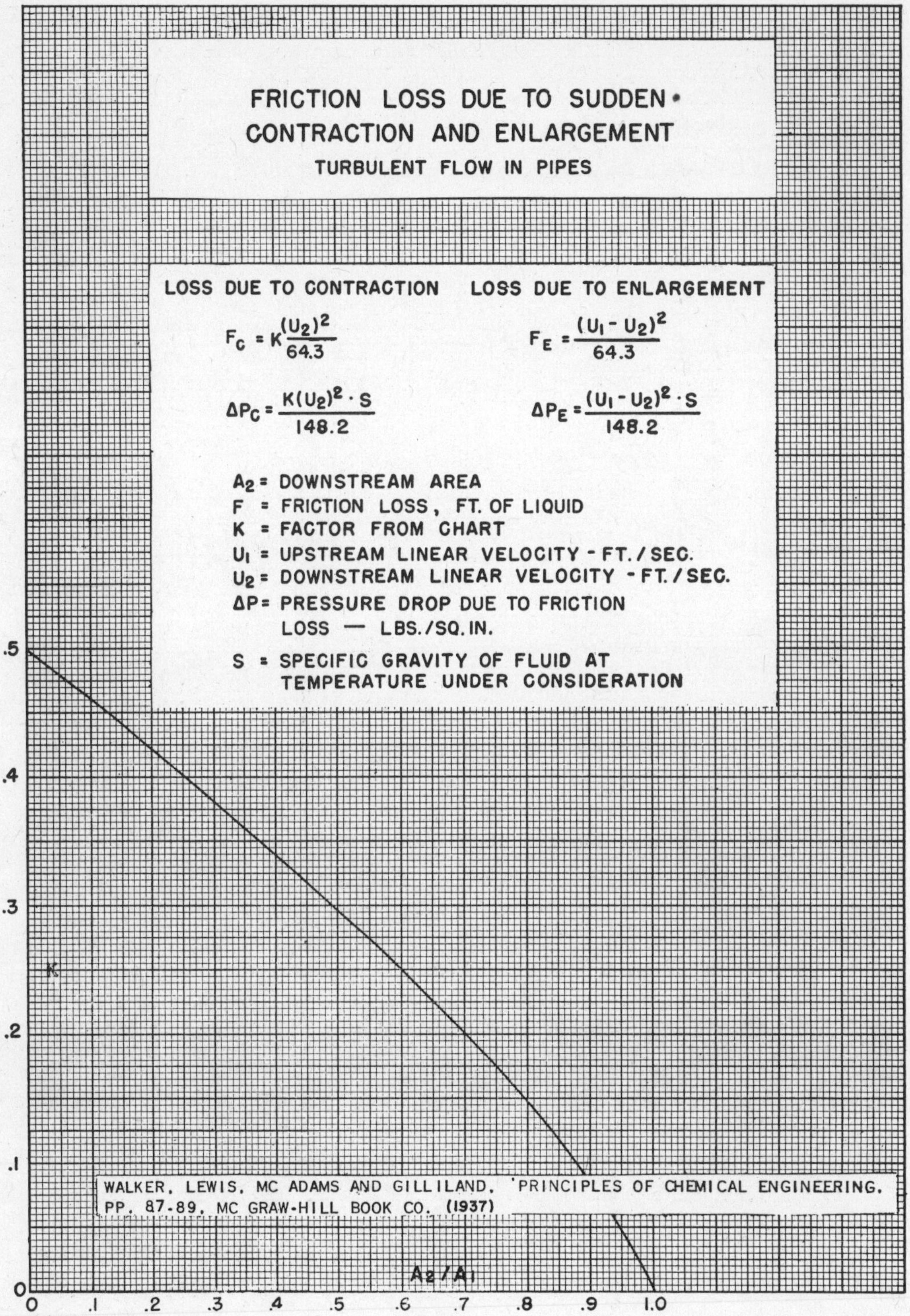

FRICTION LOSS DUE TO SUDDEN
CONTRACTION AND ENLARGEMENT
TURBULENT FLOW IN PIPES

LOSS DUE TO CONTRACTION	LOSS DUE TO ENLARGEMENT

$$F_C = K\frac{(U_2)^2}{64.3} \qquad\qquad F_E = \frac{(U_1 - U_2)^2}{64.3}$$

$$\Delta P_C = \frac{K(U_2)^2 \cdot S}{148.2} \qquad\qquad \Delta P_E = \frac{(U_1 - U_2)^2 \cdot S}{148.2}$$

A_2 = DOWNSTREAM AREA
F = FRICTION LOSS, FT. OF LIQUID
K = FACTOR FROM CHART
U_1 = UPSTREAM LINEAR VELOCITY - FT. / SEC.
U_2 = DOWNSTREAM LINEAR VELOCITY - FT. / SEC.
ΔP = PRESSURE DROP DUE TO FRICTION
   LOSS — LBS. / SQ. IN.

S = SPECIFIC GRAVITY OF FLUID AT
   TEMPERATURE UNDER CONSIDERATION

WALKER, LEWIS, MC ADAMS AND GILLILAND, "PRINCIPLES OF CHEMICAL ENGINEERING,
PP. 87-89, MC GRAW-HILL BOOK CO. (1937)

K

A₂ / A₁

.5 .4 .3 .2 .1 0

0 .1 .2 .3 .4 .5 .6 .7 .8 .9 1.0

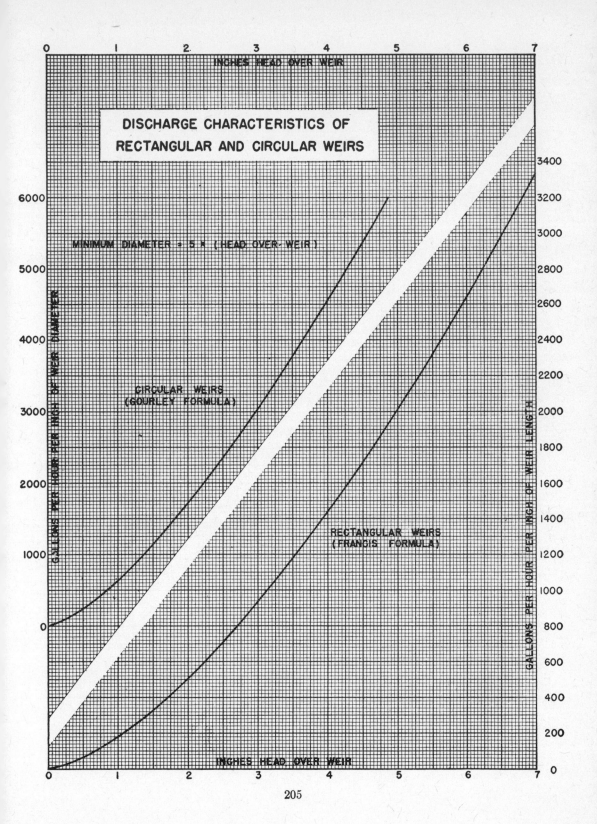

DISCHARGE CHARACTERISTICS OF
RECTANGULAR AND CIRCULAR WEIRS

MINIMUM DIAMETER = 5 × (HEAD OVER WEIR)

CIRCULAR WEIRS
(GOURLEY FORMULA)

RECTANGULAR WEIRS
(FRANCIS FORMULA)

INCHES HEAD OVER WEIR

GALLONS PER HOUR PER INCH OF WEIR DIAMETER

GALLONS PER HOUR PER INCH OF WEIR LENGTH

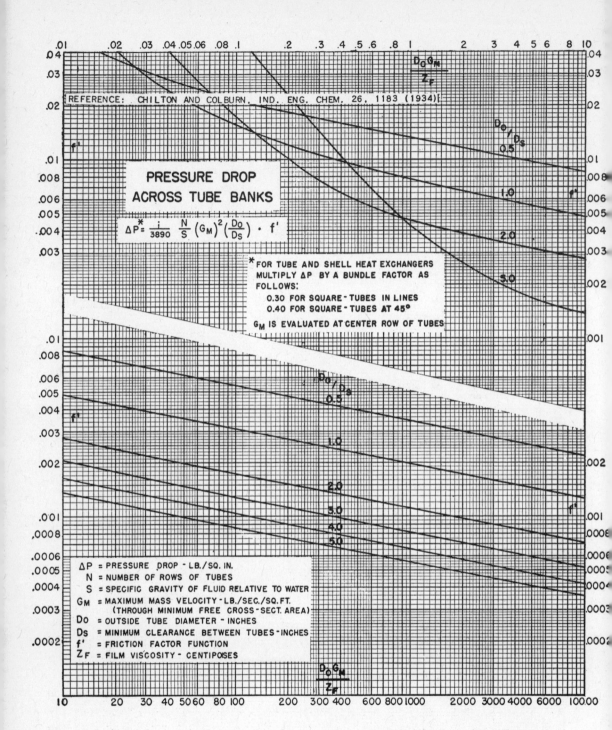

PRESSURE DROP ACROSS TUBE BANKS

$$\Delta P \overset{*}{=} \frac{i}{3890} \frac{N}{S} (G_M)^2 \left(\frac{D_0}{D_S}\right) \cdot f'$$

REFERENCE: CHILTON AND COLBURN, IND. ENG. CHEM. 26, 1183 (1934).

*FOR TUBE AND SHELL HEAT EXCHANGERS
MULTIPLY ΔP BY A BUNDLE FACTOR AS
FOLLOWS:
    0.30 FOR SQUARE-TUBES IN LINES
    0.40 FOR SQUARE-TUBES AT 45°
G_M IS EVALUATED AT CENTER ROW OF TUBES

ΔP = PRESSURE DROP - LB./SQ. IN.
N = NUMBER OF ROWS OF TUBES
S = SPECIFIC GRAVITY OF FLUID RELATIVE TO WATER
G_M = MAXIMUM MASS VELOCITY - LB./SEC./SQ.FT.
    (THROUGH MINIMUM FREE CROSS-SECT. AREA)
D_0 = OUTSIDE TUBE DIAMETER - INCHES
D_S = MINIMUM CLEARANCE BETWEEN TUBES - INCHES
f' = FRICTION FACTOR FUNCTION
Z_F = FILM VISCOSITY - CENTIPOISES

$\frac{D_0 G_M}{Z_F}$

206

Section 12

FLOW OF HEAT

Heat Transfer

The film transfer coefficient for liquids flowing inside tubes (page 211) is based on the Sieder and Tate correlation[1] which is generally accepted as the most reliable for this type of heat transfer.

The chart on page 212 for the outside film coefficient for flow across tube bundles was derived from a correlation by Chilton and Colburn[2] with the consistent units in the dimensionless terms replaced by more common units. Comparison of limited data with this correlation has indicated that the film coefficient should be multiplied by the "bundle factors" given on the chart when G_M is taken as the mass velocity at the center row of tubes. Non-uniformity of flow and by-passing between the tube bundle and shell appear to be the principal reasons for this difference.

Thermal Conductivity of Petroleum Liquids

Attempts to correlate thermal conductivity of petroleum liquids as a function of gravity in addition to temperature have resulted in contradictory trends with °API gravity.[3,4] In view of this inconsistency and since Smith[5] has shown that, at 86°F, a single value represents the reliable data better than either trend with gravity, the relation for the thermal conductivity of petroleum fractions on page 213 is shown as a function of temperature alone. This chart may also be used for pure hydrocarbons, although the data on low-boiling aromatics are about 10% higher than the curve.

Thermal Conductivity of Hydrocarbon Gases

As most data on the thermal conductivity of hydrocarbon gases were obtained at room temperature, it is was necessary to find some means of extrapolation to higher temperatures. This was done by using two different methods: (1) assumption that the Prandtl number is a constant independent of temperature and (2) employment of Sutherland's equation. As the results of the two methods became more divergent with increasing temperature, it was a question of selecting either one or the other or using an average of the two. An average was chosen

[1] Sieder and Tate, *Ind. Eng. Chem.* **28**, 1429 (1936).
[2] Chilton and Colburn, *Ind. Eng. Chem.* **26**, 1183 (1934).
[3] *Misc. Publication of Bur. Standards, No. 97*, 24 (1929).
[4] Kaye and Higgins, *Proc. Royal Soc.* **117**, 459 (1928).
[5] Smith, *Trans. Am. Soc. Mech. Engrs.* **58**, 719 (1936).

since, while it was felt that the Prandtl number was probably more reliable, the Sutherland equation gave lower and consequently more conservative values. In view of the uncertainties of these extrapolations any refinement beyond the use of a straight line was unwarranted. Consequently, the chart on page 215 gives the thermal conductivity of hydrocarbon vapors as a linear function of temperature for various molecular weights.

Logarithmic Mean Temperature Difference

In the transfer of heat between two fluids, the log mean temperature difference applies to flow that is either entirely countercurrent or entirely concurrent. Under conditions where there is a combination of these two types of flow, such as a heat exchanger with more tube passes than shell passes, Nagle[6] has shown that a correction factor should be applied to the log mean temperature difference. This correction factor is given herein by either one of two types of charts, the first on page 218 and the second on pages 219 to 221. The chart on page 218 may be more convenient to use when the factors R and A do not approach unity. If these factors are near to unity, it is necessary to use the other charts. The following example illustrates the application of these charts:

Example 1. Determine the correct temperature difference and the number of shell passes required in the heat transfer between two fluids having the following inlet and outlet temperatures:

Shell side: T_1(inlet) = 400°F; T_2(outlet) = 300°F
Tube side: t_1(inlet) = 275°F; t_2(outlet) = 320°F

$$R = \frac{T_1 - T_2}{t_2 - t_1} = \frac{100}{45} = 2.22$$

$$m = \frac{t_2 - t_1}{T_1 - t_1} = \frac{45}{125} = 0.36$$

From the chart on page 219, it is seen that one shell pass is insufficient since F is close to 0. With two shell passes F = 0.90, and this arrangement would appear to be satisfactory.[7] The corrected log mean temperature difference is:

$$0.90(\text{L.M.T.D.}) = 0.90 \times 47.3 = 42.6°\text{F}$$

The solution of this sample is also illustrated on the chart on page 218.

[6] Nagle, *Ind. Eng. Chem.* **25,** 604 (1933).

[7] While other factors may enter into the number of shell passes selected for a given design, any arrangement which results in a correction factor of less than 0.80 should be rejected.

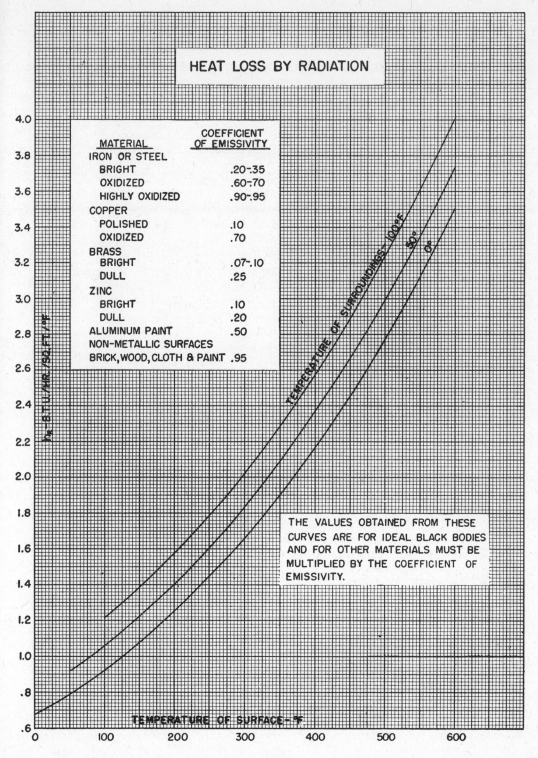

HEAT LOSS BY RADIATION

MATERIAL	COEFFICIENT OF EMISSIVITY
IRON OR STEEL	
BRIGHT	.20-.35
OXIDIZED	.60-.70
HIGHLY OXIDIZED	.90-.95
COPPER	
POLISHED	.10
OXIDIZED	.70
BRASS	
BRIGHT	.07-.10
DULL	.25
ZINC	
BRIGHT	.10
DULL	.20
ALUMINUM PAINT	.50
NON-METALLIC SURFACES	
BRICK, WOOD, CLOTH & PAINT	.95

THE VALUES OBTAINED FROM THESE
CURVES ARE FOR IDEAL BLACK BODIES
AND FOR OTHER MATERIALS MUST BE
MULTIPLIED BY THE COEFFICIENT OF
EMISSIVITY.

TEMPERATURE OF SURFACE - °F

h_r - B.T.U./HR./SQ.FT./°F

TEMPERATURE OF SURROUNDINGS - 100°F   50°   0°

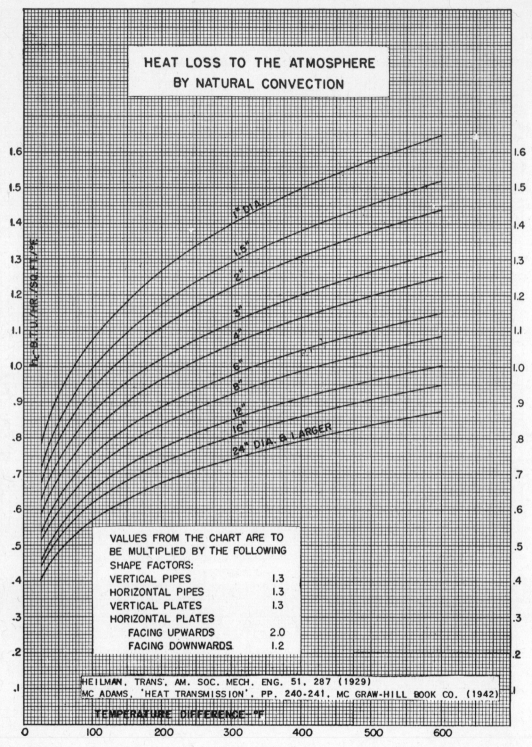

HEAT LOSS TO THE ATMOSPHERE
BY NATURAL CONVECTION

hc B.T.U./HR./SQ.FT./°F.

1" DIA.
1.5"
2"
3"
4"
6"
8"
12"
16"
24" DIA. & LARGER

VALUES FROM THE CHART ARE TO
BE MULTIPLIED BY THE FOLLOWING
SHAPE FACTORS:
VERTICAL PIPES   1.3
HORIZONTAL PIPES   1.3
VERTICAL PLATES   1.3
HORIZONTAL PLATES
    FACING UPWARDS   2.0
    FACING DOWNWARDS   1.2

HEILMAN, TRANS. AM. SOC. MECH. ENG. 51, 287 (1929)
MC ADAMS, 'HEAT TRANSMISSION', PP. 240-241, MC GRAW-HILL BOOK CO. (1942)

TEMPERATURE DIFFERENCE—°F

0   100   200   300   400   500   600

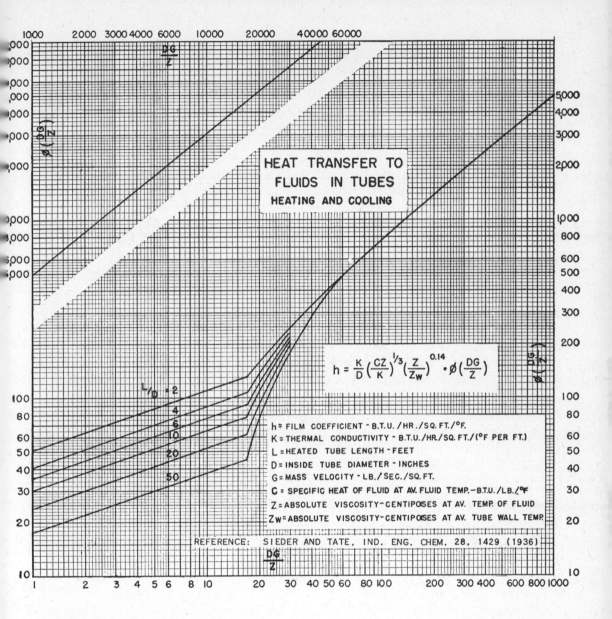

HEAT TRANSFER TO
FLUIDS IN TUBES
HEATING AND COOLING

$$h = \frac{K}{D}\left(\frac{CZ}{K}\right)^{1/3}\left(\frac{Z}{Z_w}\right)^{0.14} \cdot \phi\left(\frac{DG}{Z}\right)$$

h = FILM COEFFICIENT - B.T.U./HR./SQ. FT./°F.
K = THERMAL CONDUCTIVITY - B.T.U./HR./SQ. FT./(°F PER FT.)
L = HEATED TUBE LENGTH - FEET
D = INSIDE TUBE DIAMETER - INCHES
G = MASS VELOCITY - LB./SEC./SQ. FT.
C = SPECIFIC HEAT OF FLUID AT AV. FLUID TEMP. - B.T.U./LB./°F
Z = ABSOLUTE VISCOSITY-CENTIPOISES AT AV. TEMP. OF FLUID
Zw = ABSOLUTE VISCOSITY-CENTIPOISES AT AV. TUBE WALL TEMP.

REFERENCE: SIEDER AND TATE, IND. ENG. CHEM. 28, 1429 (1936)

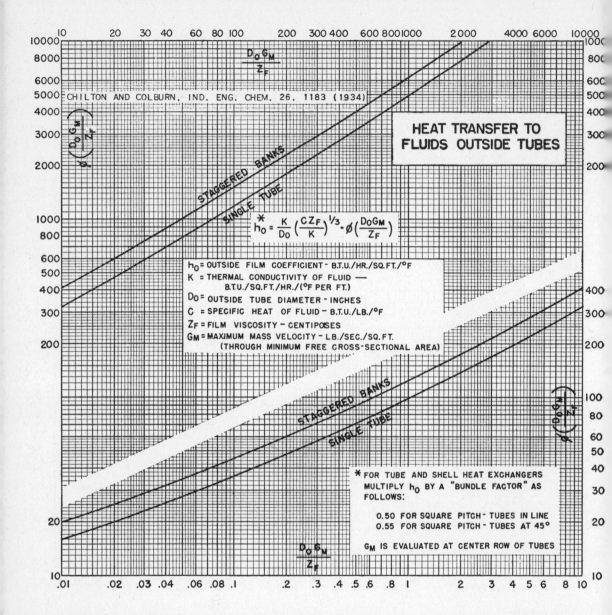

HEAT TRANSFER TO FLUIDS OUTSIDE TUBES

$$h_0 = \frac{K}{D_O}\left(\frac{CZ_F}{K}\right)^{1/3} \cdot \phi\left(\frac{D_O G_M}{Z_F}\right)$$

h_O = OUTSIDE FILM COEFFICIENT - B.T.U./HR./SQ.FT./°F
K = THERMAL CONDUCTIVITY OF FLUID — B.T.U./SQ.FT./HR./(°F PER FT.)
D_O = OUTSIDE TUBE DIAMETER - INCHES
C = SPECIFIC HEAT OF FLUID - B.T.U./LB./°F
Z_F = FILM VISCOSITY - CENTIPOISES
G_M = MAXIMUM MASS VELOCITY - LB./SEC./SQ.FT.
(THROUGH MINIMUM FREE CROSS-SECTIONAL AREA)

CHILTON AND COLBURN, IND. ENG. CHEM. 26, 1183 (1934)

STAGGERED BANKS
SINGLE TUBE

* FOR TUBE AND SHELL HEAT EXCHANGERS MULTIPLY h_O BY A "BUNDLE FACTOR" AS FOLLOWS:

0.50 FOR SQUARE PITCH - TUBES IN LINE
0.55 FOR SQUARE PITCH - TUBES AT 45°

G_M IS EVALUATED AT CENTER ROW OF TUBES

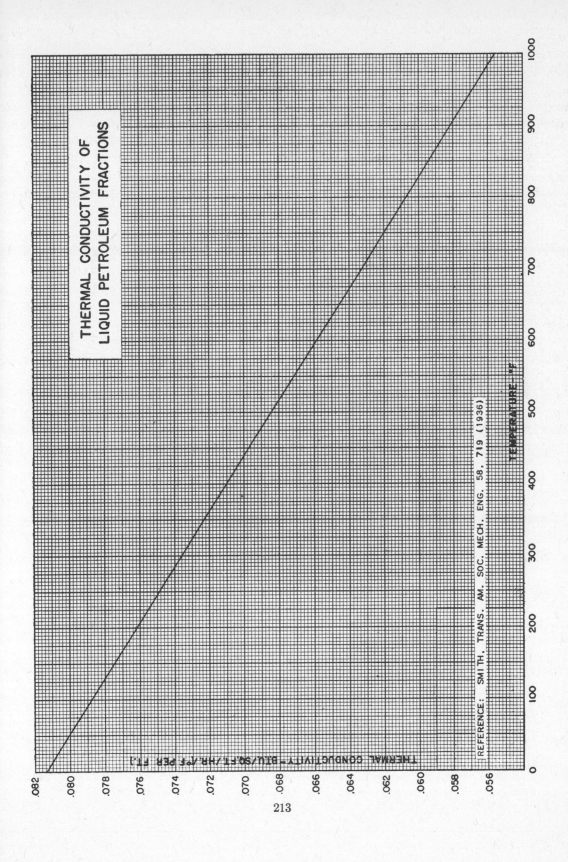

THERMAL CONDUCTIVITY OF
LIQUID PETROLEUM FRACTIONS

THERMAL CONDUCTIVITY-BTU/SQ.FT/HR./°F PER FT.)

REFERENCE: SMITH. TRANS. AM. SOC. MECH. ENG. 58, 719 (1936)

TEMPERATURE °F

213

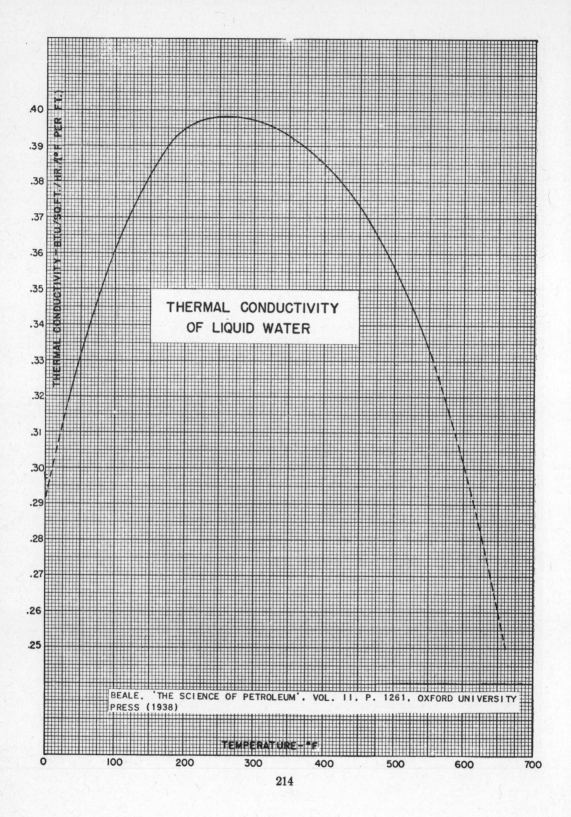

THERMAL CONDUCTIVITY
OF LIQUID WATER

THERMAL CONDUCTIVITY—B.T.U./SQ.FT./HR./(°F PER FT.)

.40
.39
.38
.37
.36
.35
.34
.33
.32
.31
.30
.29
.28
.27
.26
.25

TEMPERATURE—°F

0   100   200   300   400   500   600   700

BEALE. 'THE SCIENCE OF PETROLEUM'. VOL. II. P. 1261, OXFORD UNIVERSITY PRESS (1938)

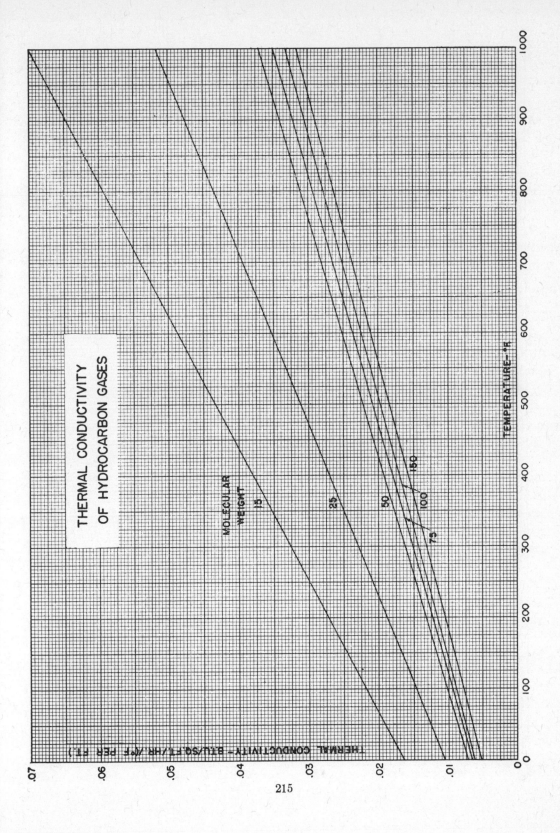

THERMAL CONDUCTIVITY
OF HYDROCARBON GASES

MOLECULAR
WEIGHT

15

25

50

150

100

75

THERMAL CONDUCTIVITY - BTU/SQ·FT/HR /(°F PER FT.)

TEMPERATURE-°R

.07
.06
.05
.04
.03
.02
.01

0   100   200   300   400   500   600   700   800   900   1000

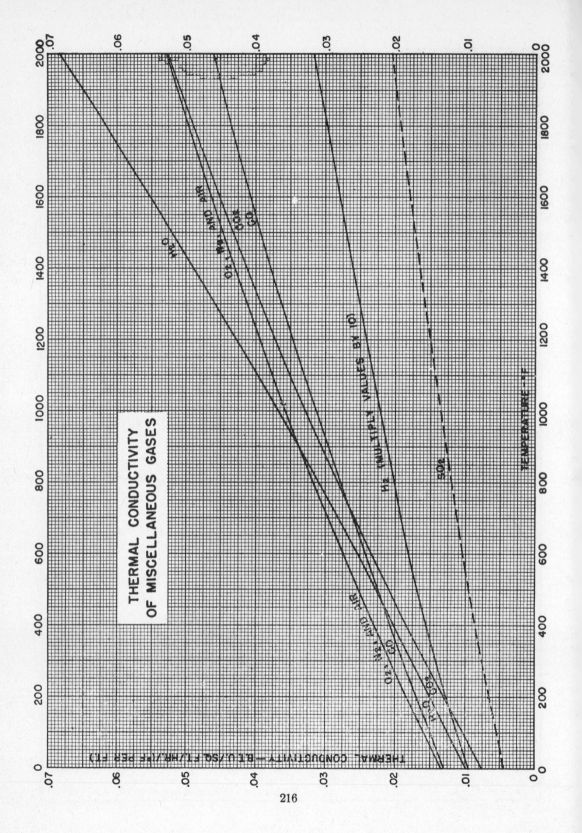

THERMAL CONDUCTIVITY OF MISCELLANEOUS GASES

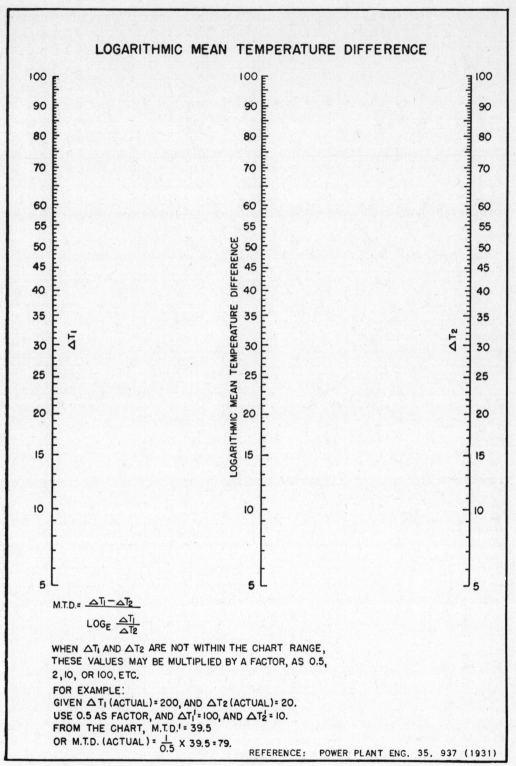

LOGARITHMIC MEAN TEMPERATURE DIFFERENCE

$$M.T.D. = \frac{\triangle T_1 - \triangle T_2}{LOG_E \frac{\triangle T_1}{\triangle T_2}}$$

WHEN $\triangle T_1$ AND $\triangle T_2$ ARE NOT WITHIN THE CHART RANGE,
THESE VALUES MAY BE MULTIPLIED BY A FACTOR, AS 0.5,
2, 10, OR 100, ETC.

FOR EXAMPLE:
GIVEN $\triangle T_1$ (ACTUAL) = 200, AND $\triangle T_2$ (ACTUAL) = 20.
USE 0.5 AS FACTOR, AND $\triangle T_1^1$ = 100, AND $\triangle T_2^{\frac{1}{2}}$ = 10.
FROM THE CHART, $M.T.D.^1$ = 39.5
OR M.T.D. (ACTUAL) = $\frac{1}{0.5}$ X 39.5 = 79.

REFERENCE: POWER PLANT ENG. 35, 937 (1931)

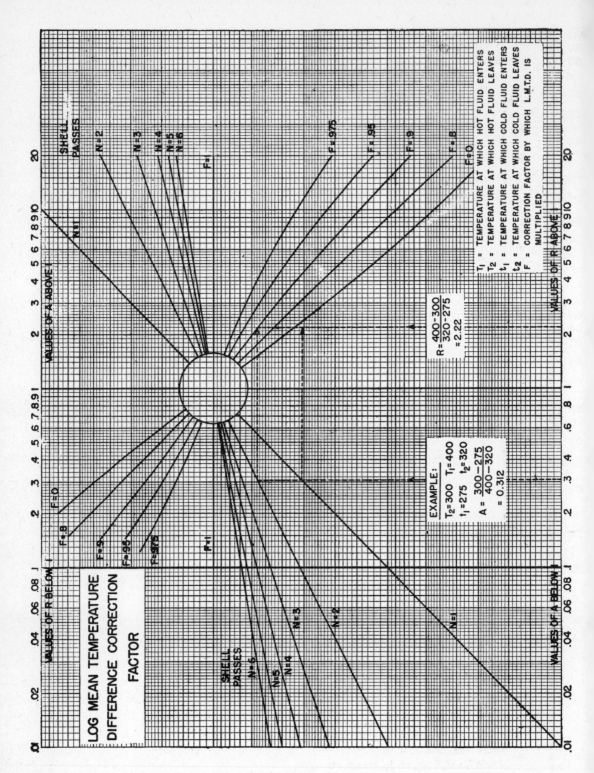

LOG MEAN TEMPERATURE
DIFFERENCE CORRECTION
FACTOR

SHELL
PASSES

N=1
N=2
N=3
N=4
N=5
N=6

F=1

F=.975
F=.95
F=.9
F=.8
F=0

F=0
F=.8
F=.9
F=.95
F=.975

F=1

N=1

SHELL
PASSES
N=6
N=5
N=4
N=3
N=2

VALUES OF A ABOVE

VALUES OF A BELOW

VALUES OF R BELOW

VALUES OF R ABOVE

$R=\dfrac{400-300}{320-275}=2.22$

EXAMPLE:

$T_2=300$ $T_1=400$
$t_1=275$ $t_2=320$

$A=\dfrac{300-275}{400-320}$
$=0.312$

T_1 = TEMPERATURE AT WHICH HOT FLUID ENTERS
T_2 = TEMPERATURE AT WHICH HOT FLUID LEAVES
t_1 = TEMPERATURE AT WHICH COLD FLUID ENTERS
t_2 = TEMPERATURE AT WHICH COLD FLUID LEAVES
F = CORRECTION FACTOR BY WHICH L.M.T.D. IS
      MULTIPLIED

218

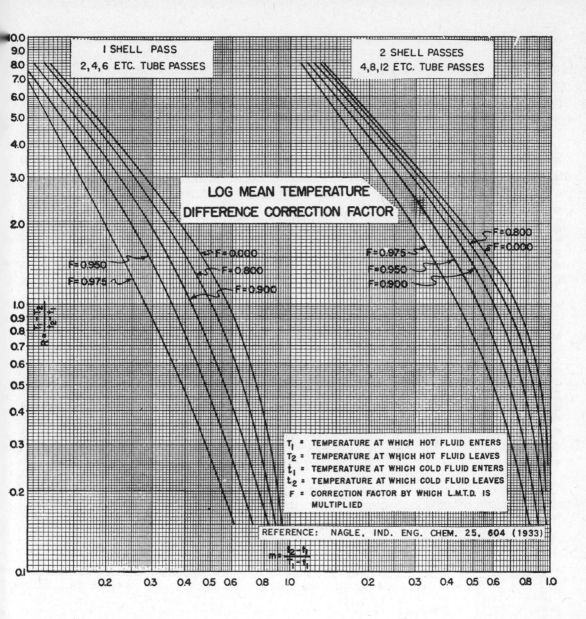

LOG MEAN TEMPERATURE DIFFERENCE CORRECTION FACTOR

1 SHELL PASS
2,4,6 ETC. TUBE PASSES

2 SHELL PASSES
4,8,12 ETC. TUBE PASSES

T_1 = TEMPERATURE AT WHICH HOT FLUID ENTERS
T_2 = TEMPERATURE AT WHICH HOT FLUID LEAVES
t_1 = TEMPERATURE AT WHICH COLD FLUID ENTERS
t_2 = TEMPERATURE AT WHICH COLD FLUID LEAVES
F = CORRECTION FACTOR BY WHICH L.M.T.D. IS MULTIPLIED

REFERENCE: NAGLE, IND. ENG. CHEM. 25, 604 (1933)

$$m = \frac{t_2 - t_1}{T_1 - t_1}$$

$$R = \frac{T_1 - T_2}{t_2 - t_1}$$

219

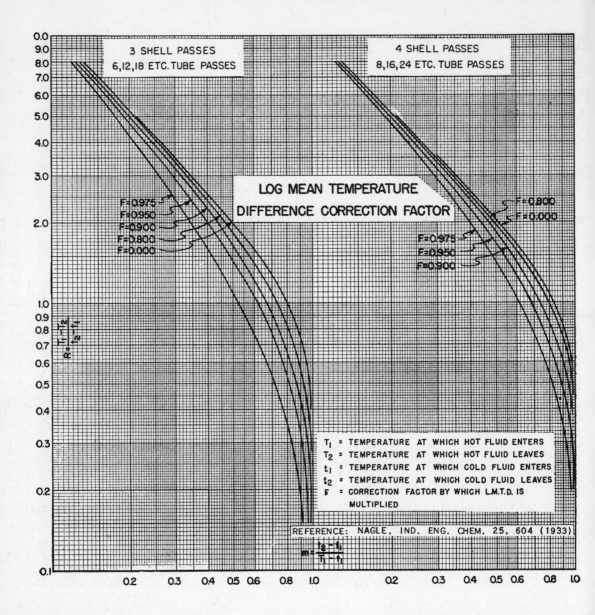

LOG MEAN TEMPERATURE
DIFFERENCE CORRECTION FACTOR

3 SHELL PASSES
6,12,18 ETC. TUBE PASSES

4 SHELL PASSES
8,16,24 ETC. TUBE PASSES

F=0.975
F=0.950
F=0.900
F=0.800
F=0.000

F=0.800
F=0.000
F=0.975
F=0.950
F=0.900

T_1 = TEMPERATURE AT WHICH HOT FLUID ENTERS
T_2 = TEMPERATURE AT WHICH HOT FLUID LEAVES
t_1 = TEMPERATURE AT WHICH COLD FLUID ENTERS
t_2 = TEMPERATURE AT WHICH COLD FLUID LEAVES
F = CORRECTION FACTOR BY WHICH L.M.T.D. IS
   MULTIPLIED

REFERENCE: NAGLE, IND. ENG. CHEM. 25, 604 (1933)

$$m = \frac{t_2 - t_1}{T_1 - t_1}$$

$$R'' = \frac{T_1 - T_2}{t_2 - t_1}$$

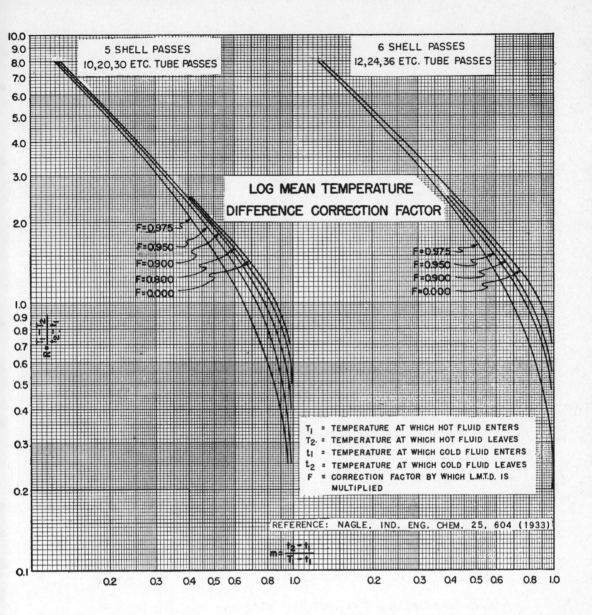

5 SHELL PASSES
10, 20, 30 ETC. TUBE PASSES

6 SHELL PASSES
12, 24, 36 ETC. TUBE PASSES

LOG MEAN TEMPERATURE
DIFFERENCE CORRECTION FACTOR

F=0.975
F=0.950
F=0.900
F=0.800
F=0.000

F=0.975
F=0.950
F=0.900
F=0.000

$R = \dfrac{T_1 - T_2}{t_2 - t_1}$

T_1 = TEMPERATURE AT WHICH HOT FLUID ENTERS
T_2 = TEMPERATURE AT WHICH HOT FLUID LEAVES
t_1 = TEMPERATURE AT WHICH COLD FLUID ENTERS
t_2 = TEMPERATURE AT WHICH COLD FLUID LEAVES
F = CORRECTION FACTOR BY WHICH L.M.T.D. IS MULTIPLIED

REFERENCE: NAGLE, IND. ENG. CHEM. 25, 604 (1933)

$m = \dfrac{t_2 - t_1}{T_1 - t_1}$

Section 13

EQUILIBRIUM FLASH VAPORIZATION

The vapor-liquid equilibrium relations for hydrocarbon mixtures of known analysis can be determined by trial and error from the equilibrium relations of the individual components and a material balance. For any component, $i(i = 1, 2 \cdots, n)$,

$$y_i = K_i x_i \tag{1}$$

and
$$X_i = x_i L + y_i(100 - L) \tag{2}$$

where y_i = mole fraction of i in the equilibrium vapor

x_i = mole fraction of i in the equilibrium liquid

K_i = equilibrium constant of i

X_i = total moles of i per 100 moles of total mixture

L = moles of equilibrium liquid per 100 moles of total mixture

Substituting $K_i x_i$ for y_i in equation (2) and rearranging

$$x_i = \frac{X_i}{L + K_i(100 - L)} \tag{3}$$

At equilibrium, the sum of the mole fractions in the liquid phase, $x_i + x_2 + \cdots + x_n$, must equal 1.00. While two variables, L and K_i, appear in the right-hand member of equation (3), there are actually three variables involved since K_i is a function of both pressure and temperature. To predict the equilibrium conditions, any two of these variables must be known and successive values of the third assumed until the sum of the x's equals 1.00. Usually, temperature and pressure are the two variables specified, and then the trial and error involves L.

Flash Vaporization of Petroleum Fractions

Although the foregoing method applies to complex petroleum fractions as well as to hydrocarbon mixtures of a comparatively few known components, it has little practical significance for petroleum fractions because of the laborious calculations required even when component analyses are available, which is rarely the case. As a result, empirical correlations have been developed for predicting equilibrium flash vaporization curves from distillation data on crudes and petroleum fractions. The flash vaporization curve is a plot of temperature against liquid volume percent vaporized, the total vapor being in equilibrium with the unvaporized liquid at constant pressure.

222

A number of empirical correlations for determining the atmospheric flash vaporization curve have appeared in the literature, but only a relatively simple correlation would seem to be justified in view of the discrepancies between the data of various investigators. The present correlation is of the same general type as those of Piroomov and Beiswenger[1] and Nelson[2] and applies to both petroleum fractions and whole crudes. For petroleum fractions, either the 10% (ASTM) distillation of the fraction itself or the portion of the crude assay (True Boiling Point) distillation corresponding to the fraction may be used for predicting the flash curve. For whole crudes, the crude assay distillation should always be used in preference to the 10% distillation. The latter should never be used if the distillation curve flattens out below the 70% point in the neighborhood of 700°F since this is indicative of cracking.

In extrapolating the atmospheric flash curves to higher or lower pressures it is suggested that the parallel method proposed by Piroomov and Beiswenger be used up to pressures of 15 psig for whole crudes and wide cuts, and up to pressures of 50 psig if the slope of the flash reference line of the fraction is not greater than 2°F/%. By this method the atmospheric flash curve is shifted parallel to itself by a temperature interval equal to the extrapolation of the 40% point[3] on the flash reference line (FRL) as a pure compound on a vapor pressure chart.

This parallel method is unsatisfactory for higher pressures, since it is known that the flash curve becomes more horizontal with increasing pressure until its slope is zero at the true critical pressure. Beyond the pressure limits recommended in the preceding paragraph for parallel extrapolation, it is suggested that a variation of the method of Watson and Nelson[4] be used, since no very elaborate method appears to be justified by the data. The 40% point on the FRL is extrapolated on a vapor pressure chart to a temperature 150°F above the critical temperature of the normal paraffin having the same boiling point as the 40% point. This extrapolated temperature and corresponding vapor pressure is then used as a focal point through which straight lines are drawn on a rectilinear vapor pressure chart (page 42) from the atmospheric flash temperatures for various percents vaporized. The flash curve at any pressure is determined from the temperatures at which the given pressure ordinate intersects these constant percent off (or quality) lines. These linear extrapolations do not apply if the true critical point of the fraction is approached since the constant percent off lines become curved and converge to the true critical temperature and pressure.

[1] Piroomov and Beiswenger, *Proc. API* **10**, No. 2, Section II, 52 (1929).

[2] Nelson, "Petroleum Refinery Engineering," pp. 242–243, McGraw-Hill Book Co., New York, N.Y. (1941).

[3] This is a slight modification of the Piroomov and Beiswenger method as they use the point of intersection between the flash and distillation curves for extrapolation.

[4] Watson and Nelson, *Ind. Eng. Chem.* **25**, 880 (1933).

Reduced Crudes

Perhaps the most direct method of predicting the atmospheric flash curve of a reduced crude (or any reduced stock) which at the same time is reasonably accurate is the following:

(1) Construct an atmospheric flash curve for the original crude.
(2) Determine the number of moles of both original crude and reduced crude per given volume of original crude.
(3) At the dew point (100% vaporized) of the original crude, assume that the reduced crude vapors are at their dew point at a partial pressure equal to their mole fraction in the total vapors (moles of reduced crude/moles of original crude) multiplied by 1 atm.
(4) Extrapolate the 40% point on that portion of the flash curve corresponding to the yield of reduced crude from the partial pressure computed by (3) to 1 atm.
(5) If the reduced crude has been stripped of light ends, its atmospheric flash curve is drawn through the extrapolated point parallel to the flash curve of the original crude between the abscissas corresponding to the yield of reduced crude.
(6) If the reduced crude has not been stripped of light ends, a smooth curve is drawn from the split point on the flash curve of the original crude to the 20% point on the flash curve constructed by (5) to approximate the front end of the flash curve of the reduced crude. Establishment of the 20% point as the point above which unstripped light ends cease to affect the reduced crude flash curve is, of course, entirely arbitrary but, at the same time, fairly representative.

While the method outlined above is empirical to a large extent, it does have some theoretical justification. If all but one drop of reduced crude were flashed, this last drop of liquid would be in equilibrium with the reduced crude vapors at 1 atm. It is then assumed that if 100% original crude were flashed at 1 atm, the last drop of liquid would have the same composition as the last· drop of reduced crude, and the latter vapors would be at a partial pressure corresponding to their mole fraction multiplied by one atmosphere. The basis for this assumption is that the temperature difference between the boiling range of the last drop and that of the vapors removed in reducing the crude is usually so great that these vapors can be considered the equivalent of steam or gas in so far as the equilibrium relations of the last drop is concerned. Making the flash curves of reduced crudes parallel to the flash curves of their original crudes was originally suggested by Piroomov and Beiswenger and appears to be fully justified by their data.

Example 1. Determine the atmospheric flash vaporization curves of an East Texas crude and its 35% bottoms (both stripped and unstripped) from the following data taken from an assay workup of the crude:

Assay (T.B.P.) Distillation   *Gravity*   *Lbs/Gal*

I.B.P., °F   —   °API

5%	122	Crude	37.4	6.98
10%	177	Overhead (0–65%)	47.7	6.57
20%	262	Bottoms (65–100%)	20.9	7.73
30%	350			
40%	443			
50%	538			
60%	636			
70%	752			
80%	(905)			

$$\text{Slope of DRL}^* = \frac{752 - 177}{60} = 9.6°\text{F}/\%$$

* Distillation reference line—through 10% and 70% points.

$$50\% \text{ Point (DRL)} = 177 + (50 - 10)9.6 = 561°\text{F}$$

The slope and 50% point of the flash reference line are determined from the chart on page 228:

$$\text{Slope (FRL)} = 6.4°\text{F}/\%; \quad 50\% \text{ Point (FRL)} = 561 - 40 = 521°\text{F}$$

The atmospheric flash curve is derived from its reference line by using the relation on page 229.

Percent Vaporized	Assay Distillation (°F)			Ratio of ($\Delta t'$)'s	Flash Vaporization (°F)		
	Curve	DRL	$\Delta t'$		$\Delta t'$	FRL	Curve
5	122	129	−7	0.40	−3	233	230
10	177	177	—	—	—	265	265
20	262	273	−11	.36	−4	329	325
30	350	369	−19	.34	−6	393	387
40	443	465	−22	.34	−7	457	450
50	538	561	−23	.34	−8	521	513
60	636	656	−20	.33	−7	585	578
70	752	752	—	—	—	649	649
80	(905)	848	+57	.33	+19	713	732

The flash reference line and the atmospheric flash curve of the original crude are shown on Figure 1. Proceeding from (1), the flash curve of the original crude, the atmospheric flash curves of the stripped and unstripped reduced crudes are derived by the method outlined in the text:

$$(2) \text{ Vol. Av. B.P. of whole crude} = \frac{262 + 538 + 905}{3} = 568°\text{F}$$

Mean Av. B.P. of whole crude = 568 − 70 = 498°F (Section 2)

Molec. wt. of whole crude = 197 (Section 3)

$$\text{Vol. Av. B.P. of 65\% overhead} = \frac{203 + 373 + 558}{3} = 378°F$$

$$\text{Slope of DRL (65\% overhead)} = \frac{495 - 139}{60} = 5.9°F/\%$$

Mean Av. B.P. = 378 − 38 = 340°F
Molec. wt. of 65% overhead = 139

	Per 100 Gal of Crude
Moles of crude = (6.98 × 100)/197 =	3.55
Moles of overhead = (6.57 × 65)/139 =	3.07
Moles of reduced crude	0.48

(3) Partial pressure of reduced crude at the dew point of the original crude

$$= \frac{0.48}{3.55} \times 1 = 0.135 \text{ atm.}$$

(4) The 40% point on the reduced crude flash curve corresponds to 65 + 0.40 × 35 = 79% or 722°F on the flash curve of the original crude.

By extrapolation from 0.135 atm. to 1 atm., the 40% point on the atmospheric flash curve of the reduced crude is 900°F.

(5) The atmospheric flash curve of the stripped reduced crude is drawn through the extrapolated point parallel to the 65–100% portion of the flash curve of the original crude. This reduced crude flash curve may be converted to percent on reduced crude by proportioning the 65–100% yield on original crude to 0–100% on reduced crude. Both curves are shown in Figure 1.

(6) The front end of the atmospheric flash curve on the unstripped reduced crude is constructed by drawing a smooth curve from the 65% point on the flash curve of the original crude to the 20% point on the flash curve of the stripped reduced crude as shown in Figure 1. This curve is also given on the basis of 0–100% reduced crude.

GENERAL REFERENCES

Edmister and Pollock, *Chem. Eng. Progress* **44,** 905 (1948).
Katz and Brown, *Ind. Eng. Chem.* **25,** 1373 (1933).
Packie, *Trans. Am. Inst. Chem. Engrs.* **37,** 51 (1941).

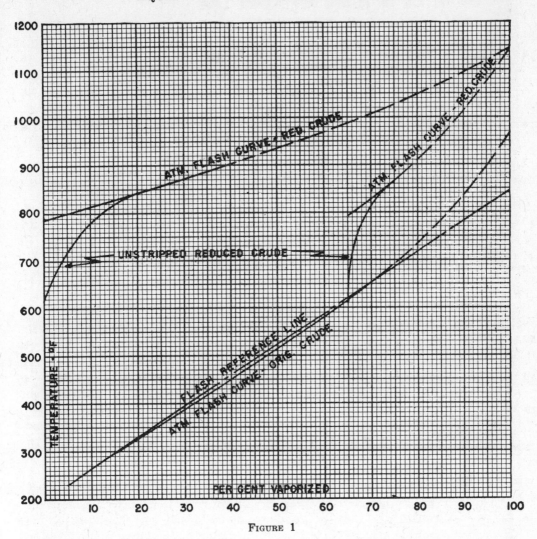

FIGURE 1

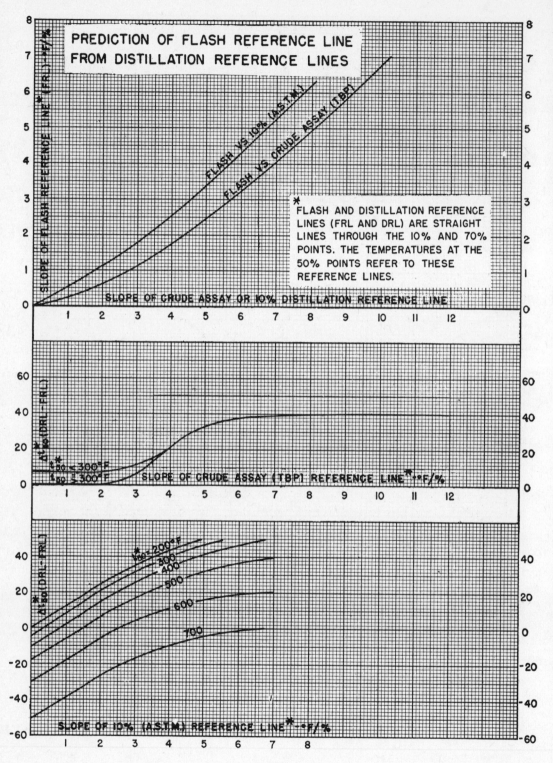

PREDICTION OF FLASH REFERENCE LINE
FROM DISTILLATION REFERENCE LINES

FLASH AND DISTILLATION REFERENCE
LINES (FRL AND DRL) ARE STRAIGHT
LINES THROUGH THE 10% AND 70%
POINTS. THE TEMPERATURES AT THE
50% POINTS REFER TO THESE
REFERENCE LINES.

228

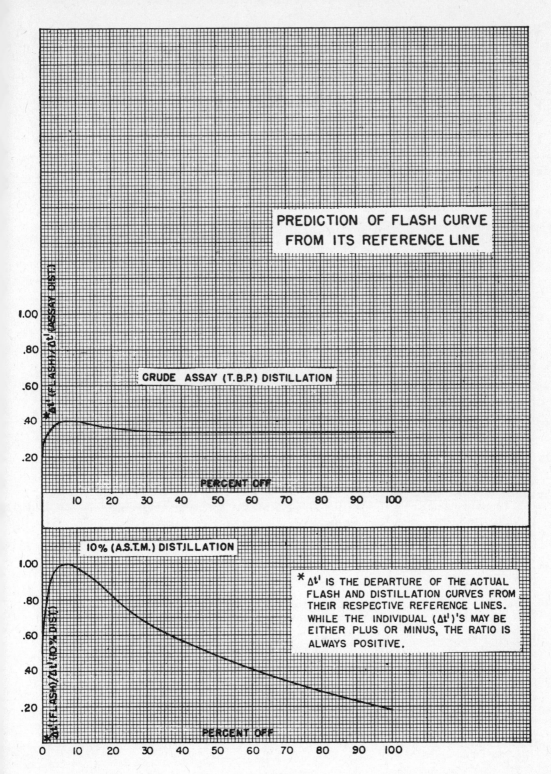

PREDICTION OF FLASH CURVE
FROM ITS REFERENCE LINE

CRUDE ASSAY (T.B.P.) DISTILLATION

10% (A.S.T.M.) DISTILLATION

* $\Delta t'$ IS THE DEPARTURE OF THE ACTUAL
FLASH AND DISTILLATION CURVES FROM
THEIR RESPECTIVE REFERENCE LINES.
WHILE THE INDIVIDUAL ($\Delta t'$)'S MAY BE
EITHER PLUS OR MINUS, THE RATIO IS
ALWAYS POSITIVE.

Section 14

FRACTIONATING TOWERS

In order to simplify the work involved in making stepwise calculations for the rectification of binary and multicomponent systems, Gilliland[1] has presented an empirical correlation between theoretical steps and reflux ratio. To use the Gilliland correlation to predict the number of theoretical plates for a given reflux ratio, the minimum number of steps at total reflux and the minimum reflux ratio are required.

Minimum Number of Theoretical Steps

When a separation is specified with respect to only two components of a multi-component mixture, the lower boiling of these two components is designated the *light key component* and the higher boiling the *heavy key component*, and the minimum number of steps can be calculated by the well-known Fenske equation[2] as follows:[3]

$$S_M = \frac{\log \left(\frac{X_{LKD}}{X_{LKW}}\right)\left(\frac{X_{HKW}}{X_{HKD}}\right)}{\log \alpha_{LK}} \tag{1}$$

or

$$[\alpha_{LK}]^{S_M} = \left(\frac{X_{LKD}}{X_{LKW}}\right)\left(\frac{X_{HKW}}{X_{HKD}}\right) \tag{1a}$$

After equation (1) is solved for S_M, the latter may be substituted in this equation along with the distribution of either key component to predict[4] the distribution of the other components, or

$$\log \left(\frac{X_{LD}}{X_{LW}}\right)\left(\frac{X_{HKW}}{X_{HKD}}\right) = S_M \log \alpha_L \tag{2}$$

Likewise,

$$\log \left(\frac{X_{HW}}{X_{HD}}\right)\left(\frac{X_{LKD}}{X_{LKW}}\right) = S_M \log \left(\frac{\alpha_{LK}}{\alpha_H}\right) \tag{3}$$

In any of the above equations, moles per 100 moles of feed may be replaced by total moles, or volume or weight units since in any of these conversions the multiplying factors cancel out.

[1] Gilliland, *Ind. Eng. Chem.* **32**, 1220 (1940).
[2] Fenske, *Ind. Eng. Chem.* **24**, 482 (1932).
[3] A table of nomenclature is given on page 243.
[4] This equation may be used for any pair of components.

When the degree of separation is specified for more than two components, equation (1) must be applied to all critical combinations of these components and the maximum S_M determined for the most difficult case. If the separation is specified with respect to the total quantity of two or more components, as in the case of Example 1, trial and error is required for the solution of S_M.

It should be pointed out that the concentrations calculated by equations (2) and (3) actually apply only to the separation at total reflux and, with the exception of the two key components, there will be some variation of the degree of separation with the reflux ratio. As the reflux ratio decreases, there is some improvement in separation between light and heavy components boiling outside the range of the key components and some deterioration in the separation of components boiling intermediate between the key components. However, in so far as the present procedure is concerned, the distillate and bottoms compositions for other reflux ratios are assumed to be the same as those calculated for total reflux.

Minimum Reflux Ratio

Gilliland[5] has proposed several different formulas for predicting minimum reflux ratio and all have the disadvantage of being composed of a number of complex terms in addition to requiring trial and error for solution. Although all these equations appear to give satisfactory results, the terms are so complex that it is difficult to be certain that there are no numerical errors in their application.

In order to apply the Gilliland method with greater facility, the following equation was developed for predicting the minimum reflux ratio of a multicomponent system:

$$(O/D)_M + 1 = \left(\frac{\alpha_{LK} I_{LK} + 1}{\alpha_{LK} - 1}\right)\left(\frac{x_{LKD}}{I_{LK}} - x_{HKD}\right)$$

$$+ \sum_L \frac{\alpha_L}{\alpha_L - 1}\left(x_{LD} - I_L x_{HKD}\right) + \sum_H \frac{\alpha_H}{\alpha_{LK} - \alpha_H}\left(\frac{x_{LKD}}{I_H} - x_{HD}\right) \qquad (4)$$

$(O/D)_M$ can be calculated for two arbitrary states of feed vaporization:

1. "Liquid" feed, corresponding to vaporization of the feed equivalent to the fraction of the feed lighter than the light key component. For the components lighter than the light key, $I_L = Z_L/\alpha_L$ and for the light key and heavier components, $I_{LK} = Z_{LK}$, and $I_H = Z_H$.[6]

[5] Gilliland, *Ind. Eng. Chem.* **32**, 1101 (1940).

[6] If components, intermediate between the two key components, are present, they are considered ei her *light* or *heavy* components depending upon which key their volatility more nearly approaches. In the case of "liquid" feed, $I_L = Z_L$ and $I_H = Z_H$ for these intermediate components; in the case of "vapor" feed, $I_L = Z_L/\alpha_L$ and $I_H = Z_H \alpha_H/\alpha_{LK}$.

2. "Vapor" feed, corresponding to vaporization of the feed equivalent to the fraction of the feed consisting of the heavy key component and lighter. For the components lighter than the heavy key, $I_L = Z_L/\alpha_L$ and $I_{LK} = Z_{LK}/\alpha_{LK}$ and for the components heavier than the heavy key, $I_H = Z_H$.[6]

After the minimum reflux ratios have been calculated for "liquid" and "vapor" feeds, the minimum reflux ratio for the actual vaporization of the feed can be calculated by direct interpolation or extrapolation. However, extrapolation beyond 50% of the difference between "liquid" and "vapor" feed may lead to serious deviations.

The first term of the right-hand side of equation (4) is the same as for binary mixtures, and the equation reduces to the equivalent of a binary mixture when all light components other than the light key have infinite volatility and all heavy components other than the heavy key have zero volatility. Under these circumstances the equation is exact when I_{LK} is taken as the ratio of the two components in the liquid phase of the feed. That is, if the feed is introduced as a liquid at its bubble point, $I_{LK} = Z_{LK}$, which is the ratio of the two components in the feed; if the feed is introduced as a vapor at its dewpoint, $I_{LK} = Z_{LK}/\alpha_{LK}$, which is the ratio of the two components in the equilibrium liquid. For intermediate stages of vaporization I_{LK} can be calculated from the flash vaporization formula, although direct interpolation of the minimum reflux ratio on the basis of percentage vaporization between the saturated liquid and saturated vapor feeds gives values only slightly in error on the conservative side.

In the case of multicomponent mixtures, equation (4) is semi-empirical since it was necessary to make simplifying approximations in its derivation. Furthermore, the exact values of the various I's cannot be calculated directly from the composition and state of vaporization of the feed, since the liquid on the feed plate is not identical to the liquid phase of the feed as in the case of a binary mixture. As a result, it was necessary to define the I's empirically for two states of feed vaporization, arbitrarily chosen to simulate a binary mixture of the two key components, and then interpolate or extrapolate to the minimum reflux ratio corresponding to the actual vaporization of the feed.

Equation (4) has been checked for a number of multicomponent systems on which the minimum reflux ratio was determined by stepwise trial and error calculations. Generally, unusual systems were chosen with respect to composition and relative volatility in order to reveal the maximum deviations ever likely to be encountered in practice. The agreement was quite satisfactory as the average deviation was less than $\pm 5\%$ and the maximum about 10%. The latter occurred at the limit of extrapolation relative to the arbitrary feed states.

Also, the minimum reflux ratio was calculated for these same systems by the Colburn method[7] with about the same degree of accuracy. It should be pointed out that the latter gave better results than equation (4) when the relative volatilities and compositions were not so abnormal as the systems selected. However, under these circumstances both methods were quite accurate as the deviations seldom exceeded a few percent, and the present equation has a distinct advantage in that it is explicit and does not require trial and error.

Both methods are quite sensitive to the selection of key components, and the selection of the wrong key components can lead to a much greater error than is inherent in either method. If the desired separation is between adjacent components, there is usually no doubt about selecting these as the key components. However, if there are additional specifications relative to other components, it may be necessary to try two or more combinations of key components to make sure that the minimum reflux ratio is sufficient to fulfill all specified conditions.

Correlation of Theoretical Steps with Reflux Ratio

As mentioned at the beginning of this section, Gilliland correlated the results of a large number of stepwise calculations on various binary and multicomponent mixtures by plotting

$$[S-S_M]/[S+1]=\phi(S) \quad \text{against} \quad [(O/D)-(O/D)_M]/[O/D+1]=F(O/D)$$

and found that all points could be represented by a single curve irrespective of the type or degree of separation. These points, along with about half again as many additional points, were replotted, and the best curve through them was essentially the same as Gilliland's original correlation.

In arriving at the coordinates for the additional points the minimum reflux ratio was calculated by equation (4); therefore these points are a criterion of the present method as well as the curve itself. In no case did the deviations exceed either 3 theoretical steps or 15%, and the average deviation was less than 1 theoretical step and also less than $\pm 5\%$. To take care of the maximum deviation it is recommended that in any design the number of theoretical steps predicted from the correlation on page 244 be increased by either 3 theoretical steps or 10%, whichever is greater.

Plate Efficiency

Because of the large number of factors which undoubtedly influence the plate efficiency of a fractionating tower, any fundamental formula accounting for even the most important variables must necessarily be quite involved. For this reason, a simple empirical correlation of the limited data on hydrocarbon mixtures seemed to be the most promising method of predicting plate efficiency.

[7] Colburn, *Trans. Am. Inst. Chem. Engrs.* **37**, 805 (1941).

Gunness[8] correlated the results of several tests on petroleum mixtures on the basis of vapor pressure of the liquid. As he points out, this is a method of indirectly correlating plate efficiency with liquid viscosity since viscosity of pure hydrocarbons and narrow boiling fractions is an approximate function of vapor pressure over a fairly wide range of vapor pressures.

In view of the consistent results obtained by Gunness, plate efficiency was plotted directly against fluidity (reciprocal viscosity) for a number of tests on commercial towers including those upon which Gunness based his curve. The curve on page 245 represents this correlation. While the overall plate efficiency exceeds 100% at fluidities greater than 9 cp^{-1}, this is not inconsistent as the flow of the liquid across the plates results in concentration gradients which may achieve a greater degree of fractionation than predicted by stepwise calculations in which the liquid is assumed to leave the plate in equilibrium with the composite vapor. Lewis[9] has shown theoretically that different combinations of liquid and vapor concentration gradients across the plate may give overall plate efficiencies as high as 200–300% when based on stepwise calculations.

There is no reason to believe that this correlation applies to mixtures other than hydrocarbons, and with the exception of alcohol-water mixtures there are too little data available to afford a comparison. Although there is considerable variation in the alcohol-water data, there is some indication that plate efficiencies are somewhat greater than for hydrocarbons of the same viscosity.

Location of the Feed Plate

As a simple approximation for locating the feed plate, it may be assumed that the proportion of actual plates above the feed will be the same as that required to effect the same separation between the key components at total reflux. That is, the number of theoretical steps at total reflux is calculated for the concentration change in the key components between the feed and distillate compositions. It is then assumed that the ratio of this to the total number of theoretical steps at an infinite reflux ratio is the same as the ratio of actual plates above the feed is to the total number of plates. Application of this method is illustrated by Example 1.

In some cases where there are critical components other than the two key components, it may be necessary to check the total reflux steps above and below the feed on the basis of these components, since the optimum location of the feed plate will be different with each pair of components. Usually the separation of components other than the key components is so complete that only the latter need be considered.

[8] Gunness, Sc.D. Thesis, Mass. Inst. Tech. (1936).
[9] Lewis, *Ind. Eng. Chem.* **28**, 399 (1936).

Packed Towers

The charts on pages 246 to 248 giving the H.E.T.P., capacity and pressure drop in packed towers are self-explanatory. Since practically all of the H.E.T.P. data were on towers less than 12 in. in diameter, caution should be used in the design of larger towers. One of the greatest sources of inefficiency in a packed tower is poor liquid distribution. If good distribution can be achieved by efficient distributors, the extrapolations may be used for larger towers with reasonable assurance.

Example 1. At an operating pressure of 100 psig determine the number of plates and reflux ratio required to separate the mixture given below so that the bottoms contain at least 90% of the butenes-2 present in the feed and at the same time have an isobutene content not greater than 5%:

Component	Feed (Mole %)
i-C_4H_{10}	40.0
i-C_4H_8	20.0
C_4H_8-1	15.0
C_4H_{10}	5.0
t-C_4H_8-2	10.0
c-C_4H_8-2	10.0
	100.0

(1) Dewpoint of Distillate and Bubble Point of Bottoms

In order to calculate the average volatilities, the dewpoint of the distillate and bubble point of the bottoms must be found by trial and error using assumed compositions. These are tabulated below.

Component	Moles Per 100 Moles of Feed			Mole Fraction	
	Feed	Distillate	Bottoms	Distillate	Bottoms
i-C_4H_{10}	40.0	39.3	0.7	0.530	0.027
i-C_4H_8	20.0	18.7	1.3	.253	.050
C_4H_8-1	15.0	13.0	2.0	.176	.077
C_4H_{10}	5.0	1.0	4.0	.014	.154
t-C_4H_8-2	10.0	1.5	8.5	.020	.327
c-C_4H_8-2	10.0	0.5	9.5	.007	.365
	100.0	74.0	26.0	1.000	1.000

As a first trial, assume the dewpoint of the distillate is 140°F at 7.8 atm (114.7 psia).

| Component | y_D | First Trial | | |
		α'_D* 140°F	F† 140°F	$\dot{x}$ $\pi y/F$
i-C_4H_{10}	0.530	1.29	8.4	0.493
i-C_4H_8	.253	1.155	7.5	.263
C_4H_8-1	.176	1.13	7.35	.187
C_4H_{10}	.014	1.00	6.5	.017
t-C_4H_8-2	.020	0.97	6.3	.025
c-C_4H_8-2	.007	0.91	5.9	.009
	1.000			0.994

* Relative volatilities to C_4H_{10} or (α')'s are used as a matter of convenience; then, the (α'_{av})'s are converted to (α_{av})'s, the relative volatilities to t-C_4H_8-2, which will be selected as the heavy key component.

† Computed from the fugacity function of butane multiplied by the relative volatilities.

Since the sum of the x's is 0.994 instead of 1.000, the assumed temperature should be lowered slightly, but the difference would be so small (less than 1°F) that the change in the (α'_D)'s would be imperceptible. Consequently, 140°F will be used as the dewpoint of the distillate.

The bubble point of the bottoms is assumed to be 165°F at 8.0 atm[10] for the first trial.

| Component | x_W | First Trial | | | Second Trial | | |
		α'_W* 165°F	F† 165°F	y Fx/π	α'_W* 160°F	F† 160°F	y
i-C_4H_{10}	0.027	1.26	10.7	0.036	1.265	10.25	0.035
i-C_4H_8	.050	1.14	9.7	.061	1.145	9.3	.058
C_4H_8-1	.077	1.115	9.5	.091	1.12	9.1	.088
C_4H_{10}	.154	1.00	8.5	.164	1.00	8.1	.156
t-C_4H_8-2	.327	0.97	8.25	.337	0.97	7.85	.321
c-C_4H_8-2	.365	0.915	7.8	.356	0.915	7.4	.338
	1.000			1.045			0.996

* Relative volatilities to C_4H_{10} or (α')'s are used as a matter of convenience; then, the (α'_{av})'s are converted to (α_{av})'s, the relative volatilities to t-C_4H_8-2, which will be selected as the heavy key component.

† Computed from the fugacity function of butane multiplied by the relative volatilities.

The bubble point of the bottoms will be taken as 160°F. The relative volatilities are averaged and converted to t-C_4H_8-2 as the heavy key in the following table:

[10] After allowing 3 lb/sq in. as the approximate pressure drop through the tower.

Component	α'_D 140°F 7.8 atm	α'_W 160°F 8.0 atm	α'_A 150°F 7.9 atm	α'_{av} $(\alpha'_D\alpha'_W\alpha'_A)^{1/3}$	α_{av}
i-C_4H_{10}	1.29	1.265	1.275	1.275	1.315
i-C_4H_8	1.155	1.145	1.15	1.15	1.185
C_4H_8-1	1.13	1.12	1.125	1.125	1.16
C_4H_{10}	1.00	1.00	1.00	1.00	1.03
t-C_4H_8-2	0.97	0.97	0.97	0.97	1.00
c-C_4H_8-2	0.91	0.915	0.91	0.91	0.94

(2) *Minimum Theoretical Steps (Total Reflux)*

The minimum number of theoretical steps by which the desired separation can be accomplished is calculated as follows:

Let $\quad\quad t$ = moles of t-C_4H_8-2 in the distillate per 100 moles of feed

$\quad\quad 10 - t$ = moles of t-C_4H_8-2 in the bottoms per 100 moles of feed

Since 90% of the butenes-2 must be retained in the bottoms, the cis-butene-2 content of the distillate and bottoms will be:

$\quad\quad\quad\quad (2 - t)$ moles in the distillate per 100 moles of feed

and $\quad\quad\quad\quad (8 + t)$ moles in the bottoms per 100 moles of feed

Using the previously assumed values of 18.7 moles of isobutene in the distillate and 1.3 moles in the bottoms, the following equations must be satisfied:

$$\left(\frac{18.7}{1.3}\right)\left(\frac{10 - t}{t}\right) = (1.185)^{S_M}$$

$$\left(\frac{18.7}{1.3}\right)\left(\frac{8 + t}{2 - t}\right) = \left(\frac{1.185}{0.94}\right)^{S_M}$$

A trial and error solution of these equations shows that they are satisfied by $S_M = 25.5$ and $t = 1.62$.

The distribution of the other components can be calculated from S_M and the distribution of t-C_4H_8-2.

i-C_4H_{10}: Let u = moles of i-C_4H_{10} in bottoms

$$\left(\frac{40 - u}{u}\right)\left(\frac{8.38}{1.62}\right) = (1.315)^{25.5} = 1075$$

$$= 0.19 \text{ moles of } i\text{-}C_4H_{10} \text{ in the bottoms}$$

C_4H_8-1: Let v = moles of C_4H_8-1 in the bottoms

$$\left(\frac{15 - v}{v}\right)\left(\frac{8.38}{1.62}\right) = (1.16)^{25.5} = 44$$

$$v = 1.58 \text{ moles of } C_4H_8\text{-2 in the bottoms}$$

C_4H_{10}: Let w = moles of C_4H_{10} in the bottoms

$$\left(\frac{5-w}{w}\right)\left(\frac{8.38}{1.62}\right) = (1.03)^{25.5} = 2.12$$

$$w = 3.55 \text{ moles of } C_4H_{10} \text{ in the bottoms}$$

The percentage of i-C_4H_8 in the bottoms will be:

$$\left(\frac{1.3}{0.19 + 1.3 + 1.58 + 3.55 + 8.38 + 9.62}\right) 100 = 5.3\%$$

In order to meet a maximum of 5.0% i-C_4H_8 specified for the bottoms, it is necessary to reduce the 1.3 moles to 1.22 moles in the bottoms. This would require an increase in S_M to 25.8 which would modify the distribution of the other components. However, the latter change is so slight that it can be neglected. The composition of the overhead and bottoms will then be:

Component	Moles Per 100 Moles of Feed			Mole Fraction	
	Feed	Distillate	Bottoms	Distillate	Bottoms
i-C_4H_{10}	40.0	39.81	0.19	0.528	0.008
i-C_4H_8	20.0	18.78	1.22	.249	.050
C_4H_8-1	15.0	13.42	1.58	.178	.064
C_4H_{10}	5.0	1.45	3.55	.019	.145
t-C_4H_8-2	10.0	1.62	8.38	.021	.342
c-C_4H_8-2	10.0	0.38	9.62	.005	.391
		75.46	24.54	1.000	1.000

(3) Minimum Reflux Ratio

Since the critical separation is between isobutene and the butenes-2, the former is naturally selected as the light key component and trans-butene-2, since it is more volatile than the cis-butene-2, as the heavy key component. Butene-1 is considered a light intermediate component because of the proximity of its relative volatility to that of isobutene; normal butane is considered a heavy intermediate component since its relative volatility is nearer to the heavy key than the light key. The following tabulation gives the necessary information for calculating the minimum reflux ratios for the two arbitrary states of feed vaporization:

Component	Type	Mole Fraction			α_{av}	"Liquid" Feed	"Vapor" Feed
		Feed	Distillate	Bottoms			
i-C_4H_{10}	L	0.400	0.528	0.008	1.315	3.04	3.04
i-C_4H_8	LK	.200	.249	.050	1.185	2.00	1.69
C_4H_8-1	L	.150	.178	.064	1.16	1.50	1.29
C_4H_{10}	H	.050	.019	.145	1.03	4.00	3.48
t-C_4H_8-2	HK	.100	.021	.342	1.00	—	—
c-C_4H_8-2	H	.100	.005	.391	0.94	2.00	2.00
		1.000	1.000	1.000			

"Liquid" feed—40% vaporized

$$(O/D)_M + 1 = \frac{1.185 \times 2.00 + 1.0}{1.185 - 1.0}\left(\frac{0.249}{2.00} - 0.021\right)$$

$$+ \frac{1.315}{0.315}(0.528 - 3.04 \times 0.021) + \frac{1.16}{0.16}(0.178 - 1.50 \times 0.021)$$

$$+ \frac{1.03}{1.185 - 1.03}\left(\frac{0.249}{4.00} - 0.019\right) + \frac{0.94}{1.185 - 0.94}\left(\frac{0.249}{2.00} - 0.005\right)$$

$$(O/D)_M = 1.88 + 1.94 + 1.07 + 0.29 + 0.46 - 1 = 4.64$$

"Vapor" feed—90% vaporized

$$(O/D)_M + 1 = \frac{1.185 \times 1.69 + 1.0}{1.185 - 1.0}\left(\frac{0.249}{1.69} - 0.021\right)$$

$$+ 1.94 + \frac{1.16}{0.16}(0.178 - 1.29 \times 0.021)$$

$$+ \frac{1.03}{1.185 - 1.03}\left(\frac{0.249}{3.48} - 0.019\right) + 0.46$$

$$(O/D)_M = 2.06 + 1.94 + 1.10 + 0.35 + 0.46 - 1 = 4.91$$

Assume that the feed is sufficiently preheated to vaporize a percentage equivalent to the distillate or 75.46%. By interpolation, the minimum reflux ratio corresponding to this feed vaporization is:

$$(O/D)_M = 4.64 + \left(\frac{75.46 - 40}{90 - 40}\right)(4.91 - 4.64) = 4.83$$

(4) Theoretical Steps vs. Reflux Ratio

Using the values determined in preceding sections for minimum theoretical steps, 25.8, and for minimum reflux ratio, 4.83, the number of theoretical steps for various reflux ratios can be predicted from the correlation on page 244:

O/D	F(O/D)	φ(S)	S	Theoretical Plates*
4.83	—	—	∞	∞
5.25	0.067	0.570	61.3	60.3
5.75	.136	.502	52.7	51.7
6.50	.223	.430	46.0	45.0
7.50	.314	.366	41.3	40.3
∞	—	—	25.8	24.8

* The reboiler is considered the equivalent of one theoretical step. With a partial instead of a total condenser, a second theoretical step also could have been deducted.

(5) *Number of Actual Fractionating Plates*

To predict the number of actual plates it is necessary to determine the average viscosity of the liquid on the plates. Since the temperature difference between the top and bottom of the tower is so small, the average viscosity may be taken as the viscosity at the average temperature. For this purpose the viscosity of butane at 150°F will be used.

Viscosity of C_4H_{10} @ 150°F = 0.216 cs $\approx$ 0.216 $\times$ 0.523 = 0.113 cp
Fluidity = 1/0.113 = 8.9 cp^{-1}; Plate efficiency = 99%

Using a plate efficiency of 99% the number of actual plates is computed for various reflux ratios:

O/D	S	Theoretical Steps	Actual Plates
4.83	∞	∞	∞
5.25	61.3	60.3	60.9
5.75	52.7	51.7	52.2
6.50	46.0	45.0	45.5
7.50	41.3	40.3	40.7
∞	25.8	24.8	25.0

The number of actual plates is plotted against reflux ratio in Figure 1.

A reflux ratio of 6.50 to 1, or 1.35 times the minimum, is selected. The number of actual plates corresponding to this reflux ratio is 45.5 so that a 50-plate tower would be required.

(6) *Location of the Feed Plate*

The number of plates above the feed is based on the proportion of theoretical steps at total reflux which would be required to effect the change in concentration of the key components between the feed and distillate. This proportion is applied to the actual number of plates (including the reboiler) to determine the number above the feed plate.

In order to take into account any appreciable difference in relative volatility above and below the feed, the relative volatility used for calculating the steps at total reflux between feed and distillate is the geometric mean of α_D and α_A or,

$$\alpha_n = \left(\frac{1.155}{0.97} \times \frac{1.15}{0.97}\right)^{\frac{1}{2}} = 1.19$$

The number of total reflux steps which would be required between the feed and distillate is calculated by the following equation:

$$\left(\frac{18.78}{20}\right)\left(\frac{10}{1.62}\right) = 1.19^n = 5.79; \qquad n = 10.1$$

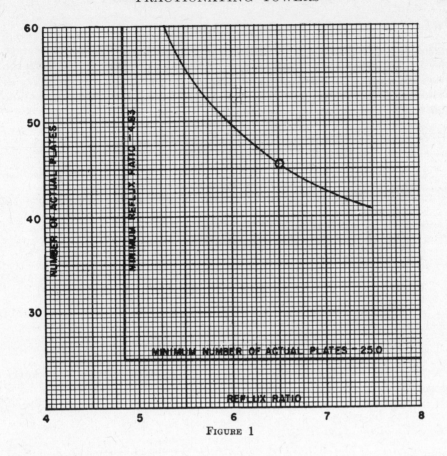

FIGURE 1

Number of actual plates above the feed would then be:

$$\frac{10.1}{25.8}(50 + 1) = 20$$

The vaporization of the feed can be taken into account by adding the fraction vaporized to n since 100% vaporization would be equivalent to a theoretical step at total reflux. This would change the proportion of plates above the feed as follows:

$$\left(\frac{10.1 + 0.75}{25.8}\right)(50 + 1) = 21.4 \text{ plates above the feed}$$

Feed lines would probably be installed above the 24th, the 28th and 32nd plates from the bottom of the tower.

GENERAL REFERENCES

Atkins and Franklin, *Refiner Natural Gasoline Mfgr.* (Jan. 1936).

Brown, Sanders, Nyland and Hesler, *Ind. Eng. Chem.* **27,** 383 (1935).

Brown and Souders, *Oil and Gas J.* **31,** 34 (1932).

Chilton and Colburn, *Trans. Am. Inst. Chem. Engrs.* **26,** 178 (1931).

Elgin and Weiss, *Ind. Eng. Chem.* **31,** 435 (1939).

Fenske, Lawroski and Tongberg, *Ind. Eng. Chem.* **30,** 227 (1938).

Fenske, Unpublished data, Pennsylvania State College.

Gilliland, *Ind. Eng. Chem.* **32,** 918, 1101, 1220 (1940).

Gunness, *Ind. Eng. Chem.* **29,** 1092 (1937).

Lewis and Wilde, *Trans. Am. Inst. Chem. Engrs.* **21,** 99 (1928).

Perry, "Chemical Engineers' Handbook," pp. 829–832, McGraw-Hill Book Co., New York, N.Y. (1941).

Sherwood, Shipley and Holloway, *Ind. Eng. Chem.* **30,** 765 (1938).

White, *Trans. Am. Inst. Chem. Engrs.* **31,** 390 (1935).

Nomenclature

X	moles of any component in distillate or bottoms per 100 moles of feed
x	mole fraction of any component in liquid
y	mole fraction of any component in vapor
D	moles of distillate per 100 moles of feed
O	moles of reflux per 100 moles of feed
O/D	reflux ratio
$(O/D)_M$	minimum reflux ratio corresponding to $S = \infty$
S	number of steps from still to distillate
S_M	minimum number of steps corresponding to $O/D = \infty$
P	number of theoretical plates; with a partial reboiler and partial condenser, $P = S - 2$, and with a partial reboiler and total condenser, $P = S - 1$
Z_L	ratio of mole fraction of any light component to heavy key component in the feed
Z_H	ratio of mole fraction of light key component to any heavy component in feed
α_D	relative volatility of any component to heavy key at the dew point of the distillate
α_W	relative volatility of any component at the bubble point of the bottoms
α_A	relative volatility of any component at the arithmetic average temperature of the dew point of the distillate and the bubble point of the bottoms
α_{av}	mean relative volatility of any component, $(\alpha_D \cdot \alpha_W \cdot \alpha_A)^{1/3}$
LK	used as a subscript to refer to the light key component
HK	used as a subscript to refer to the heavy key component
L	used as a subscript to refer to any light component
H	used as a subscript to refer to any heavy component
D	used as a subscript to refer to the distillate
W	used as a subscript to refer to the bottoms
n	used as a subscript to refer to the plates above the feed
m	used as a subscript to refer to the plates below the feed

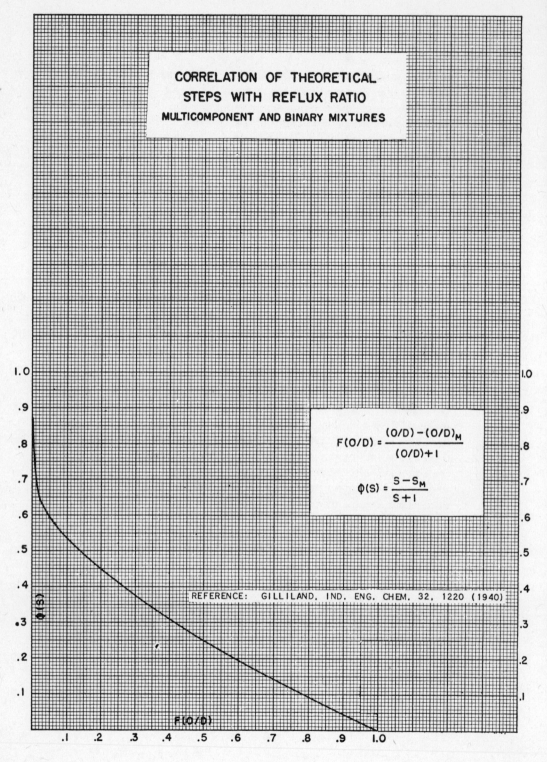

CORRELATION OF THEORETICAL
STEPS WITH REFLUX RATIO
MULTICOMPONENT AND BINARY MIXTURES

$$F(O/D) = \frac{(O/D) - (O/D)_M}{(O/D) + 1}$$

$$\phi(S) = \frac{S - S_M}{S + 1}$$

REFERENCE: GILLILAND, IND. ENG. CHEM. 32, 1220 (1940)

$\phi(S)$

F(O/D)

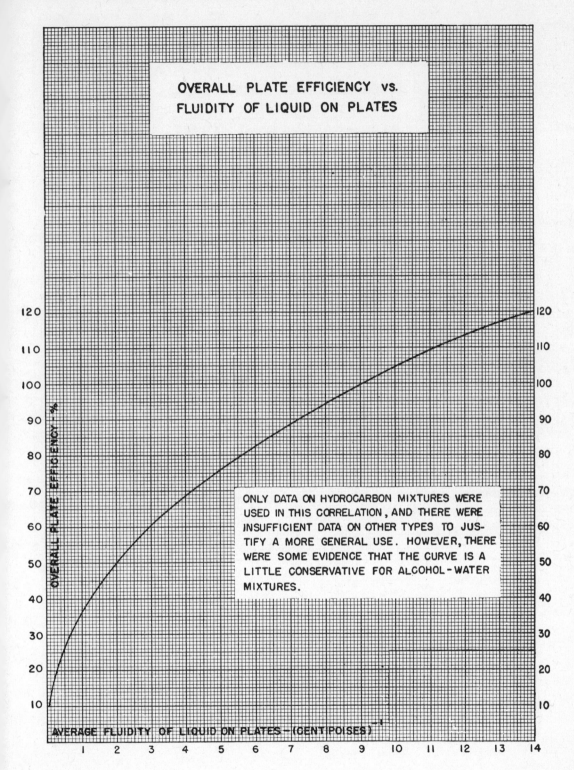

OVERALL PLATE EFFICIENCY vs.
FLUIDITY OF LIQUID ON PLATES

ONLY DATA ON HYDROCARBON MIXTURES WERE
USED IN THIS CORRELATION, AND THERE WERE
INSUFFICIENT DATA ON OTHER TYPES TO JUS-
TIFY A MORE GENERAL USE. HOWEVER, THERE
WERE SOME EVIDENCE THAT THE CURVE IS A
LITTLE CONSERVATIVE FOR ALCOHOL-WATER
MIXTURES.

OVERALL PLATE EFFICIENCY - %

AVERAGE FLUIDITY OF LIQUID ON PLATES - (CENTIPOISES)$^{-1}$

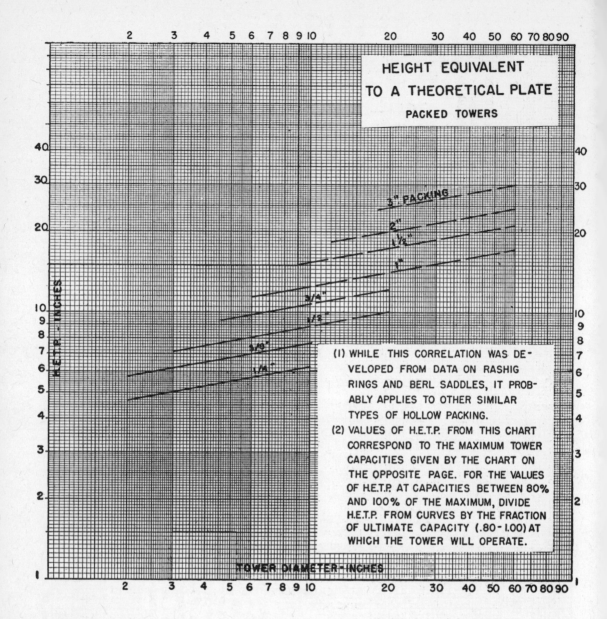

HEIGHT EQUIVALENT
TO A THEORETICAL PLATE
PACKED TOWERS

(1) WHILE THIS CORRELATION WAS DE-
VELOPED FROM DATA ON RASHIG
RINGS AND BERL SADDLES, IT PROB-
ABLY APPLIES TO OTHER SIMILAR
TYPES OF HOLLOW PACKING.

(2) VALUES OF H.E.T.P. FROM THIS CHART
CORRESPOND TO THE MAXIMUM TOWER
CAPACITIES GIVEN BY THE CHART ON
THE OPPOSITE PAGE. FOR THE VALUES
OF H.E.T.P. AT CAPACITIES BETWEEN 80%
AND 100% OF THE MAXIMUM, DIVIDE
H.E.T.P. FROM CURVES BY THE FRACTION
OF ULTIMATE CAPACITY (.80-1.00) AT
WHICH THE TOWER WILL OPERATE.

H.E.T.P. - INCHES

TOWER DIAMETER-INCHES

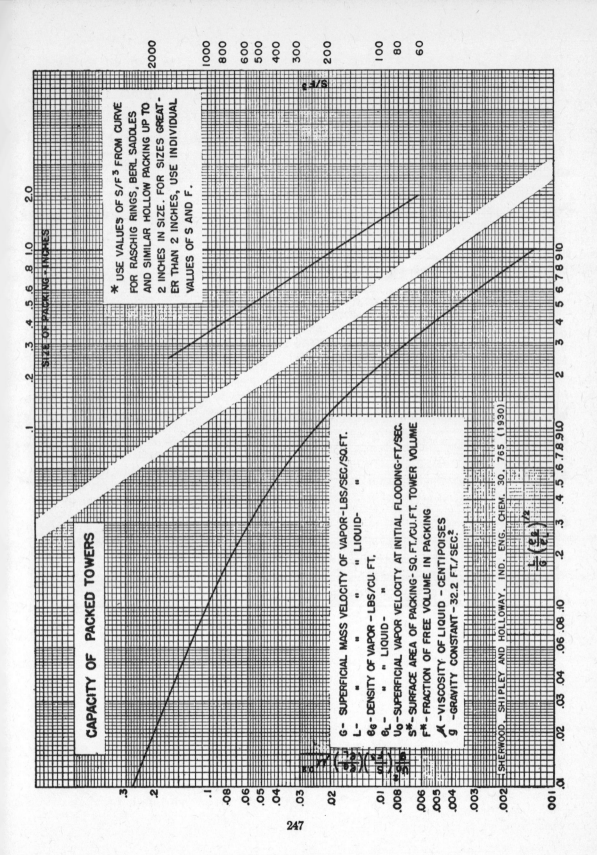

CAPACITY OF PACKED TOWERS

SIZE OF PACKING – INCHES

$G \cdot S/S$

* USE VALUES OF S/F^3 FROM CURVE FOR RASCHIG RINGS, BERL SADDLES AND SIMILAR HOLLOW PACKING UP TO 2 INCHES IN SIZE. FOR SIZES GREATER THAN 2 INCHES, USE INDIVIDUAL VALUES OF S AND F.

G – SUPERFICIAL MASS VELOCITY OF VAPOR – LBS/SEC/SQ.FT.
L – " " " LIQUID – "
ρ_G – DENSITY OF VAPOR – LBS/CU. FT.
ρ_L – " " LIQUID – "
U_O – SUPERFICIAL VAPOR VELOCITY AT INITIAL FLOODING - FT/SEC.
S^* – SURFACE AREA OF PACKING – SQ. FT./CU.FT. TOWER VOLUME
F^* – FRACTION OF FREE VOLUME IN PACKING
μ – VISCOSITY OF LIQUID – CENTIPOISES
g – GRAVITY CONSTANT – 32.2 FT./SEC.²

SHERWOOD, SHIPLEY AND HOLLOWAY, IND. ENG. CHEM. 30, 765 (1930)

$$\frac{L}{G}\left(\frac{\rho_G}{\rho_L}\right)^{1/2}$$

$$\frac{U_O{}^2}{gF^3}\left(\frac{S}{F^3}\right)\left(\frac{\rho_G}{\rho_L}\right)\mu^{0.2}$$

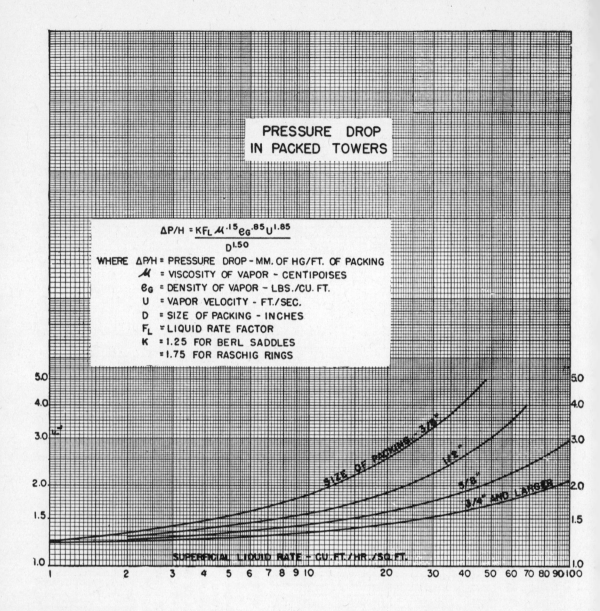

PRESSURE DROP
IN PACKED TOWERS

$$\Delta P/H = \frac{KF_L \mu^{.15} \rho_G^{.85} U^{1.85}}{D^{1.50}}$$

WHERE $\Delta P/H$ = PRESSURE DROP - MM. OF HG/FT. OF PACKING
μ = VISCOSITY OF VAPOR - CENTIPOISES
ρ_G = DENSITY OF VAPOR - LBS./CU. FT.
U = VAPOR VELOCITY - FT./SEC.
D = SIZE OF PACKING - INCHES
F_L = LIQUID RATE FACTOR
K = 1.25 FOR BERL SADDLES
= 1.75 FOR RASCHIG RINGS

SUPERFICIAL LIQUID RATE - CU. FT./HR./SQ. FT.

248

CONVERSION FACTORS

TEMPERATURE

To Convert

From	To	°C	°F	°R	°K
°C		—	1.8(°C) + 32	1.8(°C) + 459.7	°C + 273.2
°F		(°F − 32)/1.8	—	°F + 459.7	(°F + 459.7)1.8
°R		(°R − 491.7)/1.8	°R − 459.7	—	°R/1.8
°K		°K − 273.2	1.8(°K) − 459.7	1.8(°K)	—

LENGTH

To Convert

From	To	Cm	Meters	Inches	Feet
		Multiply By			
Centimeters		1.000	0.0100	0.3937	0.03281
Meters		100.0	1.000	39.37	3.281
Inches		2.540	0.0254	1.000	0.08333
Feet		30.48	0.3048	12.00	1.000

AREA

To Convert

From	To	Sq cm	Sq m	Sq in.	Sq ft
		Multiply by			
Sq cm		1.000	1.000×10^{-4}	0.1550	1.076×10^{-3}
Sq m		10,000	1.000	1,550	10.76
Sq in.		6.451	6.451×10^{-4}	1.000	6.944×10^{-3}
Sq ft		929.0	0.09290	144.0	1.000

VOLUME

To Convert

From	To	Cu in.	Cu ft	US gal	Imp gal	Cu cm	Liters	Bbl (42's)
				Multiply by				
Cu in.	1.000	5.787×10^{-4}	4.329×10^{-3}	3.607×10^{-3}	16.39	0.01639	1.031×10^{-4}
Cu ft	1,728	1.000	7.481	6.232	2.832×10^{4}	28.32	0.1781
US gal	231.0	0.1337	1.000	0.8326	3,785	3.785	0.02381
Imp gal	277.3	0.1605	1.200	1.000	4,543	4.543	0.02857
Cu cm	0.06102	3.531×10^{-5}	2.642×10^{-4}	2.201×10^{-4}	1.000	1.000×10^{-3}	6.290×10^{-6}
Liters	61.02	0.03531	0.2642	0.2201	1,000	1.000	6.290×10^{-3}
Bbl (42's)	9,700	5.614	42.00	34.97	1.590×10^{5}	159.0	1.000

FORCE

To Convert

From	To	Poundals	Pounds	Dynes	Grams
		Multiply by			
Poundals		1.000	0.03108	13,830	14.10
Pounds		32.17	1.000	4.448×10^{5}	453.6
Dynes		7.233×10^{-5}	2.248×10^{-6}	1.000	1.020×10^{-3}
Grams		0.07093	2.205×10^{-3}	980.7	1.000

DENSITY

To Convert

From	To	Sp gr	Lb/gal	Lb/cu ft
			Multiply by	
Sp gr...		1.000	8.347	62.43
Lb/gal.......................................		0.1198	1.000	7.481
Lb/cu ft.....................................		0.01602	0.1337	1.000

PRESSURE

To Convert

From	To	Lb/sq in.	Lb/sq ft	Atm	Kg/sq cm	In. of Hg	Mm of Hg	Ft of H$_2$O (60°F)
				Multiply by				
Lb/sq in. ..		1.000	144.0	0.06804	0.07031	2.036	51.70	2.307
Lb/sq ft ...		6.944×10^{-3}	1.000	4.726×10^{-4}	4.882×10^{-4}	0.01414	0.3592	0.01602
Atm.......		14.70	2,116	1.000	1.033	29.92	760.0	33.90
Kg/sq cm..		14.22	2,048	0.9678	1.000	28.96	735.5	32.81
In. of Hg ..		0.4912	70.73	0.03342	0.03453	1.000	25.40	1.133
Mm of Hg		0.01934	2.785	1.316×10^{-3}	1.360×10^{-3}	0.03937	1.000	0.04461
Ft of H$_2$O (60°F)		0.4335	62.43	0.02950	0.03048	0.8826	22.41	1.000

RATE OF FLOW

To Convert

From	To	Liters per sec	Gal per min	Gal per hr	Cu ft per sec	Cu ft per min	Cu ft per hr	Bbl per hr	Bbl per day
					Multiply by				
Liters/sec		1.000	15.85	951.2	0.03532	2.119	127.1	22.66	543.8
Gal/min.		0.06308	1.000	60.00	2.228×10^{-3}	0.1337	8.019	1.429	34.30
Gal/hr ..		1.052×10^{-3}	0.01667	1.000	3.713×10^{-5}	2.228×10^{-3}	0.1337	0.02382	0.5716
Cuft/sec		28.30	448.9	2.693×10^{4}	1.000	60.00	3,600	641.1	1.538×10^{4}
Cuft/min		0.4717	7.481	448.9	0.01667	1.000	60.00	10.69	256.5
Cu ft/hr.		7.862×10^{-3}	0.1246	7.481	2.778×10^{-4}	0.01667	1.000	0.1781	4.272
Bbl/hr ..		0.04415	0.6997	42.00	1.560×10^{-3}	0.09359	5.615	1.000	24.00
Bbl/day .		1.840×10^{-3}	0.02917	1.750	6.498×10^{-5}	3.899×10^{-3}	0.2340	0.04167	1.000

ENERGY, HEAT, AND WORK

To Convert

From	To	BTU	Gm-cal	Ft-lb	Hp-hr	Kw-hr
			Multiply by			
BTU...........		1.000	252.0	777.5	3.928×10^{-4}	2.928×10^{-4}
Gm-cal........		3.968×10^{-3}	1.000	3.086	1.558×10^{-6}	1.162×10^{-6}
Ft-lb...........		1.286×10^{-3}	0.3241	1.000	5.050×10^{-7}	3.767×10^{-7}
Hp-hr..........		2,547	6.417×10^{5}	1.980×10^{6}	1.000	0.7457
Kw-hr.........		3,415	8.605×10^{5}	2.655×10^{6}	1.341	1.000

POWER
To Convert

From	To	BTU per hr	Ft-lb per min	Ft-lb per sec	Hp	Kw	Kg-cal per sec	G-cal per sec	Tons of refrig
					Multiply by				
BTU/hr..		1.000	12.96	0.2160	3.928×10^{-4}	2.928×10^{-4}	6.999×10^{-5}	0.06999	8.333×10^{-5}
Ft-lb/min		0.07715	1.000	0.01667	3.033×10^{-5}	2.260×10^{-5}	5.402×10^{-6}	5.402×10^{-3}	6.431×10^{-6}
Ft-lb/sec		4.630	60.00	1.000	1.820×10^{-3}	1.356×10^{-3}	3.241×10^{-4}	0.3241	3.858×10^{-4}
Hp......		2,547	33,000	550.0	1.000	0.7457	0.1782	178.2	0.2122
Kw......		3,415	44,250	737.6	1.341	1.000	0.2390	239.0	0.2845
Kg-cal/sec		1.428×10^{4}	1.851×10^{5}	3,086	5.610	4.183	1.000	1,000	1.191
G-cal/sec		14.28	185.1	3.086	5.610×10^{-3}	4.183×10^{-3}	0.0010	1.000	1.191×10^{-3}
Tons of refrig		1.200×10^{4}	1.555×10^{5}	2,592	4.712	3.514	0.8400	840.0	1.000

INDEX